To Angela

Thanks for making such a beautiful daughter.

Arthur May 2011.

The Emergency Bouzouki Player

abp
Andrew Brel
Publishing

The Emergency Bouzouki Player
by
Andrew Brel

Published by Andrew Brel Publishing

7 Riverbank, Hampton Court. Surrey, KT8 9BH

Read by Charlotte Adler

Cover art by Stuart Catterson

Edited by John Oakley Smith

www.andrewbrel.com

All rights reserved

Without limiting the rights under copyright reserved above, no part of this publication may be reproduced, stored or introduced into a retrieval system, or transmitted, in any form or by any means (electronic, mechanical, photocopying, recording or otherwise), without the prior written permission of the above publisher of this book.

Printed and bound in the UK by the MPG Books Group, Bodmin and King's Lynn

Copyright © 2011, Andrew Brel

The moral right of the author has been asserted

ISBN: 978-0-9568364-0-3

The Emergency Bouzouki Player

Genesis

On the south western coast of Crete lies the harbour village of Sfakia, the southernmost point of European civilisation. To the south, the Mediterranean stretches down to the Egyptian coast and to the north, the towering foothills of the Samaria gorge loom imperiously over the few hundred stone houses they have shielded from the elements for the past thousand years. Sometime in the nineteenth century, as Greece battled for her freedom from 400 years of barbaric Islamic tyranny under the occupation of the Ottomans, my great-great grandfather Andreas Broulidakis was born in Sfakia. Andrea as the name is correctly spoken, with the 's' being silent, was a ship's captain and would certainly have given his heart and mind to the war for freedom from Muslim oppression.

Great-great grandfather Andreas' first son was born in Sfakia in 1836 and he named him Manoussos after his father in the Greek tradition of naming sons after their paternal grandfathers. Manoussos followed in the family business of piloting ships around the Mediterranean and sometime around 1870 his first-born son, my grandfather, was born in Sfakia and was named Andreas. Andreas Broulidakis continued the family tradition by becoming a ship's captain and on one of his sailing adventures to St. Petersburg, Andreas met a beautiful young Russian, Katerina, and brought her back to Sfakia where they were married in the thousand year-old stone walled church in a traditional Orthodox ceremony.

By the turn of the century Egypt was booming under Greek management and Andreas relocated there, first in Alexandria and then in Suez where my father, Manoussos Broulidakis, was born in 1916, the youngest of five children and the first-born son.

During 1936, when he was barely 20 years old, Manoussos, a tall and handsome young man fluent in seven languages, moved to South Africa where he soon found success in the construction business. When World War Two broke out, he volunteered to fight in the war against Nazi fascism, serving in the Allied Army in North Africa and later in Italy. In a slightly ironic symmetry with the family origins, he rose to the rank of Captain. After the defeat of the Nazi's, he returned to South Africa and the construction business, building high rises in Johannesburg, a booming city fast becoming a popular destination for Europeans seeking opportunity away from the post-war privations.

By the 1950s he was living a millionaire lifestyle in a luxurious home on Cyrildene Ridge that was featured as Johannesburg's 'House of the Year' in 1956. Manoussos was a successful bachelor in his forties enjoying the high life when a young beauty caught his eye at a society party. Helen Evangelou, known as Lela, was in her early twenties, a petite, determined, young lady who had recently arrived from Athens and was sharing a flat in Yeoville with her aunt, Thea Eftihia. The 20-year age difference was unremarkable at that time and before long they were married in the Greek Orthodox tradition. Their first child was born in 1958 and was named Katerina after my father's mother, in accordance with traditional Greek naming protocol.

Shortly after the birth, my father's business affairs took a turn for the worse and the house on Cyrildene Ridge was put up for sale. The buyer was L. Ron Hubbard and the house was to become the headquarters of his controversial Scientology operation in Africa.

Manoussos moved his young family to the northern suburb of Bryanston in 1960, the year in which I was born. By that time, he had left the construction industry and had started a factory in the suburb of Edenvale, using a patented plastic and fibreglass hybrid to manufacture practical items like Portaloos and refuse bins for South Africa's numerous municipalities. His factory, called Moulded Components, occupied a large steel-framed warehouse and employed several hundred black workers. Business seemed to be good and we lived in a large house with a swimming pool, two cars, three acres of garden, four servants and four dogs.

The first 10 years of my life, an upbringing graced with the many advantages of an economically advantaged middle-class lifestyle within the conventions of Greek culture, were the proverbial calm before the storm. Although I could speak English, my father insisted that Greek was to be the only language spoken in our home. Greek was my first language, my thoughts were in Greek and on my first day at Bryanston Primary School the only thing that struck me as being unusual was that none of the other children spoke Greek.

Then, toward the end of my tenth year, my destiny was to undergo a significant change. These events began on a midwinter morning in June 1971 when I was summoned to my father's office to be told that I was going on a six-week trip to our homeland. No further explanation was presented, just that I was being taken out of school and sent to Greece to learn about my background.

"But we only have a two-week holiday!" was my surprised reaction. None of the kids in my class had ever travelled overseas since international travel in 1971 was not the commonplace occurrence it was to become. On the same day, the school was told that I would be missing a month of lessons and, a week later, I was taken to Jan Smuts Airport to board an Olympic Airlines Boeing 707 for the overnight flight to Athens where I was met by my great aunt, Thea Eftihia, and taken to my maternal grandparents' home in Piraeus. From Piraeus I was collected by my mother's brother, Elias Evangelou, a bona fide Athenian with a deep knowledge and understanding of Greek culture and a significant academic familiarity with Greece's history. Elias was at that time a colonel in the Greek air force and with him as my guide I travelled the length and breadth of Greece in his white Citroën, visiting important classical locations such as Olympus and Sparta, stopping at countless Byzantine churches and monasteries along the way whilst hearing precisely detailed, elaborate stories of Greece's past glories and seeing at first hand the country I had so far only heard described. Under Elias' informed tutelage, my awareness of my Greek heritage was brought to life, especially my bloodline origins from the village of Sfakia, which was to be next on our visiting schedule.

We reached Crete after an eight-hour ferry journey from Piraeus and Elias drove us from Chania to Sfakia following the route the retreating Allied Army had taken during 1941, a journey of some 50 miles made memorable by Elias' detailed familiarity with the many legends surrounding that fascinating chapter of the Second World War. Elias manoeuvred the car down the twisting sandy road that cut precariously through the Samaria gorge until after a few hair-raising moments, with the hard braking Citroën raising a cloud of sandy dust, we pulled up in Sfakia. The fishing harbour lay to one side with the colourful fishing boats moored neatly to the harbour wall whilst, on the other side, several rows of stone houses led off a central square, the most prominent feature of which was the white-washed taverna perched on the harbour's edge. Sitting on the low wall that enclosed the paved area outside the taverna were two elderly men, both sporting the long bushy moustaches commonly worn by Cretan men. Elias ushered me towards them, saying, "Why don't you ask them if they know where your grandfather's house is?"

I strode up to them in the confident way of a 10 year-old. "Excuse me," I enquired politely,

"I wonder if by any chance you know where the house of my grandfather Andrea Broulidakis is." The man I had addressed stared back at me, his face creasing into a smile as he took a long draw on his pipe before replying, "Ah. Yes. Andrea Broulidakis. Let me show you." It was as if he had been expecting me.

The two old men walked me a short distance down a row of stone cottages and pointed to one of the doorways, telling me to knock. The door opened and an old woman dressed entirely in black came out. She took one look at me before letting out a loud wail and falling to her knees she started grabbing at my feet. I was taken aback and not sure what to do or say but Elias explained what was happening. "She is trying to kiss your feet," he said with an amused chuckle. "They think you have come back to claim the house where she now lives in and that she will be thrown out into the street." Elias calmed the woman down and led me back to the taverna. "There is a phone there," he explained. "I have instructions from your father that when you are in Sfakia you are to call and speak to him."

When my father came on the phone he sounded quite choked up. Since he was not ordinarily given to shows of emotion, I became aware that something unusual was going on. I listened as he gave me specific instructions.

"Elias will give you a bottle," he said. "I want you to go to your grandfather's house. When you are there, fill the bottle with sand and bring it back with you."

During the journey to Sfakia we stopped for refreshments at a roadside Taverna in the village of Anapolis where we sat in the shadow of a towering statue of a Cretan warrior, a ferocious looking man dressed in the traditional Cretan garb, also wearing the bushy beard and moustache of the time. He wielded a fearsome looking curved Cretan sabre in one outstretched hand while an equally fearsome looking dagger and a pistol protruded from his waist band. I asked who this fellow was and Elias smiled. "You will like this story. This is the memorial to Daskalogiannis. But we will wait until we are in Sfakia before I tell you."

Now, seated in the little Taverna in Sfakia, Elias recalled the story.

"In earlier times the Sfakiani were known not only for their warmth and hospitality, but also for the ruthlessness and the brigandry of their menfolk. They place a high degree of importance on matters of honour. They say the Sfakians were great sailors and even greater pirates, but always great warriors who played a leading part in the battles for the liberation of Crete. This man is one of the most famous. His name is Ioannis Vlachos but he was known as Daskalogiannis, which in English translates as 'teacher John.' He was called teacher because his wealthy ship owner father sent him abroad for an education. Daskalogiannis led a rebellion against the Ottoman occupiers in 1771, where with 1,300 men he fought 40,000 Turks, but eventually, the Pasha's men captured him and 70 of his fighters. On the orders of the Muslim ruler of Crete, the Grand Vizier, Daskalogiannis was skinned alive in front of his men. Throughout his ordeal he remained silent, showing no fear to his torturers and his heroic death has made him a symbol of the courage and the indomitable spirit of the Sfakian people that would eventually lead to the vanquishing of the Turks. His brother was forced to watch this barbaric torture and it drove him insane."

Similar acts of awe-inspiring courage characterised the Cretan resistance fighters during the evacuation of the under-supplied Allied troops during the Nazi occupation in 1941. The Cretan resistance fought a successful rearguard action to allow Allied troops time to withdraw southwards to Sfakia, the point from which the evacuation of thousands of Australian and New Zealand troops took place as the German forces moved southwards from Chania. After the war, many of those soldiers returned on pilgrimages to Crete to ceremonially mark the occasion of their remarkable escape, as well as to acknowledge their debt to the heroism of the Cretan people.

   I relished the tales of unconquerable spirit of the proud people of Sfakia that were presented to me during my visit to my Patritha, my homeland, reminders that our ancestors had possessed the unshakeable Cretan ethos whereby the fear of death was located below the fear of dishonour. I felt a warm glow of association with this place where people knew my name and, because of my forbears' long and distinguished history, spoke it with reverence. My name Andreas translates as 'manly and brave' and young though I was it all made perfect sense.

Ten days after my return to South Africa, on 11th August 1971, my father died from an undiagnosed heart condition, leaving the instruction that the sand I had been sent to collect from his father's house in Sfakia be sprinkled over his grave. He would, in this way, find his final resting place under Cretan soil. My mother, dressed in black and seldom coming out of her bedroom, observed the traditional forty days of mourning during which time the world I knew steadily unravelled.

One of the sayings that held my attention during those bleak and insecure days was: "You only become a man when your father dies," and in my case, at the age of 10, circumstance had visited upon me a close examination of dramatic transformation. I realised very quickly that in some prescient moment, aware of his impending death, my father had sent me on the journey to Crete to make me aware of my ancestry. That was my inheritance and this knowledge was to sustain me through the difficult times ahead during which I had no role model or reliable figure to offer guidance. It was an ever-present reminder that being a Sfakiano I would be possessed with indefatigable courage when life presented difficulty.

School days

Growing up in the suburb of Bryanston, where the average home occupied three acres, meant my upbringing benefitted from a degree of privilege. The opportunity to exercise social discrimination was available to me from an early age since our properties were big and our neighbours distant. Bryanston homes typically had separate servants' quarters to accommodate the live-in staff. Eaton Avenue, where we lived at number 28, was still a sand road. Before my father's death we had two maids in the house and two 'garden boys' who all called me 'Master' from the moment I could hear.

At a time when a bag of oranges that made six glasses of fresh juice cost 20 cents, there was virtually no significant crime in Bryanston and on hot nights we slept with the windows open without a second thought for our safety. We had four dogs, two German shepherds that lived outside and two indoor lapdogs, Maltese poodles with fluffy white fur and pink pads from never having stepped outside the house onto rough surfaces.

My mother ensured that we attended the Greek Orthodox

Church every Sunday, we spoke Greek at home and aside from our school acquaintances most of the visitors to our home were Greek. Family social outings were invariably to Greek community affairs like dinners at the nearby Greek restaurant, the Clay Oven, where classic Greek dishes were served in abundance until late in the evening while bouzouki music filled the air with an atmosphere that may just as well have been in Athens as in Bryanston. From as far back as my memory allows, I was drawn to the haunting and mysterious song of the bouzouki, the timeless carrier of tales across generations.

Education and the Afrikaans language

My first exposure to Afrikaans had happened during my days at Bryanston Primary School when I was barely five years old. When I attended my first Afrikaans class and heard the language spoken for the first time I found the guttural sound repellent. No intellectualising was necessary; it was just disagreeable and it was something that I intuitively shied away from.

When I first heard the sound of a violin at the age of three, I was immediately attracted to it and wanted to find out more about it. Even though I had never touched a violin my first answer to the question "What do you want to be when you grow up?" was always "A violin player." The sound of the Afrikaans language had entirely the opposite effect on my ear and I was intuitively I was at odds with the language.

Around the age of 11, I found an old F-Hole Harmony guitar discarded in previous years by my older sister and, with the aid of an illustrated 'Teach yourself to play the guitar in seven days' book and a tuning fork, I was able to construct a world of my own where my existence had a purpose and my life a meaning. The strings were old and rusty and pressing down on them made my fingers bleed although I had no idea that this was not a normal part of playing the guitar. I pressed on regardless, through the pain barrier until calluses formed and I was able make the strings of the guitar vibrate into a harmonious resonance. As I began to respond to that harmonious vibration so I learnt to find the centre of my own identity, an awareness of my appropriate place in the cosmic arrangement. In this way, I could transform my reality from that of a fatherless child into that pillar of the highest aspiration for any ambitious individual, which was to become a musician. It was almost like a spiritual calling, a way to live in balanced harmony with the universe.

South Africa's politically dominant Afrikaner elite, as represented by the National Party, was aware of the unpopularity of its language and culture and the ridicule that it attracted and so made every effort via its control of the education system to upgrade the relevance and the validity of Afrikaans. The educational curriculum made the learning of Afrikaans compulsory in order for a pupil to progress to the next level of schooling. (**See Note 3.**) Even with top grades in all other subjects, any scholar who failed Afrikaans had to repeat the previous year. When first presented with this information by the primary school Afrikaans teacher, Mnr. Van Heerden, I was fascinated.

"You mean if I pass all my other subjects, but I fail Afrikaans, then I will have to repeat the year?" I asked.

"Ja, dis reg," replied Mnr. Van Heerden. Even then my sense of fairness was outraged but in the way that young children must, I submitted to the expectations of the system and in due course left primary school and headed for Bryanston High School.

When considering their education policy, the South African government did not stray far from the same considerations that enabled them to draft the laws of apartheid, as someone who attended a state school, it seemed to me that the purpose of education was more about imposing Nationalist doctrine with complete inflexibility than about cultivating enquiring minds and arming them with information on the pathway towards knowledge and wisdom.

In the appointment of teaching staff it seemed that only

Afrikaners or pro-Afrikaans applicants could expect a position within the state education system. Many of the teachers at our English-medium school could not speak English at all, their only qualification as teachers being their Afrikaans nationality. Our science teacher in standard eight, a Mnr. Stulting, was an example. Even if he had any insights regarding science he was never able to share them with our class. His presence in my life brought about a new awareness.

The outrage I felt at being taught in Afrikaans was not exclusive to my experience. A few dozen miles down the road, in the SOuth WEstern TOwnships of Soweto, the same approach to education, which was to teach black children in Afrikaans, would lead to the 1976 Soweto riots which began the process of forcing the white population to accept that the black majority was beginning to find a collective voice.

My protest against this habitual abuse of educational authority took a more basic form than that of the Soweto students. It involved spit-balls and a hollow biro casing. Science lessons for the duration of my year in standard eight consisted of an exhaustive study into the physics of the trajectory of spit-balls relative to the egress of mouth-assisted air pressure. Small pieces of paper would be chewed into soggy pellets before being loaded into the end of an empty biro and fired at the back of Mnr. Stulting's neck from a variety of positions in the classroom. In a process requiring dexterity and precision we, and I must admit to having enlisted several of my classmates in this endeavour, would measure the trajectory of the spit-ball on its flight path towards its destination, making extensive mental notes on the correlation between muzzle velocity and the reaction of the unfortunate Mnr. Stulting to each direct hit. He would turn to face his tormentors with a storm of Afrikaans expletives that became ever less convincing with each successful strike. This process repeated itself during every science lesson for over six months until one day the miserable Mnr. Stulting failed to show up, his spirit broken by our unrelenting attacks on his inability to speak English. The unforeseen happy consequence of Mnr. Stulting's desertion was that we were left without a science teacher for the remainder of the year, a situation far preferable to listening to a buffoon maintaining the pretence of being something he quite clearly was not.

To my adolescent mind, spit-balling the buffoon seemed the appropriate remedy for being denied the opportunity to be taught science by a competent English-speaking teacher. I was aware that my education was suffering as a consequence of a political decision that had little to do with education and more with indoctrination. It seemed wrong to me and I would half-jokingly tell friends that I attended a Nazi school. Although I did experience some pangs of conscience in that I knew I was orchestrating a campaign of cruelty against a weak individual, Mnr. Stulting's presence in the classroom represented something so dark that any personal considerations had to be put to one side. With hindsight, my war on Mnr. Stulting's presence in the classroom was my first bona fide moment of political protest.

The Principal of Bryanston High School, Mnr. Viviers, was a sour-faced Afrikaner in his mid-forties who spoke English as if it caused him physical pain. His appointment seemed to us more an opportunity for the Afrikaner to take revenge on the English than to advance any educational agenda.

An outstanding example of Principal Viviers' ingrained meanness of spirit came one Wednesday morning before the day's assembly when it was announced that there was to be a surprise hair inspection, something which had never happened before. This involved each boy being scrutinised as they filed into the hall by the examining teacher who placed a finger above the top of the child's ear. If the hair touched or extended over the teacher's finger, that child was sent to the 'failed' group. By the end of this exercise, of the 500-odd boys who attended Bryanston High only one had passed the test. Johannes van Schalkwyk, an Afrikaans boy who was the proud possessor of a dog-bowl haircut, stood alone as having conformed to the previously unenforced regulation. Principal Viviers announced gloatingly from his pulpit that the punishment for boys breaking the hair code law was a caning. "Four of the best!" he intoned with lascivious relish in his Afrikaans accented English.

During the recitation of the Lord's Prayer as was required on a daily basis, the phrase *as we forgive those who trespass against us* sounded particularly sibilant that day as it came out of the mouths of those still inclined to repeat it. We were instructed to make our way after assembly in an orderly line to the Principal's office where we were expected to bend over and receive our four strokes of the cane. By 11 o'clock that morning no lessons had started at Bryanston High School. Instead, all educational resources were directed towards one objective; the dubiously motivated assault by one bitter individual on the buttocks of 499 of the 500 young male pupils placed in his care. I was 15 at the time and felt incensed by what I considered to be a disgusting abuse of office for apparently homo-erotic gratification by as nasty a piece of work as I had yet encountered. Certainly Principal Viviers did little to disavow me of the growing impression that Afrikaners in general were a base and vicious lot, drawn to serve the darkest impulses under the guise of Christian moral rectitude. I never joined the beating line as directed, deciding instead to walk home as quickly as possible rather than spend the day waiting in a queue to offer my 15 year-old posterior to be beaten with a cane by a grown man. He would have to make do with only 498 bottoms on this day.

The mass caning incident gave me pause to consider how far my views on right and wrong differed from the prevailing norms. I already knew with total certainty that I was in the wrong place and that there were better places to be. I believed the reason for this awareness of being different lay in my ethnic origins, so much so that I concluded that any attempt to help my Afrikaans colleagues to see the sense that I knew to be superior was not only futile but was also dangerous. So set were they in their conformist view, so untouchable by logic, that from early on I determined that my best interests lay in the return to my European roots where my version of common sense was more commonly held.

The majority of people I came across in Sixties and Seventies South Africa were conspicuously narrow-minded and mired in patterns of ignorance that even as a 10 year-old I recognised as 'just plain dumb'. Fear and submission to God belief conspired with bitterness and dark prejudice to create a uniquely South African layer of moral turpitude that left me in no doubt as to my future prospects.

Johannesburg had attracted many Greeks seeking a new life away from devastated post-war Greece and later from the war-torn Congo and from Mozambique where there had long been a Hellenic presence. Second in popularity only to Melbourne as a destination by the 1970s, Johannesburg had a Greek population of more than 100,000 people. South Africa being a country structured rigidly along racial lines, my Greek ethnicity marginalised me even within the white racial sector. On more than one occasion it was pointed out to me by Afrikaans-leaning school chums how lucky the Greeks were to be considered white at a time when people with even a hint of Mediterranean colouring might fall foul of the 'reclassification police' who had the power to re-categorise people on the grounds of their ethnicity, meaning that any previously 'white' victim of a revision of their status would be required to move out of a 'whites-only' area into a 'non-white' area.

This first-hand experience of racial prejudice left me bemused. Seemingly, the central basis of self-worth relied on proximity to 'white' status. My self-confidence arising from being Greek, with a cultural heritage well known to all scholars that dated back thousands of years meant that I viewed the small mindedness of Afrikaner prejudice with a predictably dismissive attitude. This would cause some confusion in the minds of many of my foolishly deluded young colleagues, one of whom asked me, "What do you mean you don't care if you are made non-white? How can you say such a thing?"

My own protest against Afrikanerdom started a lot earlier than those made by the victims of the Soweto riots or the prominent activists who lost their lives at the hands of the Afrikaner government, though it involved far less of a sacrifice. Protected by the economic privilege that accompanied living in the northern suburbs of Johannesburg, I had simply avoided all things Afrikaans. This was not difficult to do, particularly because the area I lived in had virtually no Afrikaans residents.

One of my earliest school lessons was that Afrikaans classes were to be avoided by any means available. Although my grades in all other subjects were mostly good, an F in Afrikaans was the one score I worked the hardest for and took the most pleasure from. In all things Afrikaans I became the schoolboy equivalent of a refusenik.

My most significant and probably the most baffling confrontation with the Afrikaner regime to date came on the occasion of the Matric Afrikaans exam. Confident that I had enough As and Bs in store for a high average, when I entered the exam hall to write the Afrikaans paper I wrote my name on the top, answered the first question in English as 'I don't understand' and approximately three minutes after the exam started, handed my paper in to a surprised examiner.

"But this is a two-hour paper!" he said.

"And I am done," I replied with a nod and left, confident in my gamble that they would not fail me on the basis of my results in Afrikaans. When my exam results arrived, with entrance to medical school hinging on a high average I saw that I had been awarded an E for Afrikaans, the minimum requirement for a pass. Not for the last time did I wonder at the Afrikaner logic. I had passed Afrikaans at university entrance level without having written or spoken a single word of it.

I remember the first day when I, like many of my generation, first addressed the issue of racial discrimination in a serious way. "The blacks are rising up in Soweto" was the first I heard of it, said in a voice prickly with fear.

On 16th June 1976, as I left school, I heard there was a serious riot in progress in Soweto and that there had been casualties. This event, recorded as the Soweto Riots, will forever be associated with the famous opinion-shifting image of the 12 year-old Hector Pieterson's bloodstained corpse held in the arms of an anguished youth while his tearful sister looks on.

The events of 16th June 1976 affected my life significantly. I was 15 years old and in standard nine, just one year left of schooling. This was the first time I became aware of large-scale social action motivated by conscience and it left a lasting impression, particularly as the victims of the reaction from the police had been children. I related strongly to the cause of the strike, originally a protest against the use of Afrikaans as the language medium used in schools, which mirrored my own resentment. I was also moved to learn of the musical component of the riots. The trigger for the police opening fire on 16th June was when the kids started to sing *Nkosi Sikelel'i Afrika*, at that time a banned hymn which at various times would become the national anthem of Tanzania, Zambia, Zimbabwe and Namibia. As more and more people joined in and the singing grew more powerful, the police opened fire with live ammunition.

In my insular existence, it seemed that I was alone in my astonishment at the closed thinking that prevailed. There appeared to be an unwritten rule in my school environment that no one spoke about 'the blacks'. Certainly I had no peers with whom to discuss this event and formulate a balanced view. The only black people in my school cleaned the swimming pool and were to be seen picking up garbage at outlying corners of the playing fields, never to be spoken to and out of range of eye contact.

At home, my frightened, staunchly Christian right-wing mother allowed no opportunity for any discussion that did not first glorify the Lord in whose wisdom she placed her complete trust and secondly the Prime Minister for his good work. The most widely held political opinion in the northern suburbs at the time of the Soweto Riots seemed to be that the blacks "should be shot and not heard".

At around this time I said to our 30 year-old garden 'boy',

"Johannes, please don't call me 'Master'. My name is Andrew. Please call me Andrew."

"Yes, Master," said Johannes.

Life as a high school student was a series of uncomfortable reminders of the distance between my developing ethical code and that of the authority figures around me. After one row too many with the deeply unpleasant Principal Viviers, the embodiment in a single individual of the characteristics I still regard as being among the most offensive that I encountered in my South African days, I left Bryanston High School at the end of 1976 to complete my final year of schooling at Damelin College, a leading private school with a good academic reputation, located in the City.

My education in Bryanston enjoyed one significant advantage. There was no South African television service until I turned fifteen and so books played an important role in the lives of many. Literature was abundant in our home and I became a voracious reader from a young age. Enid Blyton's books started the process. It was common at that time for homes in Bryanston to have a library and I gradually worked my way through the books collected by my father whose specific interests included the Second World War, biographies of Hitler and Rommel and books on the Greek War of Independence, many of which contained graphic and harrowing pictures of Turkish atrocities committed during the 400 year Ottoman occupation. These books informed me of the unspeakable behaviour that characterised the occupation of Greece by the Muslim Turks, whilst forming the basis for a lifelong interest in Islamic belief, the nature of its cause and its effect.

Once I discovered the existentialist writers, I was enthralled by the majestic power of the written word. Perhaps because my father spent time in Italy during World War Two in the Allied Forces, I became absorbed by his collection of the complete works of Alberto Moravia, which gave me a firm grounding in existentialist thinking. I would serially trawl the libraries in my friends' homes and would often finish a book in a day or two, relishing in particular those writers who gave me insight into the ways of life and value systems that made sense to me. John Steinbeck became a significant favourite. Gradually my reading led to the point where ignorance and hypocrisy were identified as the primary enemies of reason and these would be the two qualities I would work hardest at excising from myself.

Despite having completed school with grades good enough to make it into a leading medical school, I felt that whatever education I had acquired had less to do with my schooling than it had to do with the music by which I was surrounded and the books by which I was captivated. One of the most influential books in our library and one which served as a metaphor for the tragedy of South Africa's battle with forward thinking was the ground-breaking work by the brilliant South African lawyer turned naturalist Eugène Marais, 'The Soul of the White Ant.' **(See note 1.)**

In 1977 Steve Biko died. **(See note 2.)** I was 16 at the time and Biko's death and the horrible circumstances of his cruel torture by the Christian Afrikaner police had a defining effect on how I would relate to South Africa's Christians. It was the first time I had witnessed the full weight of Afrikaner anger towards criticism of their ways and it was my first taste of furious outrage at the unjust nature of the people who controlled the world in which I lived. A fellow mourning Damelin student lent me her copy of Biko's book 'I write what I like'. Taking possession of this book, high on the long list of books banned by the Afrikaner government, had a profound effect on me, not because of the book's content but by my newfound awareness of the danger that possession of a publication banned by the government entailed. Even the act of being seen carrying it around engaged significant risk of attracting the clandestine attentions of the authorities. It was already clear to me that, within certain politically radical circles, being found in possession of Biko's book could mean an extra-judicial death sentence, one of the signatures of the Afrikaner government. From this experience I drew a lesson that may have been uniquely South

African. Steve Biko and his book conveyed the importance of disguising independent thought processes in order that they might be allowed to fully develop away from the glare of persecution. The idea of 'freedom of speech' in my upbringing was laughable. Freedom of thought was only possible within a cloak of secrecy. Misinformation was a necessary social skill that I learnt to rely on from an early age to distract would-be persecutors and the possession of Biko's book had a polarising social effect within my world. Visitors to my home would be assessed on how they would react to noticing this book since all it would take would be one guest reporting me to the police for my prospects of a life away from the sinister attentions of the security police to come to an abrupt end. Biko's observation that *'the most dangerous weapon in the hand of the oppressor is the mind of the oppressed'* struck a resonant chord in my life.

By the time I left school following Matric exams at Damelin College, I was an intense 17 year-old unusually obsessed with popular music and driven largely by a need to address my dissatisfaction with the world I inhabited. Though I would have pursued a musical career on leaving school had this been an option, school-leaving career guidance aptitude tests had recommended that I was suitable to study psychiatry. My mother's consequent obsession with having a psychiatrist for a son ensured that at the beginning of 1978 I would enter the University of the Witwatersrand's Medical School, having had very little say in the matter.

Medical School

The 27th September 1978 was a Tuesday, my last day as a 17 year-old. The radio alarm clock woke me at 6am with Rick Springfield singing 'Jessie's girl' as I slipped out of bed and into the Levi jeans, T-shirt and trainers that were my daily outfit. I was struck by the gap between the concerns in Rick's life - obsessing over his friend's girlfriend - and those preoccupying mine, which seemed far weightier and much less frivolous. I was not a happy 17 year-old and I was all too well aware that this was the case.

"Andrea, your food will be ready in five minutes," came the sound of my great-aunt's voice echoing down the hallway from the kitchen. Thea Eftihia had come to live with us after the death of my father and she took care of our growing needs, did our laundry, cooked meals and asked for my opinions on God with whom she was on reassuringly good speaking terms. Our conversations would always be in Greek as even after living in South Africa for 33 years she had not been tempted to learn English.

A breakfast of fried eggs, bacon and toast soon lay waiting on the kitchen table, accompanied by a glass of freshly squeezed orange juice. Thea Eftihia sat at the far end of the kitchen table watching me eat. At exactly 6.45am, I opened the front door and set off down the bricked driveway. It was already hot enough to suggest another scorching highveld day as I hurried along Eaton Avenue towards the corner of Bryanston Drive and the Nichol Highway to wait for the 6.55 bus to Johannesburg. I made the 40-minute journey to Wits in a numbed and mindless blur, cloaked in my constant teenager's sorrow as the bus wound its way through the northern suburbs towards Braamfontein which bordered on Johannesburg's city centre. From the bus stop in Braamfontein I walked through the gates of Wits University to start another day as a medical student, on time as usual for the eight o'clock lecture.

Each day had been a carbon copy of every previous day over the past nine months of medical school life, a soporific cycle of sameness that at times tested my very will to live. The novelty of being a 17 year-old medical student had worn off and for some time now every day had seemed like Groundhog Day. The rigid order of a dull institutional lifestyle with its unremitting draining effect was entirely at odds with the hunger I felt for new information and experience as a remedy for the melancholy that consumed my waking moments. I perceived this regimented daily routine, devoid of any moments of spontaneity, as a treadmill from which I felt increasingly drawn to disembark.

The approach of my eighteenth birthday carried with it the right to vote. Much was made of this power by my fellow students who pressed on me sentiments like "Don't waste your vote". I found the notion of voting to be ridiculous. It was obvious to me that we lived in what was effectively a police state and that the illusion of democracy was no more than a sop to the gullible. The National Party had won every election since 1948 and my standard reply to those attempting to enlist my vote was, "If our vote actually meant anything, do you honestly think they would let us use it?" Though some of my fellow students made great play of their self-advertised political activism, I was unconvinced that it would make any difference until I heard a talk given by someone who would radically inform my perceptions.

The activist was Neil Aggett, a doctor who had recently graduated from the University of Cape Town. Though he was born in East Africa, he had moved to South Africa with his family as a child and finished his schooling at Kingswood College in Grahamstown. By the time I became aware of him, Neil Aggett was working in Baragwanath Hospital near Soweto where he had become involved in the social concerns of the local people. Because of his innate leadership qualities, his compassion and his articulacy he had become a spokesman on their behalf and to that end he had become fluent in Zulu. The tenuous link via a common interest in medicine made me feel somehow connected to this wild haired, wide-eyed enthusiast as he addressed a gathering of first year medical students.

He was speaking of the plight of the black underclass, the first time I had heard anyone openly discussing the subject of the way blacks were treated, using expressions such as 'impoverished underclass' and 'class struggle' that until then I had only seen in print. His position was clearly at odds with the status quo but I was spellbound, recognising immediately that I had heard for the first time the honest articulation of a properly motivated political conscience presented with intelligence and care. Neil Aggett was tremendously radiant and charismatic and I came away from his talk inspired with the intention to become better informed on the events unfolding around me.

Having heard him speak and hearing the way he was spoken of by others left me both uplifted and disturbed. I was both fascinated and terrified for him at the same time. On one hand, he was on the side of what was clearly right, an intelligent selfless man acting for the highest good against formidable odds by using his skills to help those less fortunate. On the other hand, I feared he was offering himself up to certain death by baiting the evil dragon of vicious ignorance with his intelligence and his compassion. Had events proved me wrong, my life might have taken a very different direction.

Neil Aggett was probably the most inspirational human being that I met in my time at Wits and the closest I came to finding a South African role model, though I learned from his example that the route of the martyr was not for me. I had far too much interest in developing my own life and far too little confidence in the possibility that I could do anything to challenge the stranglehold the Afrikaners had on common sense. In some measure, seeing where a medical degree had taken Neil Aggett affected my interest in staying at Wits. I was in no doubt that he was a remarkable human being who, had he lived, would have risen to the highest levels of leadership and helped make the world a better place. I followed his progress wherever I could and when I learned the gruesome details of his death, tortured mercilessly in secret rooms over an insanely long period by faceless Christian Afrikaner policemen, I found myself crying real tears.

Now, on the cusp of my eighteenth year, the end of my first year of medical school approached and with it the prospect of a further ten years of study loomed bleakly ahead. Perhaps my imminent birthday enforced an awareness of the passage of time that highlighted the degree of my discontent but I could not imagine myself surviving the further years of study required to qualify as a psychiatrist. I yearned for a say in my own destiny. Surely life had more to offer than this? Since my first goal was to be happy, choosing to step into the unknown seemed like the best alternative if I wanted to improve my prospects for balance and sanity. To mark my birthday, I resolved to change my life by exercising the one choice that I thought would make a difference. I decided to leave medical school undeterred by the consequences that the 'drop-out' label would visit on my future prospects.

I was soon to learn at first hand that the weightier the decision, the graver the consequences. Something I had not considered when making this decision was the military call up. I had no idea, perhaps the result of wishful non-thinking or because I was Greek and had no investment in a South African identity, that conscription applied to me as much as to the other white males of my age. Even though conscription was a fact of life at that time, I had blocked this possibility out of my life, caught up as I was in the bubble of my own youthful reality where truth was an absolute and every allocation of right and wrong was unchangeable.

I was reasonably certain by the age of 17 that the differing conclusions about life that separated me from the majority of my peers meant that in my view they were wrong and I of course was right. I could see no merit in any argument suggesting that any advantage might be found in conformity, representative as that was of a toxic and depraved mentality. Unfortunately for this nascent individualistic fervour, my mother experienced bitter disappointment at my decision to wreck her dreams and drop out of medical school. Along with her disappointment, she was also concerned that "the Devil might find work for idle hands" and that I might become an "idle loafer drop-out". This led her to contact the military with the news of my availability for national service and she sat down and wrote a letter to the army announcing that since I was no longer a student I would be available for the January call up. My name entered the bureaucratic system and within two weeks a white manila envelope with my name on the front and two A4 pages inside detailing my conscription arrived. I had received my call-up papers. I was to be posted to 11 Kommando in Kimberley. 11 Kommando was an infantry posting and my rank would be 'Rifleman'. It was a devastating blow.

"It will do you good," said my mother. "All the boys have to do it." It was only later that I learned that her motivation related to concerns voiced by her priest that in the absence of a father figure there was a high likelihood of my becoming 'gay'. Between them they had decided that the best thing for me was to 'become a man' in the South African Army. There was no way out. In contemplating my imminent departure to war, I felt a betrayal of unforgivable immensity had taken place.

News of my conscription caught me totally unprepared. Just when I thought I would be able to improve my life, two years of military service lay ahead, a prospect even worse than the one I was leaving behind. My first reaction was fury at being betrayed by my mother in this way, followed by an enormous vacuum of black despair in the pit of my stomach. The transition from medical student to a military conscript within weeks of turning 18 was a pill too bitter to swallow without some soothing remedy. Initially this took the form of denial built on the bedrock of spirit-wrenching rage.

Conscription affected every young white man in the country but although South Africa was a country fighting an undeclared war, people seldom spoke about it. Information on the war on the border was hard to come by since the media carried few details of the conflict beyond intermittent announcements of SADF casualties. My initial shock at receiving the call up papers never diminished. I couldn't properly assimilate the fact that I was about to set off for training as a 'fighting soldier' and that I would be subject to the life or death control of a people I despised, being lined up against people with whose position I identified and sympathised. I explored all the options of how to evade the call-up, only to eliminate them one by one until there were none left. Conscientious objection, the approach taken by Jehovah's Witnesses and those whose faith forbids them to carry arms, was acceptable to the Establishment though there was a forfeit involved. Instead of two years' national service, registration as a conscientious objector entailed a six-year sentence in the infamous detention barracks of Pretoria's Voortrekkerhoogte, an option I had no intention of pursuing.

I saw no way forward other than to leave the country. With very few exceptions, the people around me frightened me with their anger, their submission to ignorant fears and their inability to see the glaringly obvious. I learned early on that to open a discussion on the subject of the treatment of the black people and share my thoughts on the subject was to court disaster. Those who announced their opposition to the system, even in the guise of reasoned criticism, might just as well have held up a red target flag that said "shoot me".

The option of leaving for Europe or America, shining tantalisingly like a holy grail, was beyond my reach since I had no means of my own and no support towards making this happen. Every possibility for escape that I considered glimmered briefly and then faded to black. I felt like a rat in a cage waiting for the white-coated man to lean in with a syringe. How could the winds of Fate have blown me onto these perilous shores? I knew with certainty that what lay ahead was a huge mistake, a slow motion car crash in progress that I was powerless to avoid. I felt markedly different from my fellow conscripts and their apparently enthusiastic approach to the experience that lay ahead seemed to me to display a ridiculous disregard for common sense.

By the eve of my departure, I had still not come to terms with it. A mixture of anger and despair blended into outraged disbelief at the injustice and the powerlessness of my position. Everything about this felt wrong. I had no nationalistic or patriotic feelings towards South Africa, in fact I was fundamentally sceptical of those who spoke of national pride. Within the context of that time and place I saw Afrikaner Nationalism as a base emotional tool akin to a mechanism for blackmailing the susceptible into collaboration. Had I been arrested for a murder I had not committed, the feeling would have been much the same. Try as I might, I could find no merit in the prospect of military service in support or defence of the Christian apartheid policy. *(See Note 3.)*

I had arrived at an anti-Afrikaans scepticism at an early age. I learned not to trust information provided by Afrikaners or friends of Afrikaners on the basis that it would invariably be unreliable and at odds with the wisdom I recognised and pursued. This imposed on me the need to develop a reliable perception of truth on my own terms. I became especially interested in the search for absolute, incontrovertible, unarguable, factually certain truths that I could rely on to counterbalance what I saw as the 'ridiculously deluded' all around. This quest resulted in only limited success, beyond the Socratic idea that 'I know how little I know, so at least I know that much' and the sole reliable truth that formed the basis for all my moral considerations, that every action has an equal and opposite reaction.

Adam the Afrikaner

Aside from being staggered by the crudeness of the implementation of the apartheid policy, I was also quick to point out the glaring anomaly in the rationale that the Afrikaners were ever white people to begin with. Since the original Dutch settlers were all men and had arrived in the Cape without any women, it stood to reason that the first generation of locally born settlers must have had local mothers. It is also well documented that the first person to identify himself as an Afrikaner was a Nineteenth Century coloured man in the Western Cape whose name, aptly enough, was Adam.

A hundred years after establishing a farming foothold in the Cape, to escape from the overriding influence of the British, the Afrikaners gravitated northwards on the Great Trek during which they fought bitter battles with indigenous tribes on their way to the Promised Land they sought. After the Transvaal Republic was established in the 1800s, just when the Boers were consolidating their autonomy, the British returned to haunt them. *(See Note 5.)*

During the second Anglo-Boer war which lasted for three years and ended in 1902, in the course of the scorched earth policy seen by the British military as a way of routing out the Boer guerrillas from the farms from which they had been operating, the British army found that it had rounded up too many prisoners. They had a logistical problem on their hands, the results of which were undeniably shameful. In what was at first seen as a temporary measure, the captured Boer women and children were kept in concentration camps in which tens of thousands of innocents died of malnutrition and disease. It is not surprising that this probably unintentional genocide was a root cause of the bitter resentment of the Afrikaner towards the British now represented by the English-speaking South African population. I had already met this permutation of hatred, starting with the bitter Afrikaans headmaster of my English-medium high school.

To say I came to properly understand the meaning of the word 'despise' through my youthful insights into Afrikaner culture would not be inaccurate. This culture had laid the foundations of the apartheid regime and as a conscripted national serviceman, that was the culture for which I was expected to lay down my life, the culture that had produced and was upheld by such people as Mnr. Viviers, the unfortunate Mnr. Stulting and the snake-eyed Christian policemen such as Gideon Nieuwoudt and Harold Snyman, who in the most evil way had murdered decent, honourable people such as Steve Biko, Neil Aggett and a host of others. No amount of denial or tolerance management could disguise the fact that I was fundamentally at odds with a people whose values I despised and who, unless I took steps to prevent it, saw in me values that they found offensive.

On the eve of my departure to war, I saw the world around me as being awash with madness and toxic delusion. The only glimpse of sanity that sustained me was the work of the songwriters and authors in which I immersed myself to create my own denial-based reality as the day of my departure for Kimberley loomed ever closer. In an attempt to equip myself with the most insightful information on what lay ahead, I spent most of the remaining time before departure day with Leon Brummer, my friend and co-student at Damelin College and later at Wits Medical School and the only Afrikaans friend I had. Leon had two older brothers who had already completed their national service and were in a position to provide me with first hand information on what lay ahead. They generously gave me the best of their advice which included the phrases, "The army either makes or breaks you," as well as "National service is the best time in your life that you would never want to repeat." I detected a pitying look in their eyes as they relayed this information, which did not bode well.

The long-dreaded morning dawned when I was due to report to Johannesburg Station at 8am to be herded onto the troop train leaving for Kimberley. My alarm woke me at 6am with Andrew Gold's song 'Lonely Boy', a hit that played in my head for most of that morning, further underlining my sense of isolation and misery. My friend Leon borrowed his father's red Opel Manta to drive me and my small khaki rucksack containing some books, a toothbrush and a few clothes the fifteen miles from Bryanston to Milner Park and then to the railway station, a cavernous metal-ceilinged edifice of criss-crossed steel girders filled with the echoing racket of the thousands of people bustling through it. I joined the swirling mass of strained and confused looking white youngsters congregating on the platform, presenting their call up papers to the brown-uniformed officers who surveyed their flatulent bravado with surly expressions. Mothers and brothers looked on, equally tense behind their supportive smiles. My first impression was that they were all speaking Afrikaans.

I reached the front of the queue and presented my papers to a young corporal who examined the documents and directed me towards one of the carriages. I was surrounded by what seemed like tens of thousands of young men. Until then I hadn't realised the scale of the call up and had never before seen such a huge congregation of young people. Eventually I found myself seated in a carriage with a swarm of butterflies in my stomach.

To prevent myself being consumed by the horrors of the unknown

I replayed the song 'The Universal Soldier' **(See Note 4.)** which seemed most appropriate for that particular journey. I would recite the lyric from beginning to end and then start again, pacing each line carefully until its mantra-like qualities instilled in me a small degree of calm while the railway tracks clattered in the background as the train crawled the 500 kilometres southwards to Kimberley, the town commonly referred to by the name of its famous open-cast diamond mine 'The Big Hole', which is what it would prove to be. I don't remember much about the train ride to Kimberley, except for one incident that distracted me from the misery I felt. As the ageing mud-brown South African Railways carriage pulled up at one of the stations along the way, a group of Afrikaans lads moved to the open window outside which a number of barefoot black children scampered alongside the train begging for scraps or coins. My new mates used a plastic cigarette lighter to heat a five-cent coin held between two matchsticks until it glowed red and at what they thought was the appropriate moment the coin was tossed out of the window into the grabbing hands of one of the eager young beggars whose shrieks brought about guffaws of laughter from the train.

"Bloody doff kaffirs!" said someone, providing an early insight into the mentality of my new companions for the next two years.

"Welcome to the twilight zone," said a voice inside my head.

Diskobolos Training Camp, Kimberley

About six hours after we set off from Johannesburg the train rolled into Kimberley station. There I was first addressed by a name that was to form a common theme for the next two years which was 'rooif', derogatory Afrikaans army slang for a rookie. A rooif is identified by his lack of 'houding', another word that was to appear with monotonous regularity, referring to the carriage of the soldier in terms of his military training. To achieve the correct military deportment or houding, a rooif had to present a straight back, legs stiff, a raised jaw, boots boned to a mirror shine and, even more ridiculous to me, a razor sharp crease in his beret.

    The new intake was shepherded into Bedford trucks for what is known as the 'rooifie ride,' an initiation opportunity for the older soldiers to abuse the new intake. "Ja, rooif, nou gaan jy kak!" they joked as they loaded us into the Bedford. "Now you're going to shit yourselves!"

    The rooifie ride entailed the driver making hard turns to left and right, tossing the new recruits sitting on benches in the back from side to side and inducing a feeling of fear for their lives. Unfortunately, for the intended purpose the underpowered Bedford I was in barely summoned sufficient speed to produce a gentle lurch. The 30-minute ride ended on the sandy parade ground inside the camp known by the pseudo-Classical name of Diskobolos. Thousands of young men stood milling around in the sweltering midsummer heat awaiting instructions, most of us dressed in jeans and T shirts and carrying small rucksacks. Non-Commissioned officers strode around barking orders and reading out names. I was assigned to a group of twelve selected by alphabetical order and led to a berth inside a tent. The first instruction was to wait for further instructions. The first few days were spent being graded and equipped in between long periods of waiting. Hair parade was a long line winding towards a barber with a set of electric shears who gave each recruit a one-millimetre brush cut, the first time I had experienced virtual baldness. Being shorn of hair would require a closer look at the inner person, especially because outwardly we all now looked very similar. The first step in the obliteration of our individuality had been taken.

    After the hair shearing we were led to the quartermaster's section, referred to as 'Stores', where we were issued and made to sign for our basic military equipment:

Boots
Balaclava
Balkie - With the 11 Kommando insignia
Beret - Green

- Browns - Shirts
- Browns - Pants
- Overalls - Brown
- Socks - Brown
- Takkies - running shoes
- Underpants - White
- Vests - Brown
- PT Shorts
- Jersey - Brown
- Groot Jas - Long coat
- Raincoat
- Toiletries Bag
- Web belt
- Shoe Brush
- ID Book Cover
- Towels - Brown
- Sewing Kit
- Rifle R1. Black
- Bayonet - Grey
- Magazines (2)
- Cleaning Kit
- Staaldak - Steel Helmet
- Balsak - Brown duffel bag
- H-Frame Groot Sak - Rucksak
- Ground Sheet
- Chest Webbing
- Dixies - Mess kit for eating
- Waterbottle
- Sleeping Bag & Inner - Brown
- Sheets - White
- Pillowslip and Pillow
- Blankets (2)
- Hangkas - Tall locking metal unit for hanging clothes and storing rifle
- Trommel - Large green metal trunk with padlock.

The design of the bayonet was especially interesting. The top edge of the blade was smooth but the lower edge was a serrated series of rear-facing spikes like fishing hooks, obviously designed to rip flesh on its way back from a good stabbing thrust. This fearsome looking piece of equipment made me wonder just how often I would ever find myself in a life or death situation in which I would have to use it. I signed for the various items as directed and returned heavily laden to my tent to pack and lock the tower of items into the large green metal trommel where they would from then on be inspected daily.

Next came the medical examination. Medical classification determines the conscript's placement within the military. The system is graded from G1 K1 down to G5 K5, the G part relating to physical fitness and the K part relating to any partial physical defects, for example K2 which signifies visual impairment requiring glasses and requiring the subject to be within reasonable proximity to a military hospital. G1 K1 means the subject is fully fit and is suitable for deployment anywhere, whereas G5 K5 signifies a comprehensive unsuitability for military service and summary discharge. The lowest classification that would still remain in uniform is G4 K4, a classification that would involve little more than working short hours while seated in a hospital reception area. Looking back, the prevailing thought is 'if only I knew then what I know now'. I have had collapsed arches in both feet for all of my life, a condition which in some armies would be grounds for exemption. Flat feet would ordinarily result in at least a G3 rating, as someone unable to rely on the ability to walk for long periods would be considered unsuitable for front line soldiery. My lack of awareness of how the rating system works made me vulnerable to the doctor's determination to make everyone G1 K1. When my turn came to see the doctor, I raised the flat feet issue. He smiled knowingly at me as if to say, "That's the seven hundredth time I've heard that one today," and pronounced me G1 K1. "You can always come back and see me if there is a problem," he said and with that I was ushered into the next line, wondering what exactly had just happened. Only those able to produce doctor's certificates indicating an existing condition, I realised, were considered for more careful assessment while everyone else was automatically categorised as being G1 K1. Sitting in my tent that evening I fumed over my lack of awareness of this situation as I could so easily have brought along a doctor's certificate for this purpose.

The new intake slept those first few nights in tents inside the camp in our military issue sleeping bags, waiting for the start of basic training. The atmosphere amongst the troops was sparked with nervous excitement despite the unremitting dry, dusty, clinging heat of Kimberley. I spent whatever waiting time I had reading one of the paperbacks I had packed into my rucksack. Eventually, four days after arriving at the Diskobolos camp, the preliminaries were complete; we were equipped, documented, shorn with one-millimetre brush cuts and were now ready to begin 'basics'.

On the fourth morning, after breakfast parade, we were assembled on the parade ground for a speech by the Kommandant who informed us that the G1 K1 intakes would be transported to a place called 'the shooting range' to commence our training. We lined up to be shepherded into trucks for the 10 kilometre journey to the range on which there no buildings but which was instead dotted with tents. Along the way, sneering corporals hinted darkly at the perils that awaited us there.

"Ja, rooif. Now you will learn what afkak means," sneered the smarmy Corporal Lourens. Crudely translated, 'afkak' means shitting off. Shortly after we arrived we were grouped into platoons and sent, six to a tent, to prepare for inspection. There was a subtle change in the atmosphere. The feeling of brave adventure evident in the smiles and the friendly camaraderie between the stubble-topped young men was turning into something grimmer and more anxious. The majority of Afrikaans speakers congregated in large groups in stark numerical contrast to the small assembly of English speaking boys.

And then, with a roaring torrent of angry Afrikaans expletives emanating from a red-faced corporal like a thunderstorm crashing across a clear blue sky, our basic training began in earnest.

"Sien jy daar boom? Hardloop." "See that tree over there? Run."

It took just a few days at the shooting range for the enormity of my predicament to become all-consuming. I was surrounded by malodorous, half-witted, Afrikaans-speaking teenagers many of whom were missing teeth, being harassed relentlessly by half-witted, worse-smelling animal-like Afrikaans instructors, many of whom seemed to be missing important component parts of their brains. The pointlessness of running around trees, up and down slopes and then around more trees was not lost on me. Any prospective terrors in the guise of military training could not mask the reality of the worst terror of all, the mind numbing boredom that accompanies being placed in a world where all personal choice is replaced by the controlling direction of buffoons charged with physically exhausting you and breaking down any resistance to their authority. With every passing moment my spirits sank ever lower.

During these first few days I encountered people from walks of life I had never imagined. My upbringing in Bryanston had never encompassed travel to any of the low-income rural areas where generations of what were known as 'poor whites' existed. It was like having a front row seat in a surrealistic piece of living theatre. I experienced the joy of meeting and sharing a tent with Jacobus van Staden, from Balthusrus in the Eastern Transvaal. His body language was so submissive that he had the demeanour of a beaten, skulking dog. Having none of his own, he was the proud owner of set of false teeth that he kept in the upper pocket of his brown shirt, whence they would be extracted for use prior to each meal and once used would be returned, unwashed. Since he spoke no English and I would never voluntarily speak Afrikaans I never found out how an otherwise healthy 18 year-old farm boy came to lose all his teeth while so young. He snored like a tractor and he smelt of rancid sweat infused with the carbolic smell of Lifebuoy soap, a brand of soap I knew from shopping trips providing for our servants at home. Lifebuoy catered for the low income sector and its smell reflected its cheapness. Poor Jacobus seemed to me to be representative of an evolutionary stage some distance from the norm.

Until then, I had followed the path of least resistance, accepting whatever lay in store in a blend of curiosity, naiveté and a general hopefulness that I could make the best out of the situation. Now, less than a week after my arrival in what was nothing less than a living hell with all my instincts telling me to get away, I recognised a crisis point.

Seeing the decline in the conduct of those surrounding me to what to my way of thinking could only be described as sub-human, I became afraid for my prospects of surviving intact in the face of the conditions I was witnessing and in which I was participating. It was clear that allowing oneself to forego choice by conforming to the officers' instructions was a destination from which there would be no return. I equated it to voluntarily undergoing a lobotomy in the uninformed hope that maybe things might work out in the end.

Much of the conversation between the troops over the past few days had centred on the question of whether one could kill another human being if one had to. As usual, my opinion was entirely at odds with the consensus since I felt strongly that even in a war situation the decision to take another life should not be automatic but should be subject to microscopic consideration and not be entered into with only the instruction of another as the sole compass. The value of any soldier's measure is in terms of following orders without questioning them and I understood that this process of breaking down the individual's resistance to produce a form of automaton who would respond without the distraction of a functioning moral compass was not something I could be a part of. Becoming aware of this manipulation of the minds of young boys toward such an unholy purpose horrified me. I could find no justification in continuing as a compliant part of this mind-desecrating process.

Worse still was my disappointment at being shown so graphically that the value system, the ethical code we present as evidence of humankind's ascent towards civilised behaviour can be so readily unwoven after just a few days of sensory overload, turning almost anyone into an unthinking automaton ready to perform any task without compunction, be it killing or maiming. I believed that once this ability to decide for oneself had been given away, it could never be reclaimed. In the final analysis of what is right and what is wrong I saw this as being entirely wrong; submission to the will of another to the extent that you would kill at their command was to me, quite simply unacceptable.

I already held a firm position in respect of the importance of a rule of law in any social order. I understood the need to train an army to that end as well as for the defence of the nation but my issue was with the blanket conscription policy that enlisted an entire generation without consideration for the various layers of personality patently unsuited to this forced interaction. There were enough hard nuts around suited by aptitude to the role of soldiers. It was no more than appropriate that the standing army should rely on their number for its manpower requirements. I felt like a victim of mistaken identity. I had no business being there. They had no business forcing me to stay. I wanted nothing to do with their war against reason and my anger and resentment burned ever brighter. Clearly, I had been conscripted into a war and I was very clear on the nature of the enemy.

Between the running, the route marches, the food queues and the regular bouts of being screamed at by moronic imbeciles impersonating human beings, my position within the SADF soon revealed itself as a matter of life and death and, as the corporals repeatedly reminded us, a matter of life and death it was. A four per cent fatality rate among conscripts undergoing basic training in the SADF was acceptable. As Corporal Lourens declared with a leer: "Ja, troep, we can legally kill off four per cent of you fuckers in basics, no questions asked. It's up to you if you want to be in that four per cent."

What Lourens had said meant that of the thousand young men

under the control of the basic training instructors, forty could legally be worked to death and no explanation would be called for and no responsibility taken for what would be seen outside the military as, at the least, culpable homicide. I wondered how animals like Lourens chose their victims and even if, on occasion, they had deliberately killed a young boy, only to congratulate each other after the event. I had to work at not developing a pathological hatred towards the rulers of 11 Kommando, from the lowest NCOs with their pigswill morality to the Kommandant and his more refined version of the same affliction, aware that hate inevitably consumes the hater.

In essence, the challenge for the instructors was to break down each individual trainee both physically and mentally and then recreate the individual as a soldier. Taking a position contrary to the status quo would improve one's chances of making it into the permitted four per cent victim quota. With every passing moment my anger increased. The daily ordeal at the shooting range was a well-considered breaking down method that included sleep deprivation, assaults on the self-esteem, (although curiously they had a law preventing actual physical assault, probably because the fatality count may otherwise have become embarrassing even to a corporal in the apartheid army), by shouting loudly and by ensuring total physical exhaustion. The daily training regimen entailed running huge distances in the hot sun while carrying weights, being screamed into hundreds of push-ups often whilst weighted down and being guided into a wide variety of carefully designed physically debilitating activities. Many of the trainees broke down from the ordeal, collapsing in a breathless agony of vomiting and demoralisation. I came perilously close to collapse on several occasions, mostly as a result of the pain caused by running with flat feet inside military boots. I would stuff wads of tissue paper under the arches of my feet in an attempt to offer some arch support, but this was never successful.

There was a word supposed to encourage the suffering troop, 'vasbyt', which translates as 'tight bite'. Anyone who has experienced going beyond the point of physical endurance to find that the mind and the body can operate on a new higher level of pain management understands the meaning of the word 'vasbyt'. Although I was in good health and reasonably athletic, I objected strongly to being forced to obey commands, especially when the sole motivation appeared to be the perverse whim of the instructor.

On my fourth night of basic training, as I lay exhausted on my bunk bed with the sound of my Afrikaans tent mates snoring all around me, I considered my options with thoughts sharpened by the clarity that comes from staring close up at one's own mortality. The bobsled of my hopeful outlook that until now had carried me down the icy chute of least resistance was now crashing through the rails. If I allowed myself to continue being carried along by events, I was sure my very existence would be in jeopardy. This 'thief in the night' realisation had sneaked up on me that the time for action had arrived. That moment of clarity that would transform me from someone to whom things were happening into someone who made them happen. My life had been hi-jacked by people determined to mutilate it, with a determination so fierce they were prepared to kill to achieve their ends. This was the 'line in the sand' moment when in my head I declared: "So far and no further".

As I lay in the tent listening to the snoring of my malodorous tent mates I felt a strong escapist urge to start walking and not stop until I got to the coast where I would find a ship to take me to anywhere far from this morally diseased place. I visualised the process for a few moments, relishing the imaginary feeling of closure that simply walking away would bring. Then, as usual, the left side of the brain kicked in. Deserting a fighting army was punishable by death, or worse still, a long spell in the detention barracks.

Along with conscientious objection and flight, walking out was not an option. I had lasted four days so far and though I dreaded the fifth, I resolved that whatever they threw at me next I would find a contrary position if it killed me, a possibility that could not be ignored. I was angry enough to engage with my tormentors.

Within the first week of arriving in Kimberley, I had found a powerful if unlikely ally that would serve me well during the challenge ahead. Standing in one of the long boring lines in Diskobolos, I accepted the offer of a Marlboro cigarette from one of my fellow inmates and from the first lungful of that toasted Virginia tobacco flavour I was home, safe in the warming embrace of cigarette addiction. I was a natural addict, evidently born to smoke. It was nothing less than total unconditional love from the very first moment we found each other.

Before even a week had passed after tasting my first cigarette, I was a fully accredited top rate tax-paying citizen of flavour country, blossoming effortlessly into a 20-a-day smoker. In the calm moments that these cigarettes enabled, I was able to crystallise and focus my thoughts and transform them into action. Disabled as I was by circumstance, cigarettes enabled my re-acquaintance with self-control and I very quickly embraced the control element that smoking cigarettes represented. In my diminished circumstances where I no longer had the deciding say over the basic choice aspects of my life including when to go to the toilet, when to sit, when to stand or when to go to bed, lighting up and inhaling was one way in which I could regain some measure of control. That night, lying awake in my bunk bed at the shooting range and trying to contrive a working plan of action, I stepped outside into the warm evening air wearing only a pair of underpants and lit up a cigarette. Being several hours after lights out, the camp was completely silent and bright stars blinked overhead as I inhaled deeply while pondering how to improve my situation. I recalled hearing somewhere about a branch of the SADF called the 'Entertainment Corps', an elite unit comprised of top quality musicians seeing out their national service by performing shows. I wasn't sure if I was just triggering a memory of desperate hopefulness rather than actual fact however I was able to put this reservation to one side and, focussing on this spark of clarity and optimism to light my way, I decided that joining this unit would become my sole objective. I would get out of this dead end and into the Entertainment Corps. At last I had a goal. And as the enabling second part of my target setting, I resolved to withdraw from participation in what I believed was ritual abuse masquerading as military training. I flicked the butt of my cigarette onto the dusty ground and returned to my bunk buzzing with a new confidence. I thought of the Sfakiano resistance fighter and the Gestapo officer flaying him with a razor. If he could take them on, so could I. My alter ego was about to kick in.

    The following morning talk at the shooting range was that the G1 K1's of our intake were about to be shipped out to Walvis Bay in South West Africa. Morale had plummeted as a result since Walvis Bay was well known as a place with nothing to offer beyond sand dunes, broken spirits and the prospect of being sent to the border. I knew I would be unlikely to survive in that environment without being killed or acquiring permanent damage. Whatever the cost, I had to get off the list of candidates for basics in Walvis Bay. The alternative didn't bear thinking about. In the meanwhile, there was the not so small matter of surviving the shooting range to consider. The days would start at around 4.30am with a wake-up yell through the tent flap by the instructing corporal. This signalled a 30-minute call before the pre-breakfast inspection, enough time to dress in browns, prepare the bedding, tidy the kas and shave with cold water. In the course of this pre-breakfast inspection the instructor would deliberately find fault with one of the 'weaker' troops, whereupon the entire platoon would be called out to be told that they would now have to run and kak because so-and-so couldn't fold his bed linen properly. With that we would all go scuttling off amid curses toward the designated tree for the wake up run. Often the guilty party would be held back until the troops had completed the first leg of the circuit so that he would be running towards them on their return leg, thereby enabling the more committed amongst them to throw a punch at the unfortunate as they passed.

    The early morning ritual complete, we queued for breakfast, which meant a porridge concoction and half a litre of tea drunk from a Dixie, the metal holder for the military issue water bottle which fixed onto the belt. The tea was always Rooibos since somebody in Stores, no doubt related to someone who dealt in it, had decided that caffeine-free tea should become the norm. Never was a cigarette more welcome than in the breakfast queue at 6 am after running two miles and having had to watch a youngster who had already been cruelly mocked as being too thick to fold his own bedding being assaulted along the way. The tranquillising rush of cigarette smoke provided a welcome salve to the open wounds of my festering reality. The rush of clear thought that accompanied the first deep inhalation of smoke was like a recharging of hope and an anaesthetic for my pain.

After breakfast came the first parade of the day. Dressed in browns and carrying R1 rifles we would report to the parade ground for several hours of drill. "Links, jahks, links, jahks," screamed the instructors, ("Left, right, left, right"), as we were taught in groups of twelve to hold our rifles in the correct position whilst walking in step. Hour after hour we stamped around in the dust, pausing only occasionally whilst the instructor identified another victim to use as an example to instil a motivating terror in the rest of us. The customary punishment of one hundred push-ups was regarded as marginally preferable to running the gauntlet of head-on punches.

Step one of my emerging plan to escape from Diskobolos was to put in a 'verklaring' or declaration requesting a transfer. This was achieved by speaking to one of the English speaking instructors who arranged for me to be driven back from the shooting range that afternoon to HQ where I was taken to the adjutant's office and given the necessary form to fill in by his clerk. It was a meeting plotted by the fates. The adjutant was a Lieutenant Whitely, a Permanent Force member on his second star and soon to become a captain. Whitely was an ambitious young man in his early twenties, abundantly possessed of the traditional Afrikaner qualities that I had come to despise most. As it happened, the writing of that verklaring proved to be fortuitous in more ways than one. It was this document which brought me to the attention of the chief player in the Diskobolos hierarchy, Kommandant Van Rensburg. I was given the 'Application for Transfer' document and directed to a desk where I could complete the form. In the 'Reason for Transfer Request' section I wrote 'Musical Talent', suggesting that the army would benefit by transferring me to the Entertainment Corps. With the form filling duly completed I was driven back to the shooting range in one of the ubiquitous matt brown, long wheelbase Land Rovers. Within minutes of my return I heard the news. It had been confirmed that the entire intake was being shipped out over the next few days. All G1 and G2 troops would be moved to Walvis Bay to complete their basic training and troops classified G2 K2 and downwards would be transferred to Jan Kemp Dorp, the ammunition dump situated near Kimberley where they would be assigned guard duties for the next two years.

Walvis Bay

No two other words could have borne more menace. Located on the desert coast of South West Africa, Walvis Bay had the reputation of being the worst possible posting for basic training. Not only was the camp surrounded by dunes that provided an ideal opportunity for the notoriously sadistic instructors to exhaust the trainees ordered to run up and down them, but the thousand mile distance from Johannesburg meant that weekend passes would be complicated and shortened by the travelling involved. Worst of all, because of its proximity, Walvis Bay was a direct funnel for the manpower needed to protect the border, in other words, a shortcut to the abattoir.

    This was not a good time to be G1 K1. News of my inclusion in this shipment brought out the worst of my dark fears. I struggled against the cold embrace of growing terror, trying to drive it away with mantras like "Please dear Lord help me out of this", not that I believed in a listening Lord but because I had found that as a means of calming the brain of raging energy the repetition of a mantra has its benefits. So determined was I that Walvis Bay would not feature in my destiny that I resolved that if I were made to get on a plane to Walvis I would choose instead to shut down my will to live. Within hours of being transported to the airport for the flight to Walvis Bay and consumed by sheer desperation I decided to try my luck back at the HQ. I managed to wangle transport from the shooting range to the HQ under the pretence of having a verklaring in process that was due to be completed that day. The gods of good fortune were home more than once that day, firstly by ensuring that the proto-Nazi Adjutant Whitely who ran affairs at HQ with an iron fist and would in all certainty have told me to get on the plane without further delay, was absent when I showed up and then again when I was told the next most senior figure would see me. This turned out to be a career officer, Major Van Der Riet. After a short wait, I was ushered into his office. Van Der Riet stood to greet me. He was unusually tall and unusually well spoken. Crucially, he was a fluent English speaker.

"What can I do for you?" he asked.

"Sir, I think there's been a misunderstanding," I replied. "I am waiting to go to Pretoria to join the Entertainment Corps but my name appears to be on the list for Walvis Bay. It seems quite senseless to send me all the way there just so I have to come back next week to go to Pretoria. The thing is, I'm not a soldier at all. I'm a guitar player. Walvis is just a tremendous mistake, both for me and for the military. It's somewhere where I can do nothing to help the cause. Whereas in Pretoria at Entertainments Corps I can contribute by doing something I'm really good at."

Van Der Riet looked at me with a perplexed expression and, in another of the curious twists that were to characterise my time in the military, unexpectedly showed great kindness.

"I see," he said as I finished my monologue. Silence reigned for a few minutes while he pondered and my life's prospects flashed in a show-reel before my eyes.

"I'll tell you what I'll do. I'll assign you to an admin position here in the base for the moment while we sort out what happens next. At least that will keep you in the camp."

With that welcome pronouncement, I was placed on a very short list of conscripts who would stay behind to ensure the continuity of 'vital' camp services. As I walked away from Major Van Der Riet's office I felt exhilarating relief as though I had been reprieved on the steps to the gallows. I watched from the side of the parade ground as the other conscripts dressed in their browns and laden with their brown bags formed long brown lines for the rows of brown Bedford's to transport them to dusty Kimberley en route to Walvis Bay and, in some cases, death.

Eventually an instructor appeared with orders for me to wait in the duty room until the next Land Rover left for the shooting range and to be on it. When I arrived back at the range, it was unrecognisable from the place I had left. Without the teeming multitude, it looked like little more than a makeshift tent village in the middle of nowhere which in fact is what it was. The few instructors left behind quickly confronted me as to why I was still there. Their disapproval of a G1 K1 evading transfer to Walvis Bay was more than evident.

That evening while I had dinner in the mess tent with the remaining troops, all of whom were G3 or G4's destined for Jan Kemp Dorp, I was repeatedly approached by the remaining instructors asking variations in Afrikaans on "What are you doing here? Why are you not on your way to Walvis?"

The following morning as I was walking to the toilet, the obnoxious Lance Corporal Van Schalkwyk, one of the loudest and most enthusiastically Afrikaans of the NCOs at the shooting range, suddenly reared up in my path like a venomous snake and with a conspicuous lack of originality roared in my face:

"Jou rooif! nou gaan jy kak!" (You troop! Now you are going to shit!)

His sadistic intent was unmistakable. Isolated on the shooting range as we were, I was in no doubt that subservience to his authority would lead to a sequence of physically taxing demands which would last up to and include my collapse from total exhaustion. With the clarity that identifies defining moments, I recognised the opportunity to inaugurate my new campaign of non-compliance. I felt more like a big right boot hovering over an odious sweaty worm than a troop cowering under instruction from an officer. The adrenaline of confrontational aggression ran freely through my veins.

It bears mention at this point that the climatic conditions in Kimberley in January are particularly hot and dry. My medical background includes having broken my nose as an infant with the consequence of regular nosebleeds throughout my school years. I knew by experience that on hot dry days, days such as this, my nose was just a light tap away from spurting blood.

"Now you're here I'm going to see that you fokken KAK every single day. You're G1 K1! You should be on your way to Walvis Bay. You're trying to gyppo the army but never you mind. We'll start with push-ups. Give me one hundred!" he barked in his brusque Afrikaans.

"I'm afraid I can't do that," I replied, in a voice barely louder than a whisper, looking him straight in the eye, committing a grievous affront to the authority of a junior officer by speaking English.

"Wat se jy?"(What did you say?) he shouted, pumping his chest out in an apoplectic paroxysm of outrage. The thought that he would hit me crossed my mind. Instead he spluttered violently before shouting "WHY NOT?"

"Because I have to go to sickbay," I replied calmly in little more than a measured whisper.

"Sickbay? Why? What's wrong with you?"

"Blood nose" I said, still looking him straight in the eye as I tapped my nose with my right hand. Perhaps given the gravity of the moment I tapped a little too hard, because there followed an explosive discharge of blood, splattering against his face that was pressed up close to mine and then running in a steady flow down my chin. I made no move to staunch the flow, instead silently staring him down until the glazed anger in his eyes was replaced with a new look of stunned disbelief. "Not something you've seen before, you fuckpig," I thought. I suspect that in that moment of spurting blood he did not notice my hand tapping my nose, rather that his eyes had just seen a nose inexplicably explode right in his very face when he must have been close to thinking of ways he could cause that very reaction. The effect on his confidence was very much as if he believed he was somehow responsible. The colour drained from his face as his arrogant braggadocio gave way to a little-boy look of confused terror.

I was exhilarated by this newfound experience of power. I felt as if I had struck him a blow more powerful than a right hook to the jaw. He was speechless. With my shirtfront drenched with the blood still running freely from my nose, I addressed him in a whisper.

"Sickbay."

I turned my back on a thoroughly wrong-footed corporal and headed for the bathroom. After cleaning the blood off my face and neck with cold water, I spent the rest of that day lying on my bunk reading a book. I saw Corporal Van Schalkwyk only once after that. Some days later I noticed him approaching me from a distance, walking at a brisk pace in my direction. I saw him recognise me and saw an almost instant change in his stride before he abruptly turned to a new course on the other side of the road, avoiding any eye contact. I'm sure Corporal Van Schalkwyk wondered about our meeting for some time to come. This small but significant incident bestowed the added benefit of setting something of a precedent. There would be no more running around trees for me at the will of a shit-for-brains. I was not bothered again by any NCO for the duration of my stay on the shooting range. Perhaps they decided I was dangerously insane. I learned from that bizarre incident that the clash of wills in the setting of the Diskobolos HQ was usually won by the side prepared to go the farthest.

The following night was my last at the shooting range. The rows of tents with the flaps neatly tied back ready to welcome the next batch of unwary conscripts gave the place the sullen, haunted feel of an ambush. The only people there were three NCOs and me.

The majority of the NCOs we had met during those first few days had left with the troops for Walvis. One of the remaining three was from Johannesburg and since he spoke English he and I sat at the same table as we ate the army dinner. That night represented a brief respite between storms. It was the first occasion since I had arrived in Kimberley that I was able to hold a conversation with an English speaking person who did not seem to be detached from reality.

That night I realised with amazement that I had been in the army for just seven days. In that brief time I had been turned from a gentle contemplative and idealistic musical, medical student into a paranoid tightrope walker contemplating the razor's edge of my own mortality. I had travelled between the terrifying prospect of being shipped to Walvis Bay and the flood of relief that an angel had sent a kindly major to avert catastrophe with a swirl of his pen. One problem still needed urgent resolution, however. I may have evaded the horrors of Walvis Bay and beyond but I still needed to escape from Kimberley. I slept a troubled sleep that night, freed from the routine and the exhaustion of the past week but certain that whatever the next day held in store would not be easy.

I was driven back to the HQ the following morning. The camp was unrecognisable without the thousands of freshly shorn young men in their browns. I was assigned a berth in the residence section and allocated a steel framed bed perched on a shiny linoleum floor in a dormitory that housed around forty people and was linked to a communal shower room. It occurred to me that prison accommodation would be similar.

Backward Christian Soldiers

The next day was the first Sunday in HQ and gave me my first taste of Church Parade. Since this was a Christian army waging a war for God and Country, religion was a key element in the fabric of both South African society and the military.

Church parade started with the assembly of the several hundred mostly medically-unfit troops left in the camp. The regimental sergeant major faced the parade of troops and called out a denomination. Those identified moved to their allocated place.

"Dutch Reformed Church, line up to the left!" he bellowed and three quarters of the group dutifully filed to the left. Then came the call for Catholics, the Protestants, the Jews and so on until finally there were just two people still standing on the parade ground, an overweight fellow with a strange expression that looked like one of permanent disgust, and me.

"And what are you?" the regimental sergeant major barked, looking in my direction.

"Greek Orthodox," I replied.

"We don't have any Greek Orthodox here. You will go with the Catholics," he proclaimed before rounding on the other fellow.

"And what are you?" he asked the overweight soldier.

"Muslim," he said with a look of disdain.

"We have no mosques here. You will have to pray by yourself."

My curiosity as to how they approached religion was sufficiently piqued as to agree to attend the service and so although confident that I could have refused to enter any church other than my own, I went inside the Catholic section in a hall in which the service had already begun. The gist of the service became clearer as the priest, a man dressed as an officer in military uniform but wearing purple armlets, ranted apoplectically in swirling and thunderous waves of Afrikaans. I was again reminded of a theatre.

"God is great. He is the Almighty Redeemer. He is the Father of all things in heaven and here on earth. He is all-powerful. He is the creator of all that is great. And what are we without God? (Pause.) We are nothing without God. You are nothing without God. God gives us life. He created the Earth for us. For you. God created you. Why did God create you? Is there a reason why? (Pause – go to whisper) Do you think maybe God had nothing to do one day and thought, maybe I will just create man? Or do you think; yes, there is a reason. (Longer pause) You have been chosen by God to protect the Christian women and children from the Godless communist blacks. The Godless, Communist Blacks. (Slow down for emphasis) The dark heathen who will try to kill you and then rape the women and stab the little children repeatedly. But will you allow this to happen? Will you stand by and betray your duty to your families, to the little children, to your fatherland and most of all to your Lord God, the almighty saviour who created you in the image of his own son, who he loved so much he sent him to die for you? (Speeds up tempo and accelerates volume.) A painful death, crucified on the cross to save you. A death with terrible pain, nails hammered through his hands. Nails hammered through his feet. (Roar at full volume.) Crucified in agony and why? (Pause and then continue in a whisper.) Because of your sins. That's how much he loved you, to take that pain to give you a chance for salvation. Did he do all this so that now you can stand by and watch while the Godless (pause) communist (pause) heathen (pause) rape our families? (Another pause. Then start again real slow.) Will you look the other way, with a can of beer in your hand and a cigarette hanging out of the corner of your mouth while the black menace violates your family and destroys your children's lives? (Off again now – building up steadily to a righteous roar.) Or will you stand shoulder to shoulder with your Christian brothers, in a line that no man can break, against these communist animals and smite them with the vengeance of the Lord?"

This sermon was delivered to a hall filled with exhausted young men being kept awake by an NCO walking up and down the aisles looking for any opportunity to slap a dozing lad back into wakefulness.

I felt I had witnessed something ugly and deluded, the most disturbing element of which was the obvious transparency in the argument behind the hostile sermon. Were these people really so dumb that this second rate idiot-speak had them fooled? My conviction that I was in the wrong place was never clearer and my determination to rise above this idiotic brand of madness was never stronger. My objections, though, could not take the form of open attack. I was already familiar with the dangers presented by unguarded criticism of the church and its ways. Although it was some three hundred years since the Christian Church last executed critics of Christianity, (such as the 18 year-old Edinburgh College student, Thomas Aikenhead, who was put on trial for saying, "Christianity is a nonsense", found guilty of blasphemy and summarily hanged), I was only too aware that any comments questioning the church's absolute authority were likely to invite disaster.

The church, and especially South Africa's own variation, the Dutch Reformed Church, appeared to me to represent the very essence of all that was wrong with South Africa. 'Get them while they are young and then keep them through fear' seemed to be their mission, so to speak. I did not attend another church service during the rest of my two years of military service on the grounds that I was Greek and would only attend a Greek Orthodox service. My reluctance to be 'lumped in with the Catholics' meant I was soon known to be exempt from church parade. The irony is that to achieve this I had to maintain the pretence that I was extremely religious.

During the Monday morning parade, those of the intakes who were not shipped out to Walvis Bay were divided into squads of 12 and assigned an instructor corporal who would oversee our continued basic training. The group I was assigned to consisted of G4 K4's but also included two young men who seemed to have difficulty breathing and were awaiting medical discharge from the army. The likelihood of arduous training appeared to be low.

Our instruction in the days that followed took the form of basic skills such as stripping down a rifle, rudimentary bayonet skills and simple tactical instruction. This period introduced me to a dietary lifestyle that was to continue throughout my stay in 11 Kommando. It did not take long to establish that breakfast in the army was not worth attending. I preferred the extra few minutes to myself rather than standing in a long queue with malodorous phlegm-generating Afrikaners to be rewarded with a basic porridge breakfast slopped in a solid grey mulch onto my bowl, usually by a suicidal looking cook whose attention to hygiene had long since been abandoned. Instead, I used that 20-minute respite from the conveyor belt of daily programming to enjoy the day's first cigarette and a piece of chocolate or a biscuit, depending on my stocks at the time. At 11am, training would stop for tea when they would distribute Ouma Rusks. These bulky rusks soaked in tea were a part of my staple diet for many months. My attitude towards dinner took much the same turn. After two attempts at 'dinner parade', I retired in disgust. The food was simply not worth the time it took to queue for it. The first dinner parade involved a smelly stew of some kind with bits of fatty meat streaked with sinew floating in oily water, served with mashed potato that tasted like cardboard and smelt of infection. I never visited the mess hall for another meal for the duration of my stay in Diskobolos.

George the Driver

Around this time I became friendly with another Greek from Johannesburg, an 'ou-man' (an old man, as servicemen in their second year were known), who worked as the duty driver. He was known by all and sundry as George the Driver and his job involved delivering and collecting people or goods from Kimberley town in a Land Rover or sometimes a Bedford truck. George was an immensely likeable fellow who seemed able to befriend anybody, even the dumbest Afrikaners. We soon established a pattern whereby George would stop at a local drive-through take-away joint each evening on his return to camp, where he would pick up a Dagwood for me. A Dagwood was the popular local version of a club sandwich, comprising a burger, a fried egg, onion, relish and melted cheese across three layers of toasted bread. Though it was usually cold by the time it reached me, on most days this would be my only reasonable meal and being such it was always welcome. Rusks, tea, Dagwoods and chocolate provided 99 per cent of my food intake during those early months, accompanied by a steady, continuous stream of cigarettes.

Within the first two weeks back in the camp I had my first taste of guard-duty. Guard-duty involved a 12-hour shift of four hours on, four hours off, along with the often repeated information that if a guard falls asleep while on duty in a fighting army, the penalty is death. We were split into pairs and each issued with five rounds of live ammunition for our R1 rifles. I had never fired my rifle, but the thought of having live ammo added an edge of excitement to the experience. George the Driver transported my guard buddy and me by Land Rover to a tower overlooking one of the camp walls where we would stay for the next four hours. Conversation between us was limited. Mostly we smoked and drank cans of Coke, waiting for the four hours to end before returning to the guardroom where we would be able to snooze for a few hours in one of the bunk beds before being woken for the next shift. Four hours had never passed more slowly. I resolved that if ever I stood guard-duty again I would be sure to bring a book. Back in the guardroom I heard talk of the Jan Kemp ammunition dump nearby to which unlucky medically unfit troops were sent to see out their two years as sentries, working four hours on and four hours off, day in and day out. Many of these troops lost their minds to the draining madness of sleep deprivation interspersed with long periods of crippling boredom. I thought of the medically unfit youngsters in my intake who had that to look forward to. By the end of that evening, guard-duty had been added to my list of things to be avoided by all available means.

On the Friday morning of my first week back in the camp I was summoned by a messenger to attend an immediate meeting with the Kommandant. The visit to Kommandant Van Rensburg's office was a lesson in army procedure. I was brought into the HQ and told to wait on a bench outside his office until summoned. After a 15 minute wait I was summoned into the scary presence of the Kommandant. Kommandant Van Rensburg was a large man and one could tell by his appearance and his houding that he carried himself like a pure Afrikaner. To my surprise he addressed me in English.

"I have your declaration here," he said, waving the Entertainment Corps application form I had filled out in front of me. "Now, you are very lucky," he said, pausing to be certain I would fully appreciate the momentous significance of his words.

"We need a band here in Kimberley and I have decided to start our own band. I have decided that you will be in charge of it."

I remained silent, not at all sure about this development. I wasn't feeling very lucky. This wasn't what I was aiming for at all.

He continued, "I will arrange for you to have a job in our camp bookstore. You won't be doing any training. You will be an admin clerk. You can look after books in the day and at night I will arrange a band room for you with the equipment you need. In exchange, you will lead a band for functions. This is a very good arrangement for you. Congratulations."

"I see," was all I could say.

I left his office with mixed feelings. On one hand, the reassurance of being singled out from the mainstream as having a special skill did provide some measure of encouragement, but on the other I was concerned about the impact of this event on my intention to join the Entertainment Corps. I certainly did not want to spend any more time in Kimberley than absolutely necessary. In the short term though, there was no alternative to compliance and so I asked directions and made my way to the bookstore.

The bookstore

The 11 Kommando bookstore was located in a detached building some five minutes walk from the HQ admin block and close to the rear side of the main residence hall. It was a single storey brick building of around 700 square feet with a front office in which two desks stood at opposing ends and a warehouse area where floor to ceiling shelves were laden with stationery and related paraphernalia that supplied the camp's administrative needs. When I entered, a two-stripe corporal greeted me. Mark Dobson had been placed in charge of the bookstore for the final three-month stint of his military service, possibly by virtue of his degree in English. He was shortly to be transferred out and I was to be his replacement. In the mean time he was required to show me the ropes. This entailed sitting around at a desk for long periods of time drinking copious volumes of tea whilst occasionally fielding demands for stationery emanating from the offices in the HQ. I was to spend many a quiet moment drinking tea and ruminating over the world with Mark, the first articulate person I had come across in my fledgling military career. I was to attend the bookstore for normal working hours between 8am and 5pm from Mondays to Fridays until further notice. Crucially, I was given a key to the bookstore which meant I had a place to go to where I could be alone.

The second part of the Kommandant's instructions for my military service led to the band room. That evening the stern faced adjutant, Lt. Whitely, led me to a doorway attached to a large building to one side of the parade ground. The room was evidently a general-purpose storeroom filled with foam mattresses and chairs.

"We will get all this cleared out for you and you will have a key to this room. You will make it the band room and you will practise here."

Whitely was not a man one could relate to without deep suspicion. Everything about him put my senses on alert. He was around 22 years old, a career soldier. My feelings of revulsion for military service meant that I saw anyone who volunteered to join the Permanent Force as either a limited buffoon or a soldier of darkness motivated by the desire to kill and destroy. I was there because I was forced to be, on pain of imprisonment if I refused. Whitely was there by choice. He told me this with beaming pride and how he had achieved the rank of second lieutenant having graduated from the Commissioned Officers' course in Oudtshoorn. Despite his surname, he was an Afrikaner and was clearly uncomfortable having to speak English, spitting out each word as if it burnt his mouth in a way that reminded me of the headmaster at Bryanston High School. Whitely was evidently the Kommandant's right hand executive and had built his career plan around satisfying the Kommandant's every whim.

"After parade tomorrow we will ask for troops who play musical instruments to step forward and then you can choose the band," Whitely told me as he handed me the key to the band room with the assurance that it would be cleared and ready for use by the weekend.

By this time I had become aware of another curious aspect of being in the military. The rank and file hated nothing worse than one of their own separating from the common swill. I was conscious that the other troops in my section looked at me with the opposite of respect. On several occasions I was approached by Afrikaner lads whose interest in speaking to me appeared solely intended for the purpose of ferreting for information or agitating for confrontation. Walking towards me in a corridor they would veer in my direction, seemingly intent on bumping into me. Invariably, I would be addressed in Afrikaans but I would reply in English and the speaker's hackles would rise visibly before their reply followed in Afrikaans. It seemed important that I should never mitigate my resistance to the Afrikaners and their ways by speaking their language. No subtlety differentiated any of these aggressive approaches. They felt to me like hyenas scavenging for opportunity. It was not an especially advanced skill in discrimination to be able to spot these moments before they happened. If 80 per cent of communication is non-verbal then every time a contact with fellow troops occurred, I would be fairly certain as to the intention. I felt that there was an inevitability about saying the wrong thing at the wrong time that would lead to an assault of some kind.

The number of times I was referred to as 'Sout piel' (Salt willie - referring to people with one foot in South Africa, one foot overseas and the rest dangling in the brine), or a 'donnerse Engelsman' increased and so some pre-emptive tactic seemed entirely appropriate.

Fire with fire

I identified a fellow I knew to be weak-willed and the victim of several beatings, Johannes van Staden, as my confidant in disinformation. One evening, as I saw Johannes walking back to the dormitory, I offered him a cigarette and struck up a conversation. At an appropriate moment I enquired after the circumstances of his enlistment, listening patiently until he got around to asking me the circumstances of mine.

"I had a choice," I told him. "I didn't have to come to the army, because I'm Greek, but the judge said to me that if I did national service, I could avoid going to prison."

"Is it? What did you do?" asked Johannes, his face twitching with childlike interest.

"I don't know if we should be talking about this, Johannes," I replied, looking around.

"Ag come on man, what was it?" he pressed. I lowered my voice to a whisper.

"I got into some trouble last year. I was in a bar and there was, well, there was an incident."

"Ja and then? What happened?" asked my anxious listener, leaning forward insistently.

I hesitated. "Johannes, listen I don't like talking about this because I don't want people to know, so if I tell you, you must promise me that you will not tell anyone else."

"Ja, OK man, tell me." He replied.

"I'm from Jo'burg. I was drinking in a bar there with some friends at the Sunnyside Hotel. This guy started talking to me, some shit about he saw me looking at his girlfriend. I could see he was pissed so I told him to fuck off, but he kept yabbering. Really aggressive. I don't know what happened next. I have no memory of the gap between getting really pissed off and seeing this guy with four bullet holes in him and a warm 9 mil in my hand."

"Is it? Really? Why did you do that?" asked the wide-eyed Johannes.

"I have a rage issue," I said calmly. "It's a problem with losing control when I get mad. It's not the first time I have just lost it. I was expelled from four different schools for the same thing. I don't really remember much because I snap. Last thing I remember is him calling me a fuckin' Greek bastard and then after that I just remember a red mist. It's like I disappear and a different person takes over. The psychiatrists say I have a sociopathic predisposition but I am not sure what that means. I just go from being calm and in control to animal crazy in the snap of a finger. I honestly don't even remember how my 9 mil went from the holster to my hand. I just remember there was noise, flashing light, red mist and a lot of blood and somehow it made me feel really calm. I didn't actually hear a single shot go off, although the cops and the witnesses all said I fired four times. The weirdest thing is, when I realised where I was, I felt amazing, totally relaxed as if I had just had the best sleep. Anyhow, the guy was properly dead, no pulse when the medics arrived and I was arrested. Police took me to Hillbrow cells in handcuffs - not very much fun I can tell you. Hillbrow cells is one rough place. Lucky for me, though, I have a good lawyer who bailed me out the next day and he was able to say it was self-defence. One of my friends in the bar agreed to say he saw the guy take a swing at me first. Then my lawyer did what they call a plea bargain with the court and they offered me the choice between four years in prison for manslaughter or to join the army for two years of service, so here I am. Please don't tell anybody I told you all this, Johannes, I'm trusting you. It's not something I'm proud of. I just want to do my time and then get the hell out of here. And I am going to try really hard to make sure nothing goes wrong again for me." I told the story with a glazed look in my eye, falling so completely into character that by the end of this murderous fiction I almost believed myself.

"But don't you feel bad about killing the guy?" he asked.

"Look, Johannes. Why should I feel bad? He was being a doos and he asked for it. You should never provoke someone you don't know. I mean how do you know the guy your giving kak to isn't a psychopathic killer? You don't. So only a doos would try it on. If you want to be a doos then you deserve what you get. It's the law of the jungle. I didn't do anything wrong apart from shooting him which was his own stupid fault."

With the pale-faced Johannes thus primed, my reputation as a rage driven, psycho killer must have done the trick. Whereas previously oncoming corridor traffic would walk directly at me, I noticed the opposite now happening. Disinformation would continue to govern many of my confidential exchanges during social interactions with fellow troops. The less my army contemporaries knew about me, the better. I am still surprised at how readily people accept hearsay without bothering to check the facts.

The band room

With the band room cleared, the issue of equipment came to the fore. Kommandant Van Rensburg made a deal with a local Kimberley music store whereby they would provide the necessary band equipment and so one morning I was summoned from the bookstore to be driven by Whitely into Kimberly's town centre to oversee the selection of the instruments required for the band. A Shure Vocal master was first on the list, a grey PA system with two speaker towers and a six-channel 250-Watt amplifier mixer, the same PA system Elvis used for his first concerts in the Vegas Hilton. The best guitar they had in the store was a black Japanese-made Stratocaster copy which we took, along with a basic Roland guitar amplifier, a no-name copy of a Fender precision bass and a bass amplifier, a basic drum kit and a keyboard as well as three microphone stands and three microphones.

With this equipment set up in the band room, which by then had been cleared of everything excepting a tall pile of foam mattresses occupying one entire side of the room, auditions for the final position in each instrument commenced. Whitely addressed the troops at the Sunday parade with the announcement that there would be auditions for band members and that anyone with experience should present themselves at the band room after parade. And so I found myself sitting at a table at the head of a queue of several dozen troops. Many of the applicants replied to my first question in Afrikaans, so that thinned the numbers down fairly rapidly. Only one applicant could keep time on the drums, so Toby Steyn got the job. He was an Afrikaner from a farming background with a gentle, submissive disposition and a voice so soft it mitigated the guttural Afrikaans element.

The keyboard position would be hard to fill, as there appeared no one able to play even basic chords. Eventually, Corrie Fourie, an all round anonymous fellow, was appointed as the keyboard player. This was to remain a dynamic role for the duration of the band's life. One other musician appeared, a lad called Dino Theodosiou who played guitar, sang and, crucially, spoke English. Being of Greek origin, he was in from the start.

As for the bass player, none of the applicants had ever played the bass before but as the search was continuing, a wide-eyed young fellow appeared in the band room. Having established that the last remaining post was for a bass player, he said matter of factly: "I can play the bass". They all said that.

"Have you played before?" I asked.

"No," he said, "but I play the guitar and, more importantly, I'm being shipped to Jan Kemp tomorrow which means I'm more or less dead and this is my only chance of staying here."

None of the others had said that. Such disarming frankness made him an obvious choice and so Sean Wege came to join the band and one more slot in the guard's tent at Jan Kemp became available. The following days were spent between the bookstore and the band room, before returning to our bunk beds for lights out. This journey back to the dorm was the time I was at my most nervous due to the patrolling corporals looking for rooifies to practise their malignant skills on, but so far I had successfully managed to avoid any further interaction with army moments.

God

The most difficult time for me was the period after lights out when I would find myself alone with my thoughts and my fears. Invariably, reminders of the unknowns and uncertainties of my predicament would visit. The removal of control over my day-to-day affairs was difficult to come to terms with. Lying in bed at night in the period before sleep gave me a good opportunity to explore my relationship with the concept of God. The wisdom of the saying that 'if God did not exist, we would have to invent him' was never clearer.

As a young member of Johannesburg's Greek community in the 1960s my religious background was probably not that unusual for those from a similar socio-economic and racial background at that time. My mother being a devoted churchgoer, I was christened as an infant in the Greek Orthodox Church. From an early age, I was made aware that Sundays were different. From the moment I could walk, I would be dressed in a suit and tie and made to sit in a big room listening to people chanting in the confusing language that was ancient Greek. Then at Bryanston Primary I would be made to attend Sunday school classes, where, at around the age of seven, I was introduced to the story of Jonah and the whale in the same week that school lessons had introduced the principles of digestion. Putting one and one together, I raised my hand with the question "How did Jonah stay alive inside the whale's tummy?"

"Andrew, he stayed alive because he believed in God."

"But don't whales have digestive acid in their stomachs?" I asked. "And what about breathing. How did he breathe inside a stomach?"

I knew then that their child-duping game was up.

Whilst the beauty of the age-old ceremonies and the opportunity to gather one's thoughts in a calm environment were not wasted on me, the ridiculous notion that there was some invisible white bearded man in the heavens above who made every decision on the minutiae of everything from the number of grains of sand in the desert to the density of every raindrop that fell for all eternity, whilst turning a blind eye to immense and obvious suffering afflicting the majority of the Earth's occupants was, to my mind, quite obviously an argument without substance. I chose therefore to pursue my interests in spiritual growth outside of the guidance of the 'scriptures' and away from those who make a career out of validating and selling organised religion.

I found the Christians who proliferated on Johannesburg's social scene to be offensive and hypocritical, intolerant of anyone not sharing their values and brutally hostile towards any argument exposing frailties in the fabric of their belief without regard for the quality of the argument. Their version of Christianity appeared to me to be no more than a means of avoiding personal accountability whilst validating membership of a clique bonded by a self-righteousness pursued without regard for common sense. In my position, then 18 years of age, lying in a bunk bed surrounded by snoring Afrikaners, forcibly removed from all familiar surroundings and facing thoughts of death on a daily basis, I longed for the possibility that I was wrong about God and that I could say a prayer, abandon my common sense on the altar of blind faith and leave my cares and woes in the hands of a supreme, omnipotent fixer. But even in this dark night of the soul the paucity of this enterprise was evident. No amount of wishing for an imaginary friend to step forward and smite those who would oppose me could change the reality that imaginary friends remain in the realm of the imagination. Instead, I found a routine much like a mantra. This would take the form of a prayer like sequence in which I kept repeating my wishes at that moment. Usually it was: "Give me strength to get through another day", repeated over and over at a measured pace until I dozed off into a fitful sleep. I accepted, with a little sadness, the reality that I was accountable for my own destiny. This was not something I could hand over to anyone else, imaginary or otherwise.

The Muslim individual that I had met outside the church parade on my one visit to that ritual had piqued my interest in finding out more about Islam. I realised I knew very little about this religion and started my quest for information by borrowing from him a hard cover copy of the Quran. Sitting at my desk in the bookstore, with a cup of tea and a Camel to settle me in, I began reading. The start was less than riveting and before long I took to flicking through pages, cherry picking extracts. The first random phrase I memorised was: *'I was shown the Hell Fire and that the majority of its dwellers were women who were ungrateful.'* I read further:

'Oh Women... I have not seen anyone more deficient in intelligence and religion than you.'

It seemed to me that every page I turned expressed views that were entirely at odds with my 'love is the best way forward' approach. Instead, my reading was convincing me that this was a naïve, cruel, condemnatory and divisive belief system certain to bring misery to its followers whilst holding them in abeyance from the truth that would set them free. I found the story of the prophet and his wives to be particularly disturbing. Muhammad's marriage to Aisha, consummated when she was 9 and he 53 left me bemused by the glaring contradictions that Islam represents. The Muslim reverence for someone who we would more readily consider as a law-breaking paedophile serves better than any other example in illustrating the fundamental odds at which evolved western thought and Islam find each other. My last attempt to find sense in the Quran by opening it at a random page and reading what I found resulted in that tasty morsel (fourth Sura; 4.34):

'Admonish those women whose rebelliousness you fear. Shun them in their resting places and hit them. If they obey you, do not seek a further way against them.'

I closed the Quran with the belief that I had been introduced to the cruellest and most cynical of devices for entrenching the ignorant in a mire of submission from whence there was no escape. Apostasy, I was soon to learn, was punishable by death so they had more or less covered every angle. Islam does indeed mean submission, the submission of basic common sense. I related to the victims of Islam, with whom I felt I shared the experience of having been life-jacked.

The time over the next few weeks was consumed by band rehearsals and getting sufficient repertoire in working order so as to be able to perform whilst trying very hard simultaneously to not be noticed by the various officers roaming the campground. The repertoire being rehearsed was mostly popular songs of the day and the band was improving steadily though the songs we played were mostly three or four-chord tunes in 4/4 time. The set list included:

I'll meet you at midnight - Smokie
For a few dollars more - Smokie
Play that funky music - Wild Cherry
Can't get enough of your love - Bad Company
All right now - Free
Jumping Jack Flash - Rolling Stones
Satisfaction - Rolling Stones
I wonder - Rodriguez
I will survive - Gloria Gaynor
Cocaine – JJ Cale
Have to say I love you in a song – Jim Croce

A typical evening would start in the band room at 6pm and we would play through until 9.30 before getting back to the dormitory for lights out at 10pm.

My perspective of time was undergoing re-interpretation. Every day felt like a lifetime of challenge, anchored by the knowledge that two years, an incomprehensible, interminable passage, stretched out ahead. Small landmarks appeared to mark the progress along the way and one of these was the first payday. Unbeknown to me and much to my surprise I found out that the army pay list included national serviceman. About one month into the year, during a morning parade, it was announced that troops should 'aantree' later for Pay Parade. I was intrigued. Asking those around me for information proved relatively fruitless but the overall consensus was that we were in fact to be paid for our services to the nation, whatever those may have been. I was stunned by the thought that what I was experiencing was considered a legitimate enterprise for which remuneration was appropriate, as it was so much at odds with the reality of the experience. Nonetheless, I joined the queue along with the other troops. Hours passed standing in the hot sun as the line inched slowly forward until finally I was the next up. I was issued with a pay book and this was stamped and I was handed an envelope. I felt a small flutter of excitement at the prospect of receiving money until I read the amount written in ink on the front of the pay envelope. 32 Rand, or 1.006 Rand a day. I resolved not to fall again into same the trap of waiting for hours in a queue for virtually nothing and consequently my 11 Kommando pay book was never troubled by another entry for the duration of my incarceration. Subsequent payday calls provided a good opportunity to vanish into the band room as no one would be likely to come and look for me. After all, who would dodge getting paid.

Smoking

One evening in February, Sean and I were the only two to show up for band practice since the rest of the band had been detained on various duties.
 "Have you ever smoked zol?" asked Sean.
 "No," I replied though as a result of my medical school background I did have a well-informed position on cannabis and its effects. I had the good fortune to attend campus lectures at Wits by Dr. Sylvain de Miranda, who presented a drugs, addiction and rehabilitation course that formed the basis of a lifelong interest in the subject. At that stage, being cautious by nature I had never even been properly drunk, never mind stoned on marijuana. Reassured by Sean who professed expert knowledge on the subject, I decided this was a great opportunity to try smoking a joint and at that stage had nothing to lose by experimenting. There was a cassette tape machine in the band room and a collection of

tapes. Our favourite at that time was the new album by YES called 'Tormato' and that was the album playing on this occasion. Sean rolled up a joint known as a three-blader, using three pieces of Rizla paper in an elaborate process leading to the introduction of some crushed buds of cannabis mixed with a small measure of tobacco. The Afrikaans for a leaf or a blade of grass is 'n blaai', a term which made the crossing into general use among South African cannabis smokers and became blurred into the colloquial use of the word 'blade' or its Afrikaans diminutive 'blaaitjie' to describe a cigarette paper. A small piece of rolled up cardboard torn off the side of the Rizla paper pack was fitted into the lip end to form a filter referred to as a roach. Then, in a process requiring considerable dexterity, once the strip of glue on the paper had been licked the cannabis and the cardboard filter were rolled in the paper and a perfectly formed 'spliff' was ready for lighting.

"Inhale deeply and hold it in your lungs for as long as you can," directed Sean, illustrating by example. I tried the process with eventual success. For the next hour I lay on top of a pile of foam mattresses still being stored in the band room, listening to 'Tormato'.

The music seemed to take on a 3D perspective as my senses were swayed in an entirely fantastical way by the drug. The guitar playing of Steve Howe stood out as if he was standing in the room playing his instrument in a way that I had not experienced before. I heard the connection between the rhythms and the notes played in a new and seemingly mystical way. It felt much as if the cannabis had effected the left side of the brain, the logical side, impairing the preconceived receptors and in so doing allowing the right side, the intuitive instinct synapses to process the experience in an unrestrained uninhibited way. It was like experiencing the sound of music for the very first time. I became so completely entranced by the music that the unfortunate circumstances of the recent past were, for the moment, vanquished. For the next few hours, this warm feeling of connection prevailed. When the second playing of the album finished, with lights out fast approaching we rose from our stoned slumber and made our way back to the dormitory. Sean had told me the sensation of being stoned would last a couple of hours, after which there would be no noticeable effect. As I lay in my bunk that night I was still abuzz with the excitement of the experience. I resolved to treat cannabis with caution, starting with the decision not to smoke it again for at least a week to make sure there was no immediately addictive reaction.

In March, by the time the third month of conscription had passed, a routine had become established in day-to-day affairs. The days were spent in the bookstore and the nights in the band room eating rusks during the day and, on most nights, a Dagwood from the roadhouse delivered by George the Driver, all linked by the constant stream of cigarettes and instant coffee. An ongoing state of fearfulness evidently acts as an effective appetite suppressant and I never experienced real hunger. As Mark Dobson had been temporarily moved elsewhere, writing songs alleviated the boredom of days in the bookstore where I was now the sole clerk. I wrote at least one song a day mostly about isolation, dreams of an idyllic promised land or girls. I had several correspondents to whom I would write long, probably depressing letters detailing my miseries as an unwilling conscript.

I advanced my interest in cigarettes by dabbling with brands such as Silk Cut, Benson and Hedges, Marlboro, Gunston and Texan before finding my perfect partner and soul mate in the smoking process; R.J. Reynolds' finest product, the Camel cigarette. One of the slogans used to advertise the product in earlier times was: *'Nine out of ten doctors agree. Smoking is good for you'*. Another was: *'I'd walk a mile for a Camel'*. Later, I was to find out how true the latter slogan was and why. The hit on a Camel cigarette was like nothing else, leading to a numbing sensation that blocked out, albeit briefly and temporarily, any feelings of anxiety about one's predicament. Cigarettes and my obsession to reach the seemingly mythical Entertainment Corps became my twin crutches in these testing times and I would carry two packs at all times to be sure of never running out.

The band was by now capable of getting through a good 15 songs in some sense of order, a fact not lost on Lt. Whitely who made regular checks on our progress. Clearly something about me rankled with Whitely who would occasionally drop by the bookstore unannounced like a little uninvited evil pixie, during which intrusions he repeatedly brought up the unwelcome subjects of training and the border, giving me the impression that he disagreed with the Kommandant's view that I should be spared basic training. On more than one occasion he arrived at the bookstore in the morning to tell me, as if he had taken it upon himself to ensure that I did not miss out on the military training that would make me into a proper soldier, that I was to join the troops for a day of field exercises.

"You will need the training in case one day you find yourself on the border," he would reassure me. Though I was usually able to avoid his recommendations by contriving some excuse or other, one memorable day stands out.

"Today Lieutenant Visagie is taking the troops for bayonet training," announced Whitely. "You will close the bookstore and tree-aan with the troops in front of the parade ground at 8am. I have told him to make sure you are there."

I was moderately curious about bayonet training and decided for once to go along with the orders. After all, the bayonet was a highly unusual piece of equipment that had me marvelling at its advanced design with a fish hook bottom that begged the question "what for" because the obvious answer was too ugly to contemplate. At the given time, I gathered my kit from my kas and presented myself along with a troop of G3 and G4 troops for the day's training. We learned to fix our bayonets onto the end of our R1's, and then, using suspended sandbags as targets, the instructor illustrated the bayoneting procedure. Essentially, you run at the target while shouting at the top of your voice, plunge the bayonet straight in with maximum force, turn it clockwise 30 degrees and withdraw the blade with the same force. The fish hook style barbs on the bottom of the bayonet would then rip out either the sacking of the dangling sandbags or, should the case arise, the entrails of the person you were trying to kill. I ruminated for some time on the horrors of this killing skill. Was there really a circumstance in which this barbaric practice would affect the lives of any of these troops? Without realising it until I visited 3 Mil Hospital in Bloemfontein, I was 'fortunate' to have experienced this moment in South African military history because, as later became clear, ours was the last intake to be issued with bayonets.

In this cycle of bookstore monotony, band practice and the occasional twist of the bayonet, I scraped and smoked my way through the first months. With the initial three-month period of basic training almost over, talk amongst the inmates turned to the longed-for weekend pass. At first, I could scarcely believe they were going to let us go home for the weekend, remaining convinced that the goings on in 11 Kommando must be happening without the knowledge of the outside world. The thought that they would let us out to spread the details of their abusive ways confused my thinking. Not for the first time, I found myself out of tune with the prevailing mentality.

The first believable indication that the weekend pass was to become a reality came with the issuing of passbooks at morning parade. As the bookstore clerk I had forewarning of this as I received a message from Whitely to deliver a box of passbooks and an official stamp to his office. In due course I was issued with mine, which had been stamped and signed by the duty officer and quite suddenly, at four o'clock on a sunny March Friday afternoon, I found myself outside of the gates of 11 Kommando, along with a few hundred other rooifs. We weren't expected back until the following Monday night. Dress code for this outing was 'step-outs', the semi formal outfit consisting of boned dark tan shoes, a light brown shirt with tie, dark brown trousers and a brownish jacket with a balkie or unit crest worn at the top of both arms. The ensemble was finished off with the fetching green beret of II Kommando bearing the unit insignia at the front and creased to a sharp angle following many hours of wetting and pressing. Needless to say, mine was not the sharpest beret in the pack. Whatever sharp angle it did have was down to the five rand I had paid Frikkie Loubser to do it for me. He enjoyed folding berets into an angle.

The first decision I faced was how to make the five hundred kilometre northward journey back to Johannesburg. There was a train from Kimberley station, this being the preferred choice of the majority of my colleagues even though it involved a lengthy wait at the station. In my impatient state and being unwilling to waste even a second of the windfall of a weekend away from the madness, I decided to hitch hike. I walked several kilometres to the edge of town past several other similarly minded troops in step-outs until I found what appeared to be a suitably isolated stretch of road where I turned to face the oncoming traffic holding out my fisted left hand with the thumb turned up. Almost immediately a car pulled over and the first of several rides began. Almost every time I found myself at the roadside hitching the first or second vehicle passing would pick me up. It seemed at that time that the population was generally keen to help young servicemen with their travel arrangements. In less than six hours I was back home in Bryanston, eating a home cooked Greek meal prepared by my Aunt Thea and marvelling at how much had changed in the past three months. The weekend passed in a blur until I found myself back on the road to Kimberley on Monday afternoon, humming the lyrics to 'I am a man of constant sorrow'.

The grind

The day after my return to camp I was one of many troops brought in for questioning by the military police.

"Did you take your rifle with you on pass?" I was asked.

"No," I replied.

Shots had been fired from an R1 rifle from a car leaving on

weekend pass, identified as carrying troops from 11 Kommando. The shots were fired towards a township on the outskirts of Kimberley and a child was critically injured. A few weeks later we heard that a junior lieutenant had been arrested, court-martialled and demoted to private. I suspected that he was punished more for taking a weapon with live ammunition off base without the proper authority than for what he did with it - killing a black child simply for thoughtless amusement.

After I had been questioned by the military police, I was summoned to the office of the Kommandant who wanted to know whether the band were ready to commence working. Even though I said I thought we needed more practice, he informed me that we were due to perform at a function on the coming Friday night.

The occasion of our first gig on Friday 23rd March 1979 was the completion of basic training for the troops in 11 Kommando and Jan Kemp Dorp and the venue was the VTB Hall in Diskobolos, a hall with a capacity of around 1,000. An hour-long drive from Diskobolos, Jan Kemp, as it was known, was the location of a huge munitions store and an infamous posting for those limited by medical classification to guard-duty. Almost any mention of the name Jan Kemp Dorp was accompanied by a look of horror as this was not a destination for the sane.

The Kommandant had arranged a variety show in the hall and we were to be the headline act following the various amateur turns that preceded our appearance. I had been placed twice on the bill, second last as a solo act singing folk songs for 15 minutes and then with the band for our debut performance. Our audience of weary troops dressed in their step-outs must have been bewildered by what they saw which was a procession of mostly embarrassed young men being shepherded onto the stage to perform some brief attempt at joke telling or to demonstrate a magic trick of a remarkably low standard before I was introduced as a folk singer for my 15-minute set and a nerve racking 15 minutes it was, playing to a captive audience of around a thousand young men. I played 'The Universal Soldier' and 'The Streets of London' before being joined by the band for our first gig, introduced by the officer presenting the show as 'the band from 11 Kommando' and we launched into a 45 minute set. We successfully negotiated such popular standards as 'Play that Funky Music' and 'Meet you at Midnight' by Smokie, a band then enjoying extraordinary popularity with South African audiences. The reaction from the crowd when we played was more polite than ecstatic but we were able to regard the gig as having been a success.

While we were packing our equipment after the gig and feeling pretty elated by our efforts, the Kommandant came over to congratulate us and in the same breath tell us that we were to do another show that night, a party for the officers that was to be held somewhere called 'die Oversaal'. "Major Richardson is leaving the unit," said the Kommandant, "and we have decided to throw him a farewell party."

We packed the equipment onto trolleys and pushed it to the Oversaal to set up again for our second show, which turned out to be a massive drinking affair that lasted into the small hours of morning. We played for over four hours. It was a strange feeling. On one hand we wielded the power of entertainers and on the other we were lowly troops who could be ordered at any moment to do push-ups by any one of the audience. The soldier's instinct to be as anonymous as possible was completely at odds with the performer's obligation to put on a show.

The occasion was not without its bizarre overtones. 11 Kommando's Regimental Sergeant Major, RSM Smit or 'Smitty' as they referred to him, had a party trick that he performed during our break. This involved raising a pint glass to his mouth, biting off a chunk, chewing it with a solemn expression on his face and then swallowing the pieces after which he stuck his tongue out to reveal that no shards of glass remained. I supposed this was a means of establishing just how hard a sergeant major could be. Witnessing this behaviour provided me with further reassurance that I was most definitely a very long way from where I belonged.

Following our relatively successful reception that night, the

Kommandant decided that the band was ready to go to work. Forced by this show to decide on a name for our band, the members contributed suggestions. The name we decided upon was 'Winwood'.

Whitely came into the band room the following evening to announce that we were booked to perform at a dinner/dance event for the following Friday night. The 'Rooipan Community Boere Dance' would be our first professional engagement as a functions band.

On the day, we were instructed to report to the band room at noon where we met our allocated truck driver. All of the gigs we did involved travel by Bedford, the lumbering, slow, ugly brown trucks with little to recommend them that were the standard transport vehicle of the SADF. The process of loading the equipment into the Bedford took about an hour, packing instruments carefully into the back before we set off on the two-hour bumpy drive to Rooipan. Although there were two seats in the driver's cab for passengers, most of the time I preferred to travel in the back of the truck with the equipment and the rest of the band. The large pile of foam mattresses that remained in the band room doubled as effective protective insulators for the equipment, as well as providing a fantastically comfortable sleep opportunity in the back of the Bedford. Often this would provide a memorable luxury when returning late at night from a distant venue.

The Rooipan Community Boere Dance

The Rooipan Community Centre people were overjoyed by our arrival. In the farmlands around Kimberley, the Afrikaner community usually had a generous approach to visiting strangers as long as they were white and especially those bringing some gift or benefit, as was the case with our musical show. We were fed home-cooked food and shown to changing rooms. The show started in an atmosphere of enthusiastic interest. During the first set, repeated requests were made for boere-musiek, a distinctive styling of Afrikaner Country music propelled by the concertina and something alien to my musical taste, representing in my view an all round low level both musically and socially. Boere-musiek to me was like the musical equivalent of the cockroach to the animal kingdom. The evening went off well despite the potential for disaster. I noticed the Kommandant was present in civilian clothes and during a break he approached me to say, "Very good, but now you must learn some boere-musiek." I nodded in what he thought was agreement though I was thinking that what he had just said was like asking a Jewish inmate of Auschwitz to memorise 'Mein Kampf'. After the show, we stayed overnight at a nearby farm, by far the preferable choice to going back to our dormitory. After a sound night's sleep on comfortable mattresses we were woken with 'moer' coffee, the strong coffee brewed in the Afrikaans way. We spent the morning enjoying a cooked breakfast in a huge kitchen and being treated like celebrities by our host family who showed me the great respect of speaking in heavily accented English to accommodate my evident inability to speak Afrikaans.

Kellarprinz

Later that day, we were booked to perform during the 1979 Kellarprinz Wine festival held at the local rugby ground. This outdoor event was attended by thousands of hard-drinking Afrikaner farmers. Unaffected by many of the advances enjoyed in the modern world, these farmers were a rough looking lot, most wearing Veldskoene and khaki pants and sporting long beards. Evidently, the majority harboured a pathological dislike of anything English and it was not long before it became clear that our all-English repertoire was entirely inappropriate to the circumstances. Every word I sang seemed to cause them pain, not because I was particularly discordant but because even in the context of a popular song they could not stand the sound of the English language. Their glowering resentment steadily wore me down until my stomach started a sequence of stabbing pains and I began to feel physically ill. This was a truly hideous nether land to be in, a surreal moment in which I was entirely lucid but surrounded by thousands of drunken Afrikaners, many sporting truly revolting bushy beards, who in my mind could just as easily applaud my performance as turn on me in murderous rage if they had realised for one moment the nature of the thoughts I harboured. As the stomach pains worsened, I told Toby when the time came for our first break that I was feeling really sick and that he should carry on without me. I had had enough. This was a no win situation. Sean immediately developed identical symptoms and the two of us disappeared to the Bedford for a sleep on the comfortable mattresses in the back leaving the Afrikaans band members - the drummer and the keyboard player who couldn't actually play any keyboard instruments - to imitate popular Afrikaans songs. Poor Toby had to play the basic boere-musiek beat steadily for the next few hours, a feat he somehow accomplished with considerable aplomb.

Sean, my constant sidekick by then, had an uncanny ability to block out everything except the song in his head. As a musical accompanist he was quite brilliant to work with as his bass playing was structured entirely on following what I was doing on the guitar, a quality that defines the best of bass players. When we were not playing, Sean would be listening to his battery-powered cassette player, entirely absorbed in the album of the moment. He seemed to have found a habitable zone in the surrounding shadows and I was well aware of the benefits his neutral energy and unconditional loyalty provided.

Routine

Back in camp, life seemed to have settled into a new routine. The band's bookings were increasing to an average of two a week, providing much needed relief from the mundane daily patterns. I still felt a lingering insecurity and aching discontent but for the first time since arriving in Kimberley I had brief moments where I could sense the possibility that somewhere beyond the endless darkness a glimmering light was waiting to shine. My guitar playing seemed to be improving and during my days sitting in the bookstore I was writing songs at a prolific rate. On some days, two or sometimes three songs would be written up in the A4 hard covered notebook I had conscripted from bookstore stock for this purpose.

Whiling away the hours in the bookstore gave me the opportunity to brood over the unsatisfactory state of my life. My anger and sense of outrage at the injustice of being conscripted never abated. I would imagine an alternative life scenario in which I had left the country after completing my schooling and headed for the Berklee Music School in the USA where many of the musicians I was listening to worked as lecturers or were graduates. Instead, I was stuck in a place commonly referred to as the anus mundi surrounded by ugly individuals who represented most of the qualities I found least attractive in the human condition and who were empowered by a curious quirk of fate to direct my life and fortunes at their whim. The flames of outrage at this injustice burned ever brighter in my smouldering consciousness, fuelled by the bile of discontent that rose with every sight and sound of Afrikaner nationalism surrounding me.

I was sustained by my determination to get out of Kimberley and into the Entertainment Corps in Pretoria. I still knew virtually nothing about the Entertainment Corps beyond hearsay but the idea of a place where top musicians could see out their military service whilst being treated like human beings was an irresistibly appealing fantasy that I could rely on in the absence of any other faith-based placebo.

The Kimberley Boys' High School Dance

Some of the gigs that the Kommandant and Whitely were booking for us were surprisingly decent affairs. On 10th May, 1979, we were booked to perform at the Kimberley Boys' High matric dance, by Kimberley's standards a most prestigious function. The band was extremely well received by the three hundred well turned out young guests, with rapturous applause following every song. The people in the crowd were all just a year younger than I was and the opportunity to perform for a group of pleasant, nice looking young people was uplifting. Perhaps because of their vocal encouragement we all were at our very best and the band sounded really good. At the end of the evening, the headmaster came over to offer his congratulations and thanks for the "wonderful music". He handed me an envelope with 150 Rand in it by way of extra thanks. Evidently, the Kommandant had charged the school for our services, but the headmaster felt that this tip should be offered directly to the band. It became quite common at these country affairs for us to be tipped in this way. It also became clear to me that evening that the Kommandant was making professional charges for our services.

The Kommandant's turf

The following weekend we were booked to perform at a dance at Jan Kemp Dorp golf club. The golf club was a social focal point for local luminaries and commissioned officers. The Kommandant, clearly a person of some influence and something of a celebrity in the area, was an influential member and booked us to appear in this clubhouse on numerous occasions, each one a trial for the spirit. In response to the numerous requests to play boere musiek I had compromised to the extent of learning one token piece. Soon after our first gig the Kommandant had summoned me to his office to hand me a cassette called 'Boere-Musiek Favourites' with the instruction that I learn the songs, presumably so that he could bask in the band's reflected glory at the Jan Kemp Dorp golf club. Listening to the cassette was agony. To my ear this was music at the lowest level of effort, music made by the ignorant and deluded for the amusement of inbred imbeciles with no single merit to recommend it. Being made to listen to it in this way was to my mind a cruel and unusual treatment. I did manage to identify one track that was marginally less offensive than the others, a piece called 'Suikerbossie' which was rendered in the key of A major.

'Suikerbossie' was an international hit for the South African singing star Eve Boswell during the 1950s and lay so deep in the Afrikaners' musical subconscious that it may as well have been a traditional folk song. I learnt a signature riff on the guitar that hinted at the song's melody and memorised the key line, which was *'Suikerbos ek will jou heh'* which I understand to mean: 'Sugar Bush, I want to have you'. When I played this phrase repeated as a rhyming couplet on an eight-bar turnaround repeated ad infinitum, the audience would erupt into an ecstasy out of all proportion as if an evangelical transformation had occurred. If I had levitated in the middle of the song the applause would have been less. For some reason the sound of an 'Engelsman' playing Afrikaner music had a huge significance to members of the audience. I didn't care as long as it made the nights more manageable and I enjoyed the fact that it was such a contemptuously short snippet showing a suitable disregard for the song-writer's sentiments. I felt reassured that I was maintaining my high average of disdain for all things Afrikaans.

Curiously, there were some English songs that worked particularly well at these country dance affairs, two of which were Neil Diamond's 'Crackling Rosie' and 'Sweet Caroline'. As soon as either of those songs started the room seemed to pant with excitement. I soon recognised that on one level these gigs were providing me with the opportunity to learn the musical entertainer's art, a process of trial and error that eventually revealed which musical choices produced the most desirable reaction from the audience. There was a reliable guide to the lowest common denominator - the more simple the audience, the more they would respond to the basic formula country style songs of which 'Take me home, country roads' was one and Gloria Gaynor's classic, 'I will survive', was another which could be relied on to turn any evening into a riot of a different kind of abandon. Gradually I became more skilful at manipulating our audiences. If well executed, the choices in respect of song, tempo, key and delivery would produce a specific, predictable effect. Pacing the highs and lows across the course of a four hour evening would ensure that the crowd was exhausted by the end, enabling us to avoid playing on ad infinitum. This in itself was a skill of considerable complexity. The old showbiz adage holds that if you start strong and finish strong, what you do in the middle of the set is less important. The wisdom of this soon became evident.

After the golf club show, during which the Kommandant spent the evening beaming like a celebrity, we were packing up our equipment when a local farmer, Oom Kosie Wilson, approached us with an invitation to spend the weekend at his farm. When we left the camp that day en route to the gig, half of our Bedford truck had been filled with chairs and tables. The reason for this became clear when we reached Oom Kosie's farm and were asked to help offload them onto his patio. Apparently the Kommandant and Oom Kosie were old friends. The extent of the Kommandant's benevolent influence within the local community was becoming increasingly clear as I realised where the garden furniture had come from.

Every small moment of joy that music provided only made the return to the reality of the uniform and the dormitory more painful, and I still was no closer to the Entertainment Corps than when I had first applied. As the weeks dragged, on my resolve to re-invigorate the request for transfer grew stronger.

Danielskuil and the guitar solo

While some of the gigs we were booked into were a blessed relief from the day-to-day stress, some had the opposite effect. On the 6th April 1979 we appeared at the Danielskuil Military Display which was to reveal itself as a frightening experience. The crowd comprised mostly thick-bearded, glowering Afrikaners, some in military uniform but all radiating resentment towards us and me in particular as I was the one singing English words, each one of which appeared to be a dagger to their very hearts. After the first song, an officer approached me with the order to play something in Afrikaans. Though he left out the words 'or else', the threat was unmistakable. Not even Neil Diamond's diligent musical distillation of the simple country mentality could save me now. 'Crackling Rosie' fizzled and died. 'Sweet Caroline' turned sour and the face of the officer who had ordered me to play Afrikaans music turned ever redder.

"We don't want to hear any more English songs. Play only Afrikaans music here!" came his next instruction, hissed in Afrikaans through clenched teeth. 'Suikerbossie' was trotted out early in the set and kept us alive longer than might otherwise have been the case but as the set wore on and the crowd became progressively more and more drunk, the levels of their collective anger and resentment became increasingly obvious. I was in a bit of a bind as our ace in the hole, Suikerbossie, drew to a close and struggled to work out what to do next, when my performers skill greeted my survival instinct in a moment of joyous resonance. Suikerbossie was the song they liked so lets give them more Suikerbossie. Just change the tempo a little and play it in a different key.

"Suikerbossie in C, chaps. Up tempo about 10 per cent please," was my instruction to the band and off we went into an extended guitar solo. Eventually, seven minutes later, we had finished the extended version only to find ourselves back in the same position. The red-faced crowd, swilling as they danced from the glasses of 'Klippies and Coke' (the Afrikaner's national drink, Klipdrift brandy mixed with Coke) all turned towards me, staring in a threatening way that read: "If you dare speak one more word of English you are going to be minced and braai'd."

Suddenly, inspiration struck. I had a winning formula and there was no reason to change a thing.

"Suikerbossie in D, chaps," I said. "Lets take the tempo right down. This is the ballad version," and off we went on another seven-minute, three-chord vamp with extended guitar solo. I was incorporating my practice scales into the chord sequence without regard for the song's melody. By now I was starting to giggle with a mild hysteria. What a fabulous position to be in, I thought. We were torturing the crowd with the very thing they had forced us to do. There was no stopping me now. We spent the next hour and a half performing the eight bar section of 'Suikerbossie' in every shape and form imaginable at every tempo and in every key. I had played every scale I knew that worked over a three chord sequence in every speed and alternate phrasing that I could muster, all of which did nothing to disguise the fact that we had spent ninety minutes playing three chords in differing keys at varying tempos over the same bland melody, an insult to any listener with half a brain. On the occasions where I noticed suspicious looks coming my way I discovered a fantastic remedy to allay the doubts of my listeners. I would reach for the microphone and in the appropriate place bellow, with tremendous theatrical confidence 'Suikerbossie.' As if commanded by the gods themselves, this would spur the dancers onwards with a renewed vigour. "Take that you bunch of fuckwits," I thought to myself.

   I remember that night as a towering triumph. I did not end up as minced meat on their braai, but I do think they went home wondering whether someone had slipped something into their Klippies and Coke. I felt a rush of elation afterwards, thinking that I had taken my musical protest to a new high by slipping them this musical Mickey Finn.

   The following night was part two of the same event, with many hundreds of people passing through while we turned out a solid four-hour set. In a soft moment, long after midnight, one of the organisers, clearly a fan of 'Suikerbossie', took a collection for the band, walking through the room with a jug and asking guests to contribute. Watching this gesture, I thought that would at least give us some small measure of recognition for the many hours we had worked that weekend. As I followed the progress of the jug around the room, I watched almost every hand drop some cash and I started the mental arithmetic of guessing how much the jug would total. As the jug man reached the end of the crowd and turned towards the stage, I watched as Whitely intercepted him and took receipt of the money 'on the band's behalf'. I will never know how close my estimation of the amount was, as I never saw the jug again, but I was rewarded by the thought that I had been entirely accurate in my assessment of Whitely as a human being and his position as a representative of the Afrikaner race in general.

Whitely's glowering presence around the band was becoming a real obstacle to any musical progress. The back-up guitar player, Dino, whose input was not best suited to the rigours of the gigs we were being given, was clearly not enjoying the experience. He had become withdrawn in every way. When not playing he preferred to read a paperback and when playing he was seldom audible. Mostly he would just turn the volume down on his guitar and mime. The keyboard player, Corrie, was in a similar position. Musically, it was evident that Corrie knew nothing about the difference between the black notes and the white notes on the keyboard and it was on this weekend in the pits of a hinterland military display that Whitely announced in his musical wisdom the band would have to change. Dino and Corrie were summarily fired. The thought that they would have to return to military training horrified me and I tried to defend their positions for that reason. On the other hand, their musical contribution had been negligible. The main components of the band's sound were essentially my guitar, Sean's bass and Toby's drums, with me as the only singer - not a huge resource pool to draw on for four-hour shows. I never saw Corrie again, but Dino reappeared as an admin clerk in the law office at HQ and remained in the dormitory. He seemed to have a strong survival instinct and looked much happier in his new role than he had been in the band.

We had included a few guest musicians since the formation of the band and one of those was on guard-duty that weekend. Mike Selborne, a tall, dark-haired, earnest young man from the Cape, equally comfortable in English or Afrikaans. Mike had a tremendous enthusiasm that married well with a genuine sense of modesty and he brought with him the added benefit of knowing some suitably idiotic standards. He could do a cracking version of the old songs for which I had no stomach like the Tom Jones classics 'The Green Green Grass of Home' and 'Delilah' whilst playing a reasonable bit of strum guitar. He seemed ideal as a replacement for Dino. The keyboard player who replaced Corrie was Corporal Van Vuuren, our Permanent Force Bedford driver. Van Vuuren had volunteered for the position as he had a 'love of the theatre' though how he thought that might connect with what we were doing remains a mystery to this day. I thought his obvious effeminate qualities were out of place in the military, besides which I already thought that anyone who actually volunteered to join the Permanent Force, as was the case with Van Vuuren, possessed serious issues.

As it happened the nature of our set-up placed little importance on the keyboard player's role, the previous incumbent in the keyboard seat having been notable for his silent approach to performance, getting through every gig without ever actually playing a note. It also made sense to let the truck driver be the keyboard player. The one down side, as Sean pointed out to me later as he rolled a spliff in the back of the Bedford on the way back to Camp, was that we now had 'one of them' in our midst. The other down side was that Van Vuuren seemed to know even less about the placement of notes on a keyboard than Corrie but, as was becoming common, his inclusion in the band was a decision we had to live with for the moment. And so the second incarnation of the 11 Kommando band began. It seemed appropriate to come up with a new name and after an evening of collective brainstorming we arrived at 'Ricochet' which sounded to us like a suitable name for an army band.

From the moment I first boarded the troop train from Johannesburg to Kimberley, one song above all others kept popping into my head. The song was Buffy Sainte-Marie's elegy to humanity's personal responsibility for war 'The Universal Soldier' which contains the words 'He's the Universal soldier and he really is to blame.' *(See Note 4.)*

I knew every word of it and it seemed more truthful and relevant than any other three-minute ditty I had ever heard. This song provided me with the line that determined my reality; if every conscript to war took personal responsibility, there would be no more war. I believed this song represented a class of humanity which included me and to which I chose to belong no matter how costly the price of admission.

With the arrival of May came the first bitterly cold spells of winter. Walking back to the dormitory after band practice, the Kimberley wind was beginning to bite. It was much colder than any memory I had of the winter in Johannesburg. On my morning visits to the bathroom I would turn the hot water tap on to find that nothing happening. The water in the taps had frozen, presenting new difficulties to the daily shaving procedure. Shaving had a high priority in the military with a close shaven appearance being one of the requirements at the daily inspections. When the sergeant major conducted his inspections he would occasionally carry a piece of cotton wool and any troop displaying stubble would have the cotton wool run over his unshaven face and if it caught, punishment drills followed.

In the dormitory in which I was resident, hot water was in any case in limited supply. Invariably by the time I got to the bowl, there would be only cold water left. Shaving in cold water at 6am in sub-zero temperatures was bad enough, but having to break the ice in the tap to get any form of water movement presented a new challenge, one I resolved by the simple expedient of shaving last thing at night. I would return from band practice at just before lights out at 11 and have the bathroom all to myself for a leisurely shave in warm water. It was surprising to me that no one else practised this simple solution.

Left brain right brain

Most nights were made more bearable by the high quality of the spliffs rolled and passed by Sean. Some troops returning from weekend pass would bring back supplies of marijuana. George the Driver occasionally returned from his weekend passes with a collection of bank bags filled with prime buds from Swaziland which he passed on to trusted acquaintances for 10 Rand. This represented astonishing value. I acquired my first stash in this way and at the rate I was smoking it, this amount lasted for several months. On one occasion, George brought a pack with three Malawi cobs - astonishingly high quality cannabis, matured by pressing the ripe buds inside the leaves of a corn cob, tying it tightly with string and burying the package in the humid high altitude ground of Malawi for a few months. Usually Sean would undertake the task of preparing the spliff, crushing the bud into a ground up state, mixing it with some tobacco to improve its burning qualities before rolling it into a three-blader. Sean's numerous attempts at teaching me how to accomplish this discipline proved unsuccessful. I lacked the dexterity and the patience to master the complexities of the three-blader as well as the proper commitment to master a task which represented something of a double-edged sword. To roll a three-blader, the width of one of the three Rizla papers needs careful aligning so that it wraps around the other two to make a perfectly straight joint. My rolling attempts always resulted in a dismal pot-bellied slug that would fall apart if ever lit. Sean would review my efforts with a cheerful admonition as he dismantled the inept attempt at a roll-up and returned patiently to the process of demonstrating the correct procedure.

  As I became more familiar with the effects of cannabis, the novel effect of the wooziness had been replaced by a sense of warm familiarity that was entirely comforting, as if getting wasted was an effective way of escaping the present. As my confidence in being able to conduct myself whilst stoned increased, I was able to experiment with the degrees to which it impaired various abilities. The most significant area in which this effect was to play a part was in performing music. The band's repertoire had by now expanded and we were singing and playing rehearsed arrangements of over fifty songs. This required a reliable degree of motor-control over several interconnected events. The coordination necessary to play moving chord sequences whilst singing, remembering the words and maintaining tempo and pitch conformity was a relatively new skill set requiring considerable discipline and concentration.

  One freezing night in May, my curiosity, along with Sean's encouragement, led me to try playing whilst under the influence. The results were amazing. We were at a rehearsal in the band room. Sean and I had arrived early and while we were waiting for the others he suggested we smoke a spliff and try playing while we were stoned. After a few tokes on a spliff the other band members arrived and we set off on the first song. Even before the end of the introduction we were in a train wreck. I simply could not get through even one verse in the arrangement that we had rehearsed. My access to the programmed learning sequence that enabled words, chords, pitch and timing to meet in a steady and harmonious union was seriously impaired. My short-term memory was sufficiently derailed as to cause me to stop after every few bars to try to remember what came next. Mike and Toby stared at me with bemused expressions. Sean, with his prodigious insight into the effects and benefits of marijuana use, was able to stop his hysterical laughter just long enough to suggest that we tried playing the blues. We agreed on a tempo and a key and got a basic twelve bar groove started in the key of A. This improvisational approach provided instant access to a different level of music, altogether more mysterious and filled with a connection to another world.

  Without rational thought in place to connect logical events, an instinctive connection with a base musical energy replaced the familiar and produced a magical sensation of oneness with music. The experience had a train-like quality. When playing straight, I was the train driver, I chose the conductor, I loaded the passengers on board, took them on a journey, set the speed, showed them the sights, and dropped them off on the other side. I had total control. Stoned, I was a passenger on the train. Freed from the responsibilities, I had only to enjoy the ride, free to have my say at any point in the journey. The process enabled in me a whole new insight into music. I felt I was listening to myself play rather than playing for others to listen, a liberating insight into music that once learned could not be unlearned.

The two other musicians, Mike and Toby, watched us with slightly anxious curiosity as they played along. Mike was not comfortable with our pot-smoking and never participated though he never presented any judgmental stance beyond saying "You should be careful. Drugs are not good for you." Toby, who would have a toke though only on rare occasions, did not experience the same connection with the moment as either Sean or I did.

Our self-appointed keyboard player, Corporal Van Vuuren, seldom showed up at band practice since it had become painfully apparent from the first rehearsal that he was unable to respond to my direction in the execution of the keyboard part to any songs, for the reason that he had no keyboard skills in the first place. His moment in the sun had been long enough to see that he needed more sun screen than he could afford and since discussion was pointless we ignored each other. If I had argued against his inclusion at the outset, his rank and his influence with the Kommandant would have introduced an unbalanced element into the situation. I believed he did want to be a musician but, being unable to play even a basic major chord, he had no clue as to what that involved. So much of his life seemed to be based on delusional belief, this musical ambition at least demonstrated some consistency. The effeminate aspects I saw in his character suggested that even his relationship with his own sexuality relied on delusion. The most flattering observation I could make on Van Vuuren is that he had a neatly groomed moustache.

An unexpected benefit from having Van Vuuren in the band was that he had relayed to his close friend the Kommandant the 'high standards' that I imposed on the musicians in the band, which warranted a comment from the Kommandant during one of the country club gigs he had booked for us. He came over and told me he had heard many good things about how professional the band was and that this made him proud. The informal setting and his unusually relaxed disposition provided an ideal opportunity to raise the matter of my transfer request to the Entertainment Corps. Since I had caught the Kommandant in a good mood he agreed to allow my application to be sent to Pretoria, telling me to come and see him in his office on our return. It took several further reminders of the Kommandant's undertaking to support my request for transfer before I was summoned to Whitely's office to be presented with a document that proved something I had not entirely believed until that moment. The header on the document read 'Entertainment Corps'. It was written in English and it had a comprehensive list of questions relating to suitability for entrance to this esteemed division. Whitely provided me with a seat and a pen and encouraged me to start filling in the form. My excitement at the prospect of this transfer becoming a reality temporarily overshadowed my suspicion that Whitely and the Kommandant would never voluntarily allow me to leave the camp. Regardless, I eagerly filled in the details. When it came to which musical instruments I could play under 'First Instrument' I put guitar. Under 'Other Instruments' I put bass and drums and then paused at the next question.

'Do you play any unusual instruments?'

Aunt Thea Eftihia had brought me a bouzouki on a return trip from one of her annual visits to Crete some years before. It was more of a souvenir than a properly crafted instrument and my attempts to unravel its performance secrets had been hampered by an irregular neck which resisted staying in tune for longer than a few minutes at a time. Frustration with the tuning issue eventually led me to abandon my efforts and the bouzouki found its resting place hanging on my bedroom wall to serve as a decorative reminder of the mystical heritage it represented, pleasing the eye since it could not please the ear. Though I could not claim to play it, I could say that I had grown up in the shadow of the bouzouki. I certainly understood the bouzouki. I wrote the word 'bouzouki' in the blank line under the question and returned the forms to Whitely. What I had written was neither true nor untrue. I owned a bouzouki. I had tried to play it. In an emergency, I could pretend to be a bouzouki player. This was definitely an emergency.

I settled optimistically into the wait for news, which was not long in coming. The manner of its delivery was direct. I was summoned to the Kommandant's office, and arrived with my heart pounding. The Kommandant was uncharacteristically friendly, smiling as he handed me a document.

"Here is a route form for you," he said.

"You will travel tonight to Pretoria. You have an audition with the Entertainment Corps tomorrow and you will be back here tomorrow night."

My heart leapt. Suddenly things were moving and moving fast. In the blink of an excited eye, I was in Pretoria, making my way to an address inside Voortrekkerhoogte that ended with the words ENTERTAINMENT CORPS. I entered what looked to me like the most perfect place on Earth after the horrors of Diskobolos, a wooden frame building with a corrugated iron roof, probably formerly a house converted into a number of rooms for use by the military. To one side was a sign that said 'Office' and I made my way there. I saw troops milling around, smoking and looking at me. They looked so relaxed, I knew with total certainty that I was in the right place. Once I was in the office reception area I was told to wait, until presently I was called into the office of the commanding officer. This was my first meeting with Major Hayden. Although he wore a uniform, George Hayden did not have the look of a military man, his bespectacled slightly rotund exterior revealing a kind persona and a gentleness that I came to recognise as that of the honest musician. He explained the procedure to me. The army had sent through my application. He received two thousand applications each intake. Of the two thousand, he said, five would be selected. What, he asked, made me think that I would be one of those? What followed must rank as one of the more enthusiastic explosions of willingness to impress ever delivered by someone in a military uniform. I gushed on about how music was my life and that playing was the only thing I wanted to do for the rest of my days. I told the major how I was doing gigs in Kimberley all the time but was now desperate to play with more experienced musicians.

He listened sympathetically and then said, "I see from your

application form that you are a bouzouki player."

Though I could see he had an interest in this instrument, this was not, I decided, the time to be completely frank or honest.

"Yes," I replied. "I am Greek, so I play the bouzouki," as if this was a logical inevitability.

"What a shame we don't have one here for you to play," he said.

"Yes, that is a shame," I agreed, hoping not to betray my relief.

Once the interview section of the audition was complete, Major Hayden led me to a band room where a number of troops were standing about their various instruments. I was handed a Fender Stratocaster guitar and told to play along with the band over a number of standard tunes. None of this was too daunting for me, as the first two songs were familiar to me, 'Summertime' in A minor and 'Help me make it through the night' in E. When asked if I read music I answered yes, although my reading was, in fact, poor. If I could be an emergency bouzouki player, I thought, certainly I could be an emergency reader too. Luckily my busking skills, acquired during the hundreds of hours of having to improvise to audiences in and around Kimberley, enabled me to mask this limitation and I came away from the audition feeling elated and confident that I had played well enough to impress.

Before I left for the railway station to return to Kimberley, Major Hayden told me that although he would forward my application, no matter how good a musician I might be many factors influenced the acceptance of national service troops into the Entertainment Corps and there was no guarantee that I would be accepted.

"I will do my best for you, but don't get your hopes up."

As I sat in the train on the way back to purgatory, I didn't allow any negative thoughts to penetrate my cocoon of joy. It all felt right to me. I could salvage something from this sorry and degrading business by joining the Entertainment Corps and enjoying the opportunities to progress my skills that working with professional musicians would enable. Far away in the dark distance the light of hope began to flicker more brightly.

My euphoria lasted for a whole week after my return before I was summoned once more to the Kommandant's office. This, I convinced myself, was the moment where I would be thanked for my efforts with the Kimberley band and given news of my departure date for the Entertainment Corps. When I arrived in the office, Whitely was with the Kommandant who seemed particularly pleased with himself as he toyed with the letter he held in his hands.

"This Entertainment Corps have said you are not suitable," he said with a slight smile. "You see they only take in medically unfit troops. You are classified as G1 K1 and so it is impossible for you to go there. I hope you will see how good things are for you here and make the most of the opportunities you have. This is even better than the Entertainment Corps because you have everything you could want. Here you are a big fish in a small pond. It is much better for you."

I returned to the bookstore reeling from this blow and close to tears, chastising myself for having been so stupid when I went for my initial medical examination. Having flat feet is a basis for medical downgrading in the army and it is a fact of my medical history that I have flat feet. Instead of insisting that my medical report detailed this condition I had allowed myself to be steamrollered into silence by a pushy army doctor and now I had to face the consequences. For the next few hours I was inconsolable, desperately trying to find an alternative way forward until finally a helpful thought came to mind. I had one ally with some influence at 11 Kommando.

During one of the functions, Whitely had brought Major Van Der Riet over to the bandstand, announcing that he wanted to play a song with the band. Van Der Riet indicated that had a vague grasp of the melody of the Shadows' song 'Apache' and once provided with the opportunity he gave it a good go. Since he had helped me with the verklaring I had made requesting a transfer to Pretoria I was friendly towards Major Van Der Riet and encouraging about his musical abilities. Later that evening during a break he bought me a drink and we struck up a conversation. He was fluent in English and seemed uncharacteristically well spoken in comparison with the average Permanent Force member. I thought at the time that he was the first officer I had met whom I deemed worthy of respect quite probably because of the respect he showed me. In the week following that meeting, Major Van Der Riet visited the bookstore and stopped for a cup of tea, uncommon conduct given the prevailing distance between the officers and troops. He seemed genuinely interested in meeting me and hearing my opinion on his various concerns. On another occasion he phoned to ask me if I would be prepared to have an off-record conversation with him, which turned out to be a request for information on the use of drugs by the troops. This issue was becoming a real problem for the military, he said, and this was an area that he wished to research with a view to contributing towards an updating of military policy. His request was that I prepare a report on the prevalence and the nature of drug use in 11 Kommando. Major Van der Riet made it clear that his intention was to understand the issue and that any information would be treated in absolute confidence, saying he had asked for my co-operation because he felt I had the communication skills to accumulate the information he required.

    This was a request I took seriously and considered at some depth. Though I couldn't say so in the report, my own experiences with cannabis formed the basis for some of the information he received in terms of acquisition of prohibited substances as well as the effects of their use within the context of military training. Although I had seen no evidence of prohibited drugs other than cannabis I had seen plenty of demand for other mood altering substances. Some troops seemed to favour glue as the inebriant of their choice though I had also seen people drying out banana peels and smoking them. I had never heard anyone say it produced the desired effect.

    The meeting with Van Der Riet was rewarding in the sense that I felt my intelligence was being given a degree of respect, something not often experienced in the life of a lowly troop. I was able to draw on my experiences at medical school in terms of drug awareness and after I delivered my written report, felt that I earned further respect from Van Der Riet for my insights.

Having dealt with his interest, I felt I was in a position to ask if he might reciprocate with helping me with his advice. I arranged a meeting in his office during which I detailed the extent of my interest in going to the Entertainment Corps and the complications resulting from the Kommandant's and Whitely's stated intention to keep me in Kimberley.

I did consider the damaging consequences that could result if I were too open and honest in my description of events and risk him relaying my comments to the Kommandant, one of the risks being the ever-present if unspoken threat of being sent to the border. In this case, though, my assessment of him as a reasonable human being was accurate and Major Van Der Riet advised me with the same frankness as I had shown in addressing his request.

"Unless you can change your military classification you will not be able to transfer to that unit, so first of all you will need to be medically reclassified. This is not an easy process, but as you have flat feet you could apply on that basis." He went on to explain that I could make a formal request for a medical tribunal to examine me and if that was successful I would be reclassified from my G1 K1 status, thereby removing that particular obstacle from my route to Pretoria and the Entertainment Corps. He told me that the medical tribunal sat every week in 3 Mil Hospital in Bloemfontein and I would need to be referred to them by a doctor.

After this meeting I returned to the band room in a renewed state of hopefulness and spent that evening's practice session writing a new tune for the band. This instrumental piece was effectively a Shadows sound-alike with a strong melodic guitar line, which I named 'Major Van Der Riet' and which quickly become a standard feature in the band's repertoire. On the first occasion when Van Der Riet was present when we played the piece at one of our gigs, I noticed him stopping his conversation to listen. He came over at the conclusion and asked what 'that song' was. Something in the style had clearly caught his attention though I stopped short of offering to teach it to him. If Major Van Der Riet had arrived during band practice unannounced he could have found out more than he needed to know about cannabis smoking among the troops without having to ask.

Following Major Van Der Riet's advice I resolved to have myself reclassified. First, I needed to get an appointment before the tribunal and the first step on that road would be to see the camp doctor and register my condition. At the first opportunity, I presented myself at the sickbay and after a short wait I was shown into the doctor's office. I explained the problem of my flat feet, judiciously exaggerating the extent of the pain that this condition caused me. Since he had heard this tale many times in the past from troops looking to dodge army service his first reaction was dismissive. I persisted, however, eventually resorting to remote control rank-pulling to make my point.

"Actually, I am here on instructions from an officer. Major Van Der Riet told me to come and see you when he saw me hobbling on the parade ground yesterday, so this is not just me making something up," I said. This seemed to do the trick. The doctor agreed to recommend me for an appointment at the nearest military hospital where medical classifications were reconsidered, which was 3 Military Hospital in Bloemfontein.

I had never been to Bloemfontein before but the very mention of the name filled me with premonitory horror. Bloemfontein was deep in the Afrikaner heartland. It was the capital of the Orange Free State, the most Afrikaans of the provinces and a place I would never under any normal circumstances choose to visit. Despite this, I left the sickbay feeling elated since I had caused a positive action. For once my action had caused a reaction and events were in motion.

Crossing swords

On Saturday, 9th June 1979, Ricochet was booked at the Kimberley Golf Course for a dinner dance. It was our second gig of the weekend and by our usual standards it was a smart affair.

The Kommandant was present in civilian garb as was Whitely, resplendent in his step-outs with his two stars gleaming brightly on each shoulder, beret pressed to razor-sharp perfection and a mirror shine on his boned shoes that would have made any skirted damsel nervous. As usual, Whitely was attempting to impose his presence on the proceedings. He would tell us when to start the set and, had I not insisted on breaks, he would happily have kept us playing non-stop all evening. The simmering mutual antipathy was becoming an ongoing feature of every show he attended but on this night his overbearing attitude was so pronounced that it brought matters to a head. The evening was going well from the band's point of view. The crowd was responding well and the pacing of the evening was well within my measure. At the appropriate time, not least because I needed to visit the toilet, I announced the band would be taking a break. Whitely felt in some way diminished by this loss of control and promptly came on stage to tell me to continue playing. "I will tell you when you can stop!" he snarled. Buoyed by the fact that the night was going extremely well and that I was largely responsible, for the first time in the six months that I had known Whitely I openly challenged his authority by telling him that I was going to the toilet and walked straight past him. His apoplectic rage was simultaneously comical and worrying, comical because his decision-making capability was so slow that it looked as if the wheels turning in his head were affecting his balance. As he was in a smart establishment in full sight of refined civilians who might not be familiar with the more rough edged extremes of military existence he couldn't scream and rant as he might ordinarily do on the parade ground. His rage was worrying because I knew with all certainty that he would feel the need to exact revenge for this loss of face. When I returned from the toilet and went to the bar for a drink he approached and leaning over he hissed into my ear: "You're not going to get away with this." As was to be expected, the rest of the evening passed off under a cloud. After we had finished and were loading the equipment into the Bedford, Whitely came over once again.

"The only reason you are here is because the Kommandant wants a band," he growled, shaking with barely contained rage.

"I am going to make sure that every day from now on is a living hell for you. You make me sick."

I was in an invidious position. The only thing I could think of was that if I had any value as a band-leader, then taking that value away might compromise Whitely in the Kommandant's eyes. I too was consumed by a red rage at my apparent impotence in the face of such bitter provocation. I took a gamble.

"In that case," I replied, "I will not be able to play in this band and you can decide how to explain that to the Kommandant."

Though I consider that confronting a bully is the best option in a situation like that, I had no doubt that Whitely was capable without a blink of conscience of putting into place events that would have led to my death.

The ride back to camp was memorably tense. Whitely sat in front with the driver while the rest of the band travelled in the rear, stunned into mournful silence by the likely prospect of the band's demise. When we arrived back in camp, Whitely approached me yet again.

"If you resign from the band I will have you on the first flight to Walvis Bay. By the end of this week you will be on the border in a fighting regiment."

I could think of no reply but stared blankly at him until he turned and walked off and we went our separate ways, our mutual antipathy at an all time high.

Whitely's campaign of revenge started the very next day when a messenger arrived from the Adjutant's office with a note containing the week's guard-duty roster. Up until then I had avoided guard-duty on the pretext that I was needed during band practice but now I saw my name on the list for the next seven nights. I pondered this for about two seconds before setting off in the direction of sickbay. I hobbled in as if I could barely walk. The doctor remembered me from previous conversations. After a brief discussion detailing the extent of the difficulties arising from the damage to my collapsed arches, he summarily issued me with a 10-day admin duty notice, effectively a sick note excusing the bearer from any other duties except the bookstore and the band. I mentioned that I couldn't stand without support and that if I should be given guard-duty I would be in trouble. He added the words 'No guard-duty' to the document and stamped the pink slip with the appropriate official stamp. I had another 10 days' grace from Whitely's best efforts. It was as if a chess game was in progress. In the meanwhile though, there were still gigs to be done. Every weekend saw two or three gigs booked by the Kommandant, with the details delivered by Whitely.

The Pirates

On the suitably ominous date of Friday 13th July 1979 we were booked to entertain at the Pirates Angling Club dance, essentially a gathering of some 200 well-heeled farmers from the outlying Kimberley district. Whitely was there, as was the Kommandant. The atmosphere was subdued. The Kommandant's disapproval of my ongoing attempts to transfer to the Entertainment Corps was evident and as usual Whitely needed no excuse for finding reasons to make my situation uncomfortable. On that night I didn't care. Even the band had become divided over recent events. Mike and Toby had become increasingly alienated from Sean and myself, especially when we were smoking pot. In the Bedford on the way over they had both raised their concerns and advocated the merits of conformity. "All we have to do is play these gigs and have fun and the two years will pass in the blink of an eye," pointed out Mike, whose tendency towards gormlessness was never more apparent than at that moment.

Performing to hundreds of unknown Afrikaans people in these circumstances with the festering disapproval of both the drummer and the strummer pressing hard against my will to succeed, I explored one of the hallowed techniques of the long-haul entertainer in desperate times; the extended, expanded, interminable guitar solo, that was my own version of passive resistance and my revenge on everyone present. I would start the verse with a guitar solo while the band went round and round the chord sequence, while I would go through my full repertoire of scales in the appropriate key until I had exhausted every possible inversion of the notes at my command.

Sometimes I would get away with it for up to 15 minutes before the number of eyes turning to look at the band encouraged me to change key before setting off on another marathon exercise. As we travelled home in silence in the back of the Bedford at the end of the evening I convinced myself without any argument that this was the worst gig I had ever played.

Ave Maria

The following day we were booked to play a wedding in the camp hall. The occasion was the marriage of Sergeant Barnard's daughter. None of the band had ever met Sergeant Barnard or his daughter. In the absence of Whitely, the atmosphere between the band members was marginally improved from the night before and Toby and Mike made every effort to prevent my guitar solo approach. "I could do 'Delilah' if you like for the start of the set," pleaded Mike, remembering that I had previously complimented him on his Tom Jones styling. Sean, on the other hand, applied his usual unconditional support. "I loved last night's solos, man. Best gig ever. Fucking awesome playing. I was tripping."

Sergeant Barnard's daughter had a pleasant enough evening before setting off to heaven knows where on her honeymoon. Mike sang 'Ave Maria' as her wedding dance, on which I managed to keep the guitar solo down to a modest three minutes. During the breaks I seized every opportunity to commandeer food and bottles of wine from the buffet. The cabinet of my Roland JC60 guitar amplifier had a handy lip on the rear side, imminently suitable for storing a few bottles plus assorted sundry items. By the end of the evening I had amassed a sizeable stock, so much so that it was difficult to lift the amplifier for all the additional weight of concealed food. Once the gear had been offloaded back into the band room, Sean and I went back to the bookstore with the pilfered food and wine. Our party had to be in darkness in case any passing guard saw the light on and decided to investigate. We had to do without music for the same reason and our conversation had to be limited to whispers but staying up through the night eating, drinking and smoking spliffs was a welcome though brief release from the military and it did us good.

A day in the life of a bookstore clerk

By the time the first quarter of my term was completed, life in Kimberly had settled into a steady flow of predictability. Wednesday 11th July 1979 was a typical day in the life of an army bookstore clerk.

  I was woken at 5.45am by Corporal Lourens banging a tin mug on the steel frame of my bed. An icy chill greeted me as I left the warmth of my sleeping bag to slip into my clothes, browns, socks and boots. I pulled on my brown army issue jersey and set off to the washroom for the morning's ablutions. As usual there was no hot water and the cold water had icicles in it. In our dormitory arrangement, Sean occupied the bunk to my left and Dino the bunk on the other side. Both stumbled into my vision like morning ghosts. We three alone in this dormitory were grouped as 'Clerks'. Roll Call for Clerks was at 6.50am.

  On that day, Lance Corporal Meder was on aantree duty, calling names from a clip-board. As soon as my name was called, rather than falling into the breakfast parade line with everyone else, I made a discreet beeline for the bookstore, letting myself in and locking the door behind me. I fired up the electric heater and switched on the kettle. Breakfast was a cup of sweet tea made from Five Roses tea bags brought back from weekend pass, served with two Ouma rusks consumed while sitting on the floor pressed up against the heater trying to get warm in the near freezing conditions. I put my album of the week into the cassette player in the bookstore on, on this occasion Al Stewart's album 'Time Passages'.

Nourished by tea and rusks I set about the day's first task, which was cleaning up the mess in the bookstore after the previous night's revelries. The previous evening, Sean and I had returned to the bookstore after band practice to smoke and drink tea until late into the night. Having cleared away the remains of this minor revel and by now feeling wide awake, I settled down at my desk to read a paperback copy of 'The Devil is Alive and Well and Living on Planet Earth' by Hal Linsey.

At around 7.30am there was a knock at the bookstore door. Lyn had arrived. Lyn Bursough was a lance corporal in his second year who had recently returned from the border. He had been allocated the bookstore job with me for his final month before leaving at the end of July. He was pleasant enough company, relieved just to be finishing with the army. As we drank tea and chatted he asked me about a 'standing order' book in which officer's document the standing orders determining procedural requirements. I shared with him the trick of amending the page order to write new standing orders. We finished our tea and he left. Time was moving very slowly.

The bookstore was connected to the central phone system, which meant I was able to dial into various offices. The switchboard operator had the power to grant an outside line and I made every effort to befriend whoever was on duty at the time. Before long I had acquired a sufficiently formidable repertoire of phone conversational skills to ensure that my every request for an outside line was successful. Having this access to free phone use was a real treat and occasionally a life-saver when I was able to call up a friend in the outside world for a morale-boosting chat.

Oom Jimmy and Waltzing Matilda

Eventually the phone rang. This time the caller was someone asking for 'Oom Jimmy', an obscenely overweight Permanent Force lance corporal who ran what was called the 'AWOL' office, a windowless room located just a minute's walk from the bookstore that was basically an obscure and pointless lost property graveyard for items of little or no value that had gone astray. Oom Jimmy was a 'poor white' Afrikaner who had been given a meaningless job in the army by the Kommandant to provide him with some relief from total poverty. Loyalty towards their own underclass was common amongst the Afrikaners and members of that poor white underclass were often moved about geographically into irrelevant civil service jobs and accommodation in low income housing projects which would ensure their voting loyalty in areas where the National Party wanted to be especially certain of retaining their influence. The Kommandant almost certainly initiated the AWOL office as an excuse to create the job for Oom Jimmy. He didn't go as far as putting in a phone line, however, and so on the few occasions when anyone wanted to speak to Oom Jimmy they called the bookstore and I would call him to the phone. I tried many times to engage him in conversation but he spoke very little English. Then again, he spoke very little Afrikaans either. His vocabulary indicated a degree of mental retardation. Oom Jimmy was severely challenged, cripplingly obese and physically repulsive with three grotesque warts battling for prominence amidst an assortment of black-headed boils disfiguring his neck and face. He was slow-witted and coarse but the worst thing about Oom Jimmy was his smell. He stank with a viciousness that gave me cause to review my understanding of the very concept of smell. His was a malignant rotting-flesh reek so offensive to the nose that a single whiff would bring an involuntary retching impulse to even the strongest stomach. In another circumstance it may well have been declared a dangerous weapon. I reached the AWOL office to find it locked and so was fortunately spared a blast of Oom Jimmy's stench.

  My daily measure of the passage of time came through the songs I lost myself in. I would listen to whatever music I could lay my hands on and on this day I had borrowed an album, on cassette, from one of the English speaking troops. When I returned to the bookstore, I put it in the player. It was a Larry Norman album. I soon dismissed the first few songs as they were no more than variations on 'I love Jesus. Yippee. Lets all love Jesus.' But then the fourth track, '666' caught my ear, an intelligent gospel song by the mellifluous Larry, a born-again Christian with a lovely voice and a percussive finger picking style. This song had something about it. I was motivated to get my guitar out of its case and work out the picking sequence. Whilst engaged in this endeavour Mike arrived at the bookstore door. He always appeared slightly nervous when addressing me, choosing his words carefully in a way that I noticed did not apply when he spoke to other people. Mike told me he had just been talking to someone about the wedding gig we were booked for that coming Saturday and had found out that the bride's name was Matilda. Bursting with excitement at the very thought, he announced what he obviously considered a brilliant idea for making the wedding memorable. "We should do 'Waltzing Matilda' as the opening waltz!" he declared momentously.

I looked at him. "That's good thinking, Mike," I said, lost for any alternative reply.

He bustled off in his ecstatic cloud and I put on a cassette of 'Questions' by the Moody Blues.

'Why do we never get an answer, when we're knocking at the door, with a thousand million questions about hate and death and war?'

Seeing that the hands of the clock had reached 9am, the current yardarm for the first spliff of the day, I rolled a half a single-blader. This involved crushing and cleaning a small bud from my modest but high-quality stash and rolling it into a single Rizla paper, filling less than half of the length of the paper. This would effectively provide one good toke before burning away, a quantity that was optimum to my requirements. At the rear of the bookstore was a window that could be opened slightly to blow away the lung full of used smoke. A Camel left burning in the ashtray at the front of the bookstore made me reasonably confident that the smell would not give me away. With the comforting buzz of the cannabis making its cheering way through my central nervous system, I returned to my desk and carried on working out the finger-picking routine that I had chosen as the day's guitar exercise, disregarding any recent mention of 'Waltzing Matilda'. By the time 10 o'clock had arrived, I had mastered the Larry Norman finger picking exercise and was now feeling restless and in need of a little social distraction. I decided to pay a visit to Dino in the law office, which was located in the main HQ building. Dino had somehow secured the job of law clerk, specialising in the expert form filling which had made him invaluable to the camp hierarchy. We enjoyed a cup of tea sitting at the desk in his office chatting about the various comings and goings in our lives.

As I was leaving, attempting the same exit anonymity as had accompanied my arrival, I walked straight into the twisted Corporal Lourens. Seeing me apparently unburdened by any task, he ordered me to help him carry tea for the officers. In my lightly stoned state, buzzing pleasantly from my nine o'clock half-blader, the prospect of serving tea to officers was less than appealing but I made the most of it by pocketing at least half of their rusk allocation. With the tea serving task complete, I made my way back to the bookstore, pockets bulging with freshly commandeered Ouma rusks, enjoying the sensation of having struck another small metaphorical blow against the evil regime.

Back at my desk in the bookstore, the phone rang. It was Sean, calling all the way from the Post Office room five hundred metres away.

"Why don't you make a little better and I'll come and visit you?" he suggested, using one of the many code words for a joint. I rolled a single-blader this time and waited for him to show up. Although it was only two hours since the day's first toke, I found that the effects of the cannabis were showing a diminishing return with the first toke of the day being much more rewarding than the subsequent intake. I had also noticed that eating just after smoking caused a marked decrease in the efficiency of the cannabis, sobering me up more or less straight away, something I never thought to include in my report to Major Van der Riet.

   Although the bookstore was half a kilometre from the main HQ building, walking and smoking simultaneously was an offence posing its own risks, even beyond the fact that what we were smoking was an illegal substance. The way round it was to light a cigarette in case we were approached so that we would appear to be smoking the cigarette. The agreement was that who ever was holding the joint in the event of a bust would be required to swallow it, causing the miraculous disappearance of the evidence. On this day however none of that was necessary and having had a good few draws on a most satisfactory spliff we returned to the bookstore. It was lunch-time and Sean had to return to the Post Office room so I was left alone in the bookstore for a few moments before the door opened without the usual courtesy of a knock and there stood Oom Jimmy.

   He had seen the note I left for him regarding his phone message so I showed him to the phone, any feelings of sympathy for his abject condition alternating with total revulsion promoted by his nauseating stench. Flies buzzed in intoxicated formation around his head, seemingly unnoticed by the object of their attraction. He was like a living cartoon caricature of a fat, smelly, ugly idiot. I made another cup of tea while Oom Jimmy grunted through his mono-syllabic call and left, closing the door behind him. As soon as he had left I opened the door again to allow fresh air into the room since Oom Jimmy's vile legacy of stink had superior lingering properties that would require the smoke from several Camels to counteract the fallout. I had the radio on when the song 'Knock Knock Who's There?' sung by Mary Hopkin came on, causing my mood to take a severe downturn. Invariably the songs that come into people's lives have a governing effect on their emotional state but this song was especially saddening, causing me to wonder what musical production skulduggery enabled such a frail and pretty voice to transmit such sadness.

   I spent the next half hour sitting back in my chair daydreaming, fantasising that the phone was about to ring and that the genial voice of the Kommandant himself would boom: "Pack your bags. Your transfer has come through. Congratulations and I hope you enjoy the Entertainment Corps." The phone suddenly rang to shatter my reverie. Sadly it wasn't the Kommandant calling with glad tidings, it was Lt. Cilliers with a request for stationery.

With the weekend gigs coming up we had a band practice scheduled for that afternoon. Mike had wangled an early start for us from Whiteley on the pretext that we would have to learn 'Waltzing Matilda' with which he was apparently now obsessed.

At 1.35pm, Mike phoned to say he was ready so I locked up the bookstore and set off for the band room. We tuned up and ran through a few standards, trying to get into the mood for the wedding. A fun-filled and rewarding run through was in progress until we were rudely interrupted by an unwelcome visitor; a new officer in the camp, Lt. Wright, announced himself as duty officer saying he had come directly from Whiteley's office with orders for me.

"I have tonight's guard-duty roster from Lt. Whiteley and you are on it. You must report to the guardroom at five o'clock."

My spirits plummeted. I had got away with it for so long but now it seemed Whiteley had timed his move to perfection by springing it on me at the last minute so as to limit the time available for coming up with a viable excuse. There seemed to be no way out. In my sudden despondent state there was no point carrying on with the band practice. The last thing I needed was to be a party to the playing of 'Waltzing Matilda' so, much to Mike's disappointment, I called an end to the rehearsal and returned to the bookstore for solace. Sean accompanied me and we sneaked in unseen, locking the door behind us. While I made yet another cup of tea, Sean rolled another spliff to top up the cannabinol levels. I had to present myself at guard parade at five o'clock that afternoon complete with rifle and helmet. I had exhausted every possible device for avoiding guard-duty and it infuriated me that Whiteley's malignant persistence had finally paid off.

En Garde

Guard-duty starts with an assembly of the twelve guards who work in pairs. The guards assemble in the guardroom before the evening's festivities kick off with a roll call and a bit of flag-raising. The order to salute the flag started me giggling at the ridiculous nature of this ritual but luckily the duty officer didn't take issue over my hysterical fit. After the flag saluting ceremony we returned to the guardroom to read the roster. Mike Selborne had been put on duty along with me, one of Whiteley's little niceties. Ours was the 10pm to 1am shift.

The duty office was right next door to the guardroom, so I called in to see if George the Driver was there. He was, and he laughed at the news that I was finally doing guard-duty. "So Whiteley managed to get you in the end," he chuckled, my ongoing conflict with Whiteley being no secret amongst those who knew me.

"Luckily I have something to cheer you up," he said, producing an impeccably rolled three blader. George and Sean were closely tied in first place as the best joint rollers in Diskobolos. "Best Durban Poison," he assured me. We walked out along the perimeter fence and smoked the entire joint. I had a few hours to kill before my turn on duty arrived so to reciprocate I invited him back to the band room. George was a keen drummer and but for fate would gladly have been drummer in the band. Mike needed no persuading that a session in the band room was a better option than snoozing in the guardroom before standing guard and so he joined us. For the next few hours, we ran through songs at full volume, enjoying the moment as much as possible with George thrashing away at the drums, Mike playing the bass while I made every effort to squeeze more noise out of my amplifier than ever before.

With half an hour to go before our turn of duty, Mike and I returned to the guardroom. We clocked in, kitted ourselves up, took our rifles from the rack and set off to 'guard' the camp. I walked straight to the bookstore, convincing Mike along the way that they would not execute us for deserting our post as at least we would be manning some post or another.

"It's just that our posts will be two chairs in the bookstore," I explained. For the best part of the next three hours we listened to the Rolling Stones, smoked cigarettes and drank tea before timing our arrival back at the guardroom perfectly.

Our second shift was to be at 4am to 7am. By now I was so tired that I passed out on the guardroom bunk provided for this purpose, storing my rifle in the gun rack. I was awoken at 3.45am, feeling pretty rough. Mike and I put on our helmets, picked up our rifles and set off back into the night. This time we headed straight for the band room. Mike assured me he would wake us before seven and with that I passed out into grateful unconsciousness on the stack of foam mattress. Mike woke me at five to seven and we stumbled back to the guardroom in time to make the seven o'clock check in. Cereal and milk were left on a table for the guards coming of shift and we helped ourselves before, without realising that the fates were up to no good, I collected my rifle from the rack and went back to the bungalow for a shower and a shave. I made my way back to the bookstore at 8.30am and rolled a single-blader. I lit it and set off walking across the open ground towards the HQ, when unexpectedly a Major appeared headed straight towards me. I didn't even bother putting it out, just concealing it in my hand as I walked past him. I had arrived at a new point of not caring at all. Had he approached me, I had in mind to swallow the remnants of the spliff and take the approach of "who are you going to believe, me or your lying eyes?"

Having finished the mini-spliff, I returned to the bookstore and put on a Bob Dylan album to start another day in my own little private hell as the words *"Well I would not feel so all alone, everybody must get stoned,"* drifted from the cassette player. The next two weeks flew by in series of carbon copy days that seemed to merge into one long dark night of the soul. At least I had managed to avoid further guard-duty.

On Friday 27th July I woke at 6am All the other clerks had stood guard last night, but I had been excused on this occasion on the basis that I had a sick note resulting from a worryingly serious attack of abdominal pain. My kidneys ached horribly, largely as a result of my unbalanced diet. I was surviving on the three '-ines', caffeine, nicotine and adrenaline, living mostly on Nescafe, Five Roses tea, Camel cigarettes and Ouma Rusks supplemented with the occasional junk food meal and high doses of red meat on the occasions when we were fed at gigs. I felt so unwell that I had brought the bookstore electric heater back with me and placed it next to my bed in readiness for the early morning cold. This meant a better start to the morning, with warm socks and a warm shirt resulting from being draped over the heater. I dressed then shaved in ice-cold water before picking up the heater and making my way to the bookstore for 6.30am. There was no roll call that morning as the rest of the clerks had been on guard-duty which meant they could have an extra hour's sleep. I had settled down with my book and a cup of tea when at 6.40am there was a loud knocking on the bookstore door. Thinking no one could know I was in there I decided not to open it.

The knocking continued aggressively and then moved to the windows. Someone was really determined, knocking so loudly I thought the glass pane might break. I sensed that such urgency could result in somebody breaking down the door so after five minutes of stressing while the knocking showed no signs of lessening I decided to open the door.

There stood the dreaded AO2 'Blikkies' Blignaut, the acting regimental sergeant major. Blignaut was a tall broad man with a pot-belly that hung in a quivering roll over his belt. Possessed of a roaring voice and an anachronistic handlebar moustache that curled in a walrus style up to his rubbery earlobes, this deeply disturbed man-mountain was bellowing at me in window-rattling Afrikaans.

"What the fucking hell are you doing in here? Today is a parade day. Get back to your bungalow and get dressed in your step-outs. I will be looking for you on the parade ground and today you are going to kak!"

I had learned to avoid parades wherever possible, not least because standing around with a bunch of cowed idiots stepping into positions on the shouted commands of jumped up morons was my idea of an entirely disagreeable activity. I was not sure why Blignaut came looking for me on this day - perhaps Whiteley had tipped him off that my marching skills were insufficiently developed or perhaps someone had seen me entering the bookstore and reported this earth-shattering event to the brain-free Blignaut. Anyhow, I had been busted and so would now have to be seen to be obeying. I set of at a brisk pace towards the bungalow and out of Blignaut's sight, burning with anger and feeling more than a little sorry for myself. My kidneys were hurting and I was determined not to go on parade. This was a less than ideal time to pick a fight with the acting regimental sergeant major so I walked into the dormitory, making certain that Blignaut was out of sight before heading back to the bookstore where I quickly unlocked the door to let myself in and locked the door again. I took the heater into the back room and lay down next to it, drifting off into slumber whilst the sounds of the day's parade carried across the parade ground to provide a gentle soundtrack to my snoozing.

At around nine o'clock, once the parade had finished I went to the sickbay. I had been expecting the return of the X-rays of my feet, which were to determine my appointment for a medical tribunal. The doctor looked them over and made a note detailing a booking for me to attend an examination at the hospital in Bloemfontein. I returned to the bookstore where there was a message from Whiteley requesting a selection of books. I was busy putting this order in place when the doorway darkened with the immense shadow cast once again by Blignaut.

"So, you think you can laugh me off?" he yelled. "We will see how loud you laugh now." He paused for full effect. "You will be on guard-duty the whole weekend!" he roared then glared at me, his massive belly quivering sympathetically as he turned on his heel.

I said nothing, knowing that we had been booked for two gigs by the Kommandant who was unlikely to let any mere regimental sergeant major countermand his orders. Blignaut lumbered away and I made my way to Whiteley's office with the books he had requested.

Whiteley was waiting in his office. So was Blignaut. Clearly Whiteley had just told him that I had gigs that weekend and as I entered the room I was met with two pairs of eyes filled with a desperate festering hatred.

"So you laugh me off with guard-duty as well?" continued the corpulent Blignaut, shuddering under the weight of his rage. "Now you will have seven days of extras, starting on Monday." By extras he meant punishment involving following the orders of an officer during an extra hour of drill. Again I said nothing. I knew my current admin duty sick note still had four days left to run. I left the stationery order with Whiteley and returned to the bookstore, feeling terribly down. Waging constant war against petty minds was a tiring business.

The kidney problem which I felt was connected to my prolific caffeine intake had enforced moderation, but now seemed like a good moment to return to the comfort of hot tea. I made the first cup in two days but felt a stabbing pain in my kidneys almost directly after the first sip of tea reached my stomach. I realised I had not eaten since the previous day and decided to treat myself to one of my dwindling supply of powdered chicken soup sachets, a cherished delicacy at that time and on some days my sole source of nourishment. On this occasion it soon had me feeling better. Luckily there were no visitors to the bookstore that morning and I had the chance to sit quietly and reflect. My thoughts were of white clouds sailing effortlessly through bright blue skies to the restful whisper of a gentle rustling breeze.

Shortly before noon the phone rang requesting my presence at an orders group in HQ. All HQ personnel had to attend and as a bookstore clerk, this included me. We convened in the courtyard of HQ where tea was served and the Kommandant led a meeting inviting comments on various administrative issues. I felt nauseated by proximity to the officers. Every one of these people turned my stomach, being to my mind willing acolytes in the service of a great evil. It was all I could do to conceal my revulsion and contempt behind an expression of indifference. Once the meeting concluded, I made my way back via the sickbay. The nurse, Mrs. Dreyer, had asked me for two Koki pens from the bookstore, which in a minor act of bribery I gave her before asking if she knew when my appointment at 3 Mil was likely to be.

"Between three weeks and a month," she replied. This was distressing news as I was not sure I could keep going for that much longer. I returned once more to the bookstore, drank three glasses of water and sat quietly projecting positive images into my conscious mind.

I imagined myself lying in the sun next to my swimming pool and then jumping into the cool water, drinking Steelworks cocktails with my motocross buddies at Kyalami Country Club or lying on the beach in the warm sunshine at Sedgefield. None of these images lasted long enough to entirely support the weight of the black despondency hovering over me.

Someone knocked on the door and Mike entered, his smiling face for once a welcome sight. Despite our many differences I felt a certain affection for Mike and his hearty good cheer, regardless of his lowbrow taste in popular music. He demonstrated an intuitive and well-intentioned concern for my wellness despite the many occasions in which I was dismissive of his wishes.

"Hey man, let's go and set up the equipment for the gig tonight," he proposed, and within a short time I was back in the familiar routine of setting up equipment and getting into character as a performer, which brought about the welcome return of a small measure of wellbeing.

I filled every available moment of the passing days with writing songs. This took the form of a lyric with a chord sequence written above. I wrote in a stream of semi-consciousness style, mostly expressing the sorrow and isolation representative of my parlous state of mind, writing more in desperate haste than in pursuit of a craftsman's perfection. During the evening rehearsals I often would try running through the day's new songs with the band. Though inevitably some worked better than others, some worked well enough to be included in the main set.

One, called 'Insensitivity' became a popular favourite in the band set as well as in my solo routine.

The opening verse went:

'All the joy in the world
On a scale next to the pain in the world
Doesn't weigh the same at all
See this world's so divided and confused
One thing's sure, some will win but most will lose.
How can you feel life. Unless you're opened up to see
The price that you will pay for your Insensitivity.'

With tensions between myself, the world and the people around me steaming up to new levels of pressure, the time spent with the band was among very few opportunities for respite from the struggle of being constantly on the defensive. My relationship with the musical realm felt like the only thing worth living for and the only time I felt anything less than anger or bitter raging despair was when I was playing music.

Along the way the band had become more capable and our repertoire consisted of four hours of cover versions and a half hour set of my original songs. In addition to developing the arrangements for the band I had also been expanding my solo folk-song playlist which by now enabled me to put on a reasonably convincing 20-minute set that included a finger-picking arrangement of 'The Universal Soldier'. I would frequently perform the song as a party piece during band breaks and my performance of this song often generated considerable applause from uniformed soldiers. I was sure they were clapping despite the message of the song and not because of it.

Another audience

On the evening of 28th July, we were booked to perform at a club in the centre of Kimberley but by some arrangement with the owner of the 'Tom Cat' Restaurant, the details of which were never clear, we were told to leave early for our gig and fit in a daytime appearance in the open air that morning.

"How would you like to do a gig in the open air for the people?" asked Corporal Van Vuuren, our Permanent Force driver, 'keyboard player' and confidant of the Kommandant. It was a lovely sunny day and I was in no position to refuse. Before long we found ourselves setting up on a sidewalk in downtown Kimberley. I noticed many strange looks from the town folk passing by. We were after all in browns and this was a civilian area.

The gig being neither a dinner nor a dance, our usual set list was inappropriate and so I decided to treat it as an alternative song gig and take the opportunity to play some of my own songs. With sound check completed, we went around the corner for a cigarette before kick off. When we returned I was taken aback by the size of the crowd that had gathered in anticipation. Up until that point our audiences had been exclusively white but when we returned to where we were to play there were hundreds of people waiting for us to start playing, most of them black. We started our set and as I looked around at the crowd I realised from the reaction from the people in the crowd that most of them had probably never seen electric amplified instruments before, let alone heard the sound of a band performing popular music in a rock style. The looks on the faces in the swelling sea of humanity was amazing to behold. Their eyes were sparking with excitement. The atmosphere was uniquely electric as, for the first time in my life, I looked out over a sea of wide-eyed, open-mouthed, predominantly black faces.

Something about the crowd's fascination made the sound all the more interesting. It seemed the music communicated something more than mere rhythms, words and melodies. Part of my folk set was a version of 'The Eve of Destruction' the 60s protest song by

Barry McGuire and we had it on the bands set list that day.

'So you tell me over and over and over again my friend. You don't believe – we're on the Eve of destruction.'

When we reached the end of the song, a smartly dressed black man approached me and started to shake my hand. Smiling from ear to ear, he pumped away at my hand saying "Thank you, thank you, thank you," seemingly unable to stop himself. He carried on as if waiting for his cue to stop. It occurred to me that this was first time a black man had ever shaken my hand.

Looking around at a sea of faces all gazing happily in my direction while I stood in army browns singing and playing songs encouraging social upheaval I experienced a new and inspiring insight into the irony that was to characterise my military training. During the course of our one-hour show I had noticed a number of people taking pictures. At one point, a professional looking photographer was virtually under my nose, snapping away. Several weeks after the event, while I was in the band room for rehearsal the duty officer arrived carrying a brown manila envelope with my name written on the front. It had been dropped off that evening at the guardroom by a civilian requesting that it be passed on to me. Inside was a set of six high quality black and white photographs capturing the event in crystal clear detail. I never found out who the photographer was or how he knew to send me the photos. The sight of a white person entertaining black people by playing protest songs while in military uniform was probably a first for the good people of Kimberley, let alone the sight of a soldier having his hand shaken at unusual length by an apparently euphoric black person. My first reaction was to wonder if this might be a set-up by the Kommandant and Whiteley or whether it was a more direct message from State security demonstrating that they were keeping an eye on me. I uneasily dismissed such thoughts as having more to do with my growing relationship with paranoia, the inducement of which was another signature of the security apparatus of the apartheid regime.

3 Military Hospital, Bloemfontein, August 1979

As Mrs. Dreyer had estimated it took three weeks before I was summoned back to the sickbay to be told by the doctor that my appointment for a medical at 3 Mil had come through. I was to leave the following week for my appointment on 7th August 1979. I asked if this was the tribunal and he explained to me that it was not. The next stage was to be an examination by a doctor at 3 Mil and if the doctor felt it appropriate, then I would be recommended for the tribunal. I coated his every word with my own blind optimism. It felt like this was a huge step towards shaping my destiny. After all this time, I was close to changing the script of my unhappy circumstances in Kimberley.

It was deep winter by now and the nights had become bitterly cold. Days dragged by as I counted the hours until my trip to Bloemfontein. I was given the appropriate travel document, a route form, and a train ticket from Kimberley Station to Bloemfontein. The train departure was at 6am. George drove me to the Station with the sun still rising above the frozen horizon and dropped me at the station with a warm Hellenic handshake. "Good luck bro, I hope it works out for you."

Bloemfontein is about 150 kilometres from Kimberley, less than three hours by train. From Bloemfontein station I made my way through the sprawling military compound. The whole of Bloemfontein seemed like one big military camp and I felt under constant scrutiny with every step. More than once I saw officers look up sharply as I walked by. My houding was not convincing although I was investing considerable effort in achieving the appropriate stiffness in my walk, as befitted a SADF soldier.

Eventually I found my way to the hospital, a big complex with numerous interconnected wards all serving differing purposes - Accident and Emergency, Tropical Illnesses and so on. My route form led me to a general admissions ward, where I was told to wait until the doctor called me. My nervousness grew with every passing moment. I was smoking at every opportunity and pacing about anxiously until finally I was summoned into the office of Doctor Muller. Appearing before Dr. Muller felt much like going onstage for a performance. The same stomach tingling nervousness that visited just before show time and the same set of small routines kicking in once the curtain rose. Dr. Muller remained seated behind his desk in the brightly lit surgery when I entered, his attention directed at the form at which he scratched away with a black biro. Something about his demeanour made me think of the Gestapo.

"Sit!" he commanded, still without looking up. I moved towards the single chair located in front of his desk. As I sat, he completed signing the document in front of him with a flourish, placing it into a tray to his left. He was a sour faced, thin-lipped individual, in his late twenties. For the first time he looked at me, briefly, before turning to retrieve a file which I recognised as my military file. He opened it and began reading. I sat in silence for the few minutes it took before he finally addressed me.

"So you have problems with your feet?" His tone seemed to invite a reply and I launched into one.

"Yes, doctor, I have flat feet."

"Lots of people have flat feet, what makes yours so special?"

I could sense the conversation drifting away from my best interests and so went into what I thought would be a charm offensive based on my estimation that being a doctor, this fellow would also be possessed of some degree of intelligence.

"Doctor, I know a bit about medicine. I was a medical student at Wits, and so I have some idea about the condition." He interrupted me with a quizzical look.

"You were at Wits were you? Why did you leave?"

"I decided that Medicine was not for me. You see I want to work as a musician and that's really why I am here. I have been accepted by the Entertainment Corps, where I can pursue something I am good at. But the problem is that I am G1 K1 and so I can't be transferred as they only take lower medical classifications. As I have flat feet, I want to be reclassified so that my transfer can go through. I should really have been classified G3 at the first medical because of the flat feet. At the end of the day it's the best way forward for all concerned. To be completely honest, I have no value as a foot-soldier. I haven't done any basic training. I haven't even fired my rifle yet. I am totally unsuited to being a troop. I just play in a band in Kimberley when I could be playing at a much higher level and be a far greater asset to the army if I was in the Entertainment Corps in Pretoria."

I thought I had provided him with ample information to see that the best way forward for all concerned was to agree my immediate reclassification and enable my transfer with all haste. The dark look on his face as he digested my words was the first indication that I may have miscalculated both the man and the moment.

"So your feet don't really cause you problems?" he asked in a manner that indicated no answer was required. "I see here on your file that you played sports for Southern Transvaal, but I don't see any record of any physical disability."

The tone of his voice rang with finality. Muller started scribbling away on a form as the room filled with ominous silence. He placed the form into an A4 manila envelope and lighting a tube of red seal, dripped a small puddle of wax on the envelope then pressed a stamp bearing an intricate design into it, sealing both the envelope and my fate.

"Take this back to your camp," he said in Afrikaans, avoiding my eyes as he handed me the envelope. The interview had taken less than ten minutes. I left the office stunned as this had not gone at all as I had envisaged. So much time and hope had been invested in a moment that had turned out to be something entirely alien to my projections. I had arrived expecting to meet a doctor but I was leaving having met an army captain, a serious miscalculation on my part. Fearing the worst, I made my way back to the Bloemfontein railway station and during the lonely journey back to Kimberley I was left to ruminate that perhaps honesty is not always the best policy. As I sat on the train with the envelope on my lap, knowing in my heart that the contents were not in my favour, I was overcome by the need to end the agony of wondering what Dr. Muller had decided for my future. Being stamped with the ornately detailed and intimidating red seal, the envelope containing the folder could not be opened. Interfering with official documentation was bound to contravene some military ruling promising limitless punishment. I examined the seal closely. It had the military medical insignia on it. The proverbial light bulb flashed on top of my head. I remembered seeing an identical seal in a box filled with the various seals used for various military purposes in one of the bookstore storage units. From that point my plan unfolded with ease. I could open the envelope, read the contents of the file and once back in camp I could go straight to the bookstore, locate an identical brown envelope, re-seal the file into the envelope using the stamp with the medical insignia and present myself at the HQ office as if I had arrived there straight from the station. It was unlikely that anyone would notice the five missing minutes that this enterprise would involve. With this plan in place, I went down the rocking corridor of the railway carriage and into the toilet where I locked the door behind me and tore open the envelope. With my heart racing fit to overtake itself I opened the file to locate the new entry from 3 Military Hospital. My heart sank as I read the words, written in Afrikaans.

"This troop attended medical examination for the purpose of physical evaluation. The troop has complained of flat feet but following examination and evaluation I find that the troop is physically fit. There is no evident ailment to warrant further consideration. The troop appears to be trying to avoid military training. I recommend that he be returned to active duty immediately."

So much for medical school camaraderie, I thought grimly.

The rest of the journey was spent reeling from the blow of my own bad judgment though it was marginally reassuring to realise that my familiarity with the Afrikaner character would not require amendment. The joyful heart that had propelled me towards Bloemfontein that morning was returning to Kimberley station with burnt edges, blackened by bitter flames of resentment.

Back in the bookstore, I quickly located the Medical Corps seal. It only took a couple of minutes for me to re-label a new A4 manila envelope and then light the end of the bar of the red wax to re-seal the envelope, now minus the damning page that would have scuppered any chance I had of ever reaching the Entertainment Corps. Though disaster may have been temporarily averted, I was well aware that the battle was far from over.

Sending in the cavalry

After the disappointment of the interview in Bloemfontein with Dr. Muller I sank into deep numbing depression. All roads out of Kimberley seemed blocked now that the sustaining hope that this trip had represented was gone, along with any motivation to do anything other than smoke cigarettes and lie in the back of the bookstore reading books. The monthly weekend passes only served to remind me how time was passing by while my life stood still. Then another of the significant transforming moments in this story occurred. It happened on my next weekend pass.

   My mother was socially active in Johannesburg's Greek community and the local Orthodox priest and other estimable members of the Greek Community would join the guest list at her frequent Saturday night dinner parties. During the August weekend pass she arranged a dinner party to introduce me to Philip Steenkamp, a friend who had recently joined their social circle who, my mother assured me, was a general in the SADF and worked in Pretoria.

   "Are you sure he's a General?" I enquired, unconvinced.

   The dinner party took place and I met Philip, an amiable fellow with a good command of English. General Steenkamp was clearly enchanted by the extravagant Greek hospitality being lavished upon him and his wife. I was seated on his right and we chatted sporadically through the evening, during which I outlined my hopes of being transferred from Kimberley to the Entertainment Corps in Pretoria.

Although I found the presence of an army officer of such high rank in my home a little surreal, I was well aware that his position carried powers far greater than those dominating life within the Kimberley set up. I made every effort to create a positive impression on someone who might prove influential on the outcome of my quest and the dinner party ended with Philip's jovial assurance that he would do what he could to assist my transfer to the Entertainment Corps.

The next day, my weekend pass ended and I was back on the road to Kimberley, hoping for a car, any car to stop and take me and my cargo of four cartons of Camel cigarettes, a sealed box of freshly baked Greek biscuits and an apprehensive heart back to the purgatory of Diskobolos. 'I am a man of constant sorrow' was the song playing on repeat in my head.

Palliation

The sub-zero winter nights drew to an end in August and with the coming of Spring a new era dawned over the band room in 11 Kommando HQ. I was sitting in the band room with Sean enjoying the newly arrived evening warmth and, as was often the case in our conversations, the subject was cannabis and the various methods by which it might be ingested. Up until then my experience was limited to smoking joints, mixed with tobacco to help achieve a steady burn. I had established my tastes in respect of the degree to which I benefitted from smoking pot was for small amounts, one or two tokes, which put a hazy glow on the proceedings, enough to create an effect but not too much to impair any feeling of control.

On this occasion, Sean outlined the merits of the bottleneck pipe, sometimes referred to as a chillum though that is technically a small clay cannabis pipe originating in India. He explained that it provided a far more intense hit as a greater quantity of cannabinols reached the lungs. Because the smoke output when exhaling a lungful from a neck or a chillum is far greater than that from a joint, finding a place to light up a great reeking pipe with as obvious a smell as Oom Jimmy on a Summer's afternoon presented something of a challenge. We quickly decided against the band room as an appropriate location as a single surprise visit from Whiteley would spell all-encompassing disaster. After a lengthy process of location elimination we eventually agreed that Sean's place of daily work, the Post Office room, was the best venue. Being a Post Office clerk, Sean held a key to this Secure Area and thus we had easy access to it. The Post Office room was located in isolation to one side of the parade ground, a few minutes' brisk walk from the main HQ. It was a prefabricated wooden structure filled in part by a large table and some shelving units. A harsh fluorescent tube filled the area with a hospital glare at all times of day. The biggest risk of being caught in our illegal endeavour was the possibility of being observed crossing the darkened parade ground to get to the Post Office hut. We walked at a brisk pace, as if on a mission to collect post. Once inside, Sean lit a candle to ensure the glow of the fluorescent light did not give away our presence and for the first few minutes I kept a vigilant lookout for any signs of our presence having being detected. Once assured that this was not the case, I watched Sean assemble the ingredients for the pipe.

He held in his hand the neck of a one-litre Coca Cola bottle that had been cleanly broken off in a straight line some four inches from the top. He handed it to me to hold while he rolled some of the silver paper from a cigarette pack into a strip and then into a spiral which he stuffed into the lip end of the bottle neck with two broken off matchsticks in the centre of the spiral to enable air to pass through. This, he explained, is called a gerrik. Holding the pipe vertically he packed some tobacco from a cigarette against the silver paper spiral with his index finger, telling me that the tobacco buffer between the burning embers and the smoker's lungs is known as backstop. Then he filled the pipe with enough cannabis, cleaned of sticks and seeds and mixed with a small amount of tobacco, to make six joints. Once he was satisfied that the apparatus was properly assembled, Sean explained the etiquette.

"You'll be fireman and I'll be the buster. The fireman lights up the pipe, then after that the buster gives the pipe to the fireman and fireman has a hit and hands the pipe to the person on his right, then it moves on around the circle."

He showed me the correct manner of holding the pipe, in the palm of his clenched hand with the burning end encircled by the thumb and index finger. Preparations complete, I struck two matches held together, scraped the sulphur off as Sean had shown me and held the flame against the cannabis. Sean took an immense draw. The green buds crackled and turned a fiery orange as he sucked the air through. Once his lungs had filled he removed the pipe from his mouth and made a point of illustrating the effort he was putting into holding the smoke in his lungs. He held the smoke in for the best part of a minute before he exhaled it in a huge stream that quickly filled the entire room and made him look as if smoke was coming out of his ears.

Since I was the fireman, my turn had arrived. I tried bravely to inhale a similar quantity but found the demands on my throat to be beyond my means and burst into an extended coughing fit. It was to take several attempts before I was able to see the benefit in this method of smoking. Clearly there was a benefit; unlike the smoke from a joint which delivered a moderate hit that enabled most motor functions to continue in some working order, this 'hit' left one completely zonked within seconds. The benefit was that it was a pretty effective means of coping with military service.

We sat about in the Post Office room for an hour or so until we were able to walk straight once more, then made our way back towards the dormitory. That experience confirmed to me my interest in pot smoking was best served by mini joints.

The winged matchbox

As the pot smoking increased in regularity, habit brought with it a slackening of the caution essential when undertaking such high-risk behaviour. One Wednesday evening, Sean told me he had met a fellow in the Post Office room who had some Durban poison, the particularly renowned brand of cannabis that benefits during maturation from the heat and humidity of coastal Natal. He also had a brick bong, an imaginative way to smoke being a brick into which a one inch deep, one inch wide bowl had been ground on one end for loading the crushed buds into, with a thin hole drilled to the other end to which the smoker's lips would be attached. The primary benefit of a brick bong was that the intense heat generated by the combustion of the buds would be cooled by its passage through the cold clay of the brick, thereby avoiding the scorched lung phenomenon. Sean was adamant that I should try this new and exciting experience.

That Wednesday night we were to all meet in the Post Office room to savour both of these exotic delights, the Durban poison and the brick bong. When I arrived some time after nine o'clock, I noticed there were already five or six other troops there. They had clearly been smoking for some time as the air in the room was dense with cannabis smoke which could be smelled from afar. I immediately felt uneasy. There were too many people, there was too much noise and too much smoke. As I was in the process of deciding how best to make my excuses and leave, the door suddenly flew open and harsh zigzagging beams of torchlight broke the candle lit ambience.

"Military Police! Nobody Move!" boomed a loud voice.

Someone turned the light switch on and bright fluorescent light filled the room. I felt my heart had stopped beating as time stood still. Having just arrived I was closest to the door. Two military policemen had moved in next to me and all eyes were on a troop who stood frozen in disbelief with the smoking brick bong in his hand. Talk about being caught red-handed. As my mind raced through the many possibilities that the moment held, I remembered that I had a matchbox containing a bud of cannabis in my pocket. Life changing disaster seemed unstoppable.

Before I could do anything the two military policemen barged past me and made for the troop standing with the incriminating brick which still oozed smoke from the glowing embers embedded in its surface. The poor guy seemed uncertain whether to breathe out the lungful of smoke or keep it hidden in his lungs. A third MP stationed himself in aggressive stance at the door, removing any possibility that anyone might make a dash for it. The two MPs inside the room took the brick bong from the startled troop and began systematically searching him, turning out each pocket in turn and closely examining the contents. I had my hand in my pocket, holding the cannabis-filled matchbox while trying desperately to figure out how to make it disappear. Dropping it in the brightly lit room was not an option as the guard at the door had me firmly in his sight. I would never be able to open it and swallow the contents before they stopped me. It was only a matter of time before they completed the body searches on each of the troops ahead of me and my turn came. And then the miracle happened. As if in slow motion one of the lads ahead of me turned towards the door, his hand over his mouth leaving no one in doubt as to his intentions. As he brushed past me with all eyes on him, I followed in his wake and as he vomited all the evenings' misfortune onto the concrete parade ground outside, I tossed the matchbox into the darkness. As it flew out of my hand, the MP closest to me shouted in Afrikaans "He's thrown something." He ordered me to stand still and turned his torch in the direction where I had tossed the matchbox. I rode the waves of panic that threatened to overwhelm me with whatever calm I could muster as he flashed the torch-light. It seemed impossible that he would not find the matchbox as I had not been able to throw it very far. Another of the MP's approached me.

"What did you just throw?" he asked.

"Nothing," I said. "I've just finished work in the bookshop and I came here to drop off some post. I had no idea there was anything going on."

He looked at me in amazement, probably not expecting such a

firm and confrontational approach to his authority.

The MP with the torch distracted my interrogator when he called back, "I can't find anything!" Seizing that moment of confusion I looked determinedly directly at him and with as firm a tone of voice as I could muster, said:

"This has nothing to do with me. You're doing a good job here. I am going now. Carry on."

I turned and started to walk away across the parade ground. With every step I expected to hear them call me back, but somehow the spell of his disbelief lingered until I had made it to the shadows at the far end of the parade ground. Once there, I sprinted back to the dormitory and into the safety of my bed. Never would I have imagined arriving at an army bunk bed with such joy. I barely slept at all that night, feeling that somehow a mysterious benign force had intervened to guide my fate. I resolved that in gratitude for this small miracle I would take a month off smoking.

Sean didn't return to his bunk that night and it was only later the following morning when he arrived at the bookstore that I heard that all five of the lads in the room had been taken by the MPs to the guardroom and held in a cell until the Kimberley police arrived. This took several hours. They were then charged with the criminal possession of cannabis and released into the custody of the MPs who returned them to the cells for the rest of the night before releasing them in the morning pending charges. My feelings of sorrow for Sean at being busted for something that meant so much to him were matched only by my sense of relief that I had somehow escaped this life-disfiguring experience.

Later that evening, under cover of darkness, I went back to the post office room to work out how the MP had not found my matchbox of cannabis. I looked in the area where I had thrown it and sure enough there it was, squashed flat with the cannabis still inside it. The MP with the torch must have been standing directly on it as he swivelled his torch-beam. By this slender thread of incredible coincidence, I was spared a criminal record and a six-month sentence in detention barracks.

Sean getting busted was big news in the camp. Whiteley, with his characteristic turn of mental speed, soon made the brilliant connection between one band member being a pot smoker and the rest being involved as well. That evening when I was there alone practising scales he suddenly appeared in the band room.

"I see Wege has been caught with drugs," he said in his insinuating sibilant monotone. "Are you also taking this stuff?"

"Lieutenant Whiteley that is a completely ridiculous idea. Of course not."

"Did you know he was taking drugs," he continued.

"No. He never said a thing and we certainly never saw any evidence of drug taking. I think that must have been his first time."

I had already flushed my small stash down the lavatory and ensured that there was no trace of any cannabis anywhere in my possession, just in case. When I met up with Mike later that day he told me he had also been questioned and asked whether any of the other band members were smoking pot, which he too denied. At least we had some solidarity during that difficult time. Sean seemed curiously unmoved by the experience, as if it was an inevitability for which he had long been prepared.

"Legalise it, don't criticise it," had been his most frequent comment on the subject of cannabis.

As the ramifications of the bust dawned on me, my determination to escape from Kimberley reached a new high point. The thought that the joys of pot smoking which made the time in Kimberley barely passable were in jeopardy and knowing I would be in the glare of the spotlight of suspicion for the foreseeable future, I knew that one way or another I had to make the situation change.

The answer came to me in the bookstore the following day. I had to get back to the medical board and convince them to reclassify me and then restart the transfer process. I felt certain that without the hope that this possibility would provide, my defences against the incoming arrows of crippling despair would be entirely overwhelmed. It was abundantly clear to me that I would have to do whatever it took, without limitation, to bend the situation to my will. My conviction to succeed at any price was absolute. Like my Sfakiano ancestor, I was facing an inquisition by fortune flaying the skin of my will with a barber's razor and just as he had done, I would have to stick resolutely to my will to disregard the fear.

The Miracle of Wounded Knee

I concluded that my flat feet remained the best route to reclassification. The problem was that I had already been to the sickbay for this condition and the doctor had already referred me to 3 Mil. New evidence would be needed before I could expect to convince him to send me for a second time.

  The solution was simple. I needed to present a fresh injury, one to make them see that there was an insurmountable problem with my feet. To achieve this injury I considered various options, one of which was to break a bone myself. I found out that those pursuing this option favoured soaking the chosen limb in vinegar as this apparently softened the bone, making it easier to break. I soon decided against this remedy, settling instead on what appeared to be the simplest and most effective way forward, which was to stick with the flat foot theme. I would arrange a truck to drive over my foot, crushing a part of it sufficiently to support the argument that I had collapsed arches.

  It seemed clear to me that given the condition of denial that accompanied the two previous instances where a military doctor was unable to see the absence of an arch in my flat feet, I needed to present a scenario that confirmed beyond any debate that my feet were in fact, unquestionably, flat. The logically sound conclusion was that there could be no better illustration of a flat foot than the presentation of a foot that had literally been flattened.

  I did not enter into this arrangement with myself before giving considerable thought to the consequences. I was aware that the possibility of a lifelong injury to my foot would compromise the sporting activities, which I had always considered one of life's treasures. Nonetheless, all factors considered I found that the best option available to move my desire to leave this place forward was to cause an injury to myself that would necessitate medical reclassification. I felt like a mountain climber trapped alone on a freezing mountain with an arm jammed under an immovable rock, faced with the choice of either cutting off my own arm to live or staying trapped and dying.

Once the decision had been made, fired up with the clarity of purpose I went directly to the duty office in search of George the Driver. Fortunately he was in when I arrived, sitting with his feet up on the duty room desk like a cowboy, smoking a Texan plain whilst awaiting his next driving duty.

"George, I have a big favour to ask you."

"Sure Andy, anything," he replied with his usual congenial smile.

"I need to get back to 3 Mil for reclassification so I can go to the Entertainment Corps. Unless I can show some new reason, I won't be able to go and so I need to damage my foot a little. I have decided that the easiest way is for you to drive a Bedford over my foot."

"What?" spluttered George, causing the cigarette to go flying from his mouth. "Are you mad? I can't do that."

Eventually after much cajoling, convincing and the exchange of five crisp 10 Rand notes, George turned up outside the bookstore in a Bedford.

"Are you absolutely sure about this?" he enquired, his expression mired in uncertainty.

"George if I had a better option, believe me, we wouldn't be here."

I took a deep draw on a Camel, stubbed it out with my right foot in what I considered would probably be its last useful act, extended my foot to beneath the Bedford's left front wheel and called out "Go!"

George gunned the engine and the Bedford lurched forward. I took a deep breath and waited for the pain. As I braced myself for the pain, I had a flashback to water-skiing on the Vaal River on a cold day, anticipating the instant body shock caused by jumping into icy water.

I felt a bump as the truck passed over my foot, then nothing. There was no pain at all from that direction although something somewhere was hurting. George stopped the truck, jumped out and ran around the cab.

"Did it work?" he asked with a worried expression. We both looked down at my foot. There were no symptoms of any damage whatsoever but my knee was starting to throb painfully. I pulled up my trouser leg. There was an angry looking scrape to the side of my kneecap. Evidently the edge of the heavy metal bumper had caught my knee a glancing blow. Though the inflated rubber tyre had not caused any damage at all to the foot, the unforeseen impact of the Bedford's fender certainly had.

Within an hour, my knee had swollen up most encouragingly to almost twice its normal size whilst simultaneously turning a reddish-black colour. I was on a wave of excitement, the disappointment of discovering my miscalculation with the tyre replaced by this new sign of miraculous provenance. As if any further confirmation of its divine origins were needed, the injury was virtually painless. Pausing only long enough for one more cigarette and another strong cup of instant coffee, I hobbled to the sickbay. What with the adrenaline of the day's events still pumping through my veins along with the caffeine, on this occasion I was not on the defensive.

"What's the matter this time?" asked the doctor wearily, unaware of the formidable historical weight of determined willpower confronting him. I set off in a flat monotone, presenting a depressed pain-riddled version of misery.

"I am sorry to bother you doctor, I really didn't want to come, but its just that, well, as you know I have flat feet and I don't like to make a big deal of it which is why I'm still G1 K1, but I had to go on parade this morning and that meant standing on my feet for an hour. Then my feet started hurting and then the pain went to my knee and it got so bad that I told the corporal something wasn't right, but he told me not to be a moffie so I didn't say anything more but then my leg started to hurt so badly I couldn't walk any more. Then I fell over and then my knee went all black and now I can hardly walk at all so I thought I better show you."

With a dramatic gesture delivered with a performer's timing, I pulled up my trouser leg to present the doctor with a gloriously swollen, purple-black, gangrenous looking knee. I watched his face turn pale. Clearly his medical training had not prepared him for a foot related injury as complex or as gruesome as this and he could not fill out the forms for 3 Mil quickly enough, pausing only for long enough to say:

"In the meantime, please stay off your feet until we arrange your visit to 3 Mil."

Another 14-day admin duty slip was handed over, another 14 days for Whiteley to review his ongoing inability to impose his will. I left the sickbay limping but elated. Step one of the reclassification ambition had been ticked off the list.

The miracle of the knee was made especially spectacular by the fact that the swelling virtually disappeared soon after I had limped theatrically out of the doctor's room. By that evening the knee was almost back to normal size and within days the discolouration had faded away completely, like a flower that had come into sudden bloom in the hothouse of the doctor's rooms.

I felt certain that his report in the medical file for 3 Mil would reflect the gravity of the injury whilst I was left to reflect the irony of the foot-crunching operation going wrong and yet achieving the desired result anyhow. I wondered what mysterious forces had engineered such an improbable outcome. Once more I was on the waiting schedule for the reclassification board, armed this time with the knowledge gleaned from the previous encounter. Between the monthly weekend passes and the gigs occupying the rest of the weekend, the time, for once, flew by.

Practical piety

On the morning of 15th August I woke up abruptly just before 6am after a restless night. This was the day of Sean's appearance in the Kimberley magistrate's court on a charge of possession of a prohibited substance. As he set off dressed in his step-outs I wished him luck and without waiting around for the daily roll call, waded through freezing early morning mist down to the bookstore. My lack of attention to military protocol had reached new heights and most mornings I ignored roll call completely, leaving it up to one of the guys to think of an excuse on my behalf.

Once in the bookstore, I put on a Jim Croce tape and curled up next to the heater. Barely had 'Time in a bottle' finished playing when suddenly the door rumbled with angry pounding. Lt. Pitout appeared in the doorway, a threatening look on his face as he shouted in Afrikaans: "Corporal Lourens is looking for you in the bungalow. Get there immediately!" I made my way back to the bungalow to face up to Lourens who accused me of sleeping in the bookstore as I had not been seen in the bungalow all night. By this stage in my relations with low ranking non-commissioned officers, I had achieved a level of detachment that gave me an almost perverse pleasure in fearlessness. Nothing in the situation represented any real threat. More relevantly, I was consumed by feelings of utter contempt, marvelling at how Lourens and his kind managed to avoid seeing themselves the way I or any other sane person saw them. One of Dylan's lyrics articulated my ever-present feeling of revulsion for Corporal Lourens:

'I wish that for just one time, you could stand inside my shoes. You'd see what a drag it is to be you.'

"Look. I slept here last night. I have a lot of work to do for the Kommandant in the bookstore, so I got off to an early start. Why on earth do you think I would want to sleep in the bookstore when I have such a comfortable bed here?" I said in a measured tone.

"Today we have drill and you will be there," he warned. "Has the Kommandant booked you for any shows this weekend?" I strained to think, but I knew this was a weekend when most of the camp except for the clerks had leave.

"No, we don't have any shows this weekend," I was forced to admit.

"Good, then you can do the Friday, Saturday and Sunday shifts on guard-duty."

Not a good way to start the day, I thought. Drill and guard-duty were already looming ahead and it was not yet seven o'clock in the morning. Worst of all, my last 14-day admin duty slip was due to expire that day. Then again, I told myself, a lot can happen between now and the five o'clock guards' roll call. As for drill, I had not done any since the shooting range so this was both a bit of a blow and a bit of a novelty. I collected my rifle from my kas and fell in with the clerk's squad for drill on the parade ground. I saw Dino in the crowd and took up a place next to him. We hadn't had a chat with each other for some time so this was a good opportunity to catch up on the recent news.

"It's a real bitch that we are the only ones in the camp who don't get a pass this weekend," he observed to my ready agreement. We marched a few paces further.

"Listen," I said. "We're the only Greek Orthodox here and no one else has a clue what our holidays are. The Jewish guys get religious holidays all the time so why don't we make up a holiday and go and see the Dominee. There are Greek Saints' days almost all the time. Let's just find one that works for this weekend."

Dino needed very little persuading.

"Leave it to me," I said. "I'll call my aunt straight after parade. She knows all the Greek Saints' days."

As soon as drill ended, nursing the strain in my right arm from the unaccustomed weight of an R1, I went with Dino to the bookstore to phone my aunt. Luckily, I was given an outside line without any query and after a brief conversation with Thea Eftihia I established that the Repose of the Virgin Mary fell on the 15th August which as destiny would have it was that very day.

"We'll have to say it's a four-day fast ending on Sunday," I suggested as Dino nodded in enthusiastic agreement. We set off for the Dominee's office. The Dominee, the name given to the purple-cloaked Dutch Reformed Church ministers, was responsible for organising the religious services in the camp and was the embodiment of all that was most convincing in Afrikaner hypocrisy. We knocked at his office door for several minutes, prepared to tell him our little fiction about Greek religion. It took us a while to realise that he wasn't in his office. Undeterred, we agreed to go to our respective workplaces and stay in touch if we came up with any ideas. Less than an hour later Dino arrived at the bookstore with news.

"Your friend Major Van Der Riet is in HQ now. I just saw him go into the adjutant's office. Let's go talk to him about the holiday. The fast, I mean."

Van Der Riet heard our request with his usual polite grace.

"A four-day fast? That sounds like hard work. I will see what I can arrange for you," he assured us. Dino retired to the law office and I returned to the bookstore to top up the cannabis levels, this time with a single-blader. As I inhaled the aromatic smoke standing by the window at the rear of the bookstore, I thought of Sean and wondered how his court appearance was going. A Jackson Browne album was playing and the song 'For a Dancer' kept me entranced. I played the track over and over, enchanted by his prescience and memorising every word:

*'I don't know what happens when people die
can't seem to grasp it as hard as I try
It's like a song I can hear playing right in my ear
That I can't sing, but I can't help listening.'*

A knock on the door interrupted this reverie. It was George the Driver, responding to the message I had left for him at the duty room. I had remembered that he was the third Greek Orthodox in the camp and so explained to him the possibility that we Greek boys might be given a special pass for religious reasons.

"But there's no Greek holiday this weekend," he said.

"Yes there is. The Repose of the Virgin Mary - you know, the four-day fast that starts today which is why none of us have eaten anything so far today, okay?"

George's eyes widened with unconcealed admiration.

"If you pull this off I'll drive you home in my car," he promised.

At tea-time, as I sat listening to the Jackson Browne album for the umpteenth time, a breathless Dino arrived again.

"We have leave from 12pm today until 6am on Tuesday morning!" he proclaimed in triumph, holding up a notice from the Kommandant's office. Once more guard-duty would have to wait, I reflected with a warm glow of accomplishment as I hurriedly packed my rucksack and George and I were on the road back to Johannesburg.

"See you later, Corporal Lourens," I thought with a smirk. "Much later."

Easy money and a new guitar

Occasionally at some of the gigs we would be given cash, typically for playing requests or for playing beyond the agreed finishing time. One song, 'Michael row the boat ashore,' recorded by a popular South African singer at the time, Richard Jon Smith, evidently had some special meaning for the citizens of Kimberley because it was a frequent request invariably met with disproportionate euphoria when performed. I could not bring myself to sing this song as it represented something below my minimum tolerance level, along with two similar low-brow favourites 'Brown Girl in the Rain' and 'Ra Ra Rasputin'. Mike, however, was more than happy to give it a go. His shameless desire to please knew no arbiter of taste. Eventually this became the song he performed better than any other, his party piece, which would almost always result in financial reward for the band. I would encourage requests that we play the song with inducements for cash, along the lines of "If you write your request in the back of a 20 Rand note we will play it for you." If no money was forthcoming, I would not play the song. The crowds soon learned. Eventually the small sums being paid in this way added up to enough to enable me to consider investing in a new guitar.

During my monthly weekend passes, I would visit the music store in Johannesburg, TOMS music shop run by Eddie Boyle, a former professional musician whom I had known since school days when he frequently regaled me with stories of the professional musician's life and showed me the latest gear. The object of desire was the newly released Ibanez Artist guitar, a double cut-away rosewood, solid-body, electric guitar with two humbucking pick ups, much better than the Stratocaster copy that I had in Kimberley and a top dollar professional instrument. During this unexpected weekend pass, having brought in my earnings from the gigs, I was able to pay Eddie the full price in cash and left with a brand new guitar.

It was like having a new family member from the moment I opened the case and marvelled at the smell of its finely lacquered sunburst finish. When I hitch-hiked back to Kimberley with it on Monday evening I felt as if I was not travelling alone. This instrument represented much more than an inanimate wooden object to me. It was invested with an almost holy presence, one capable of uplifting my life and enabling me to feel closer to where I wanted to be. After band practice I would take it back to the dormitory and sleep with it next to my bed. I would play on it for as long as six hours each day, always taking care to clean and polish it afterwards. I am sure many guitars have meant a great deal to a great many players through the years and this guitar was no exception.

19

28th September was my nineteenth birthday and also the unhappiest I could remember. I awoke in my dormitory bed with a feeling of overwhelming melancholy. There was a world out there in which people were living full and meaningful lives and many wonderful things were happening though none of them were happening to me. I felt like a prisoner serving a grotesque sentence and this day just served to mark how much time I was losing in this place, time that I would never get back. My eagerness to get my life moving was matched only by my frustration at being restrained by the unfortunate circumstance of my internment. The only thing for it was to break my recent resolution not to light up a spliff before

10am. Sean joined me for the first birthday spliff in the bookstore shortly after 8am. The song playing on the radio was we puffed away was 'Guitar man' by Bread:

'Who draws the crowd and plays so loud? Baby, it's the guitar man.'

The day was spent in a haze of pot fuelled melancholy, the only upside of which was my resolution to never have another birthday in a position as low as this. My birthday dinner was a mug of powdered chicken soup.

The days that followed faded into one another in a blur of sameness, drawing me ever closer to the inevitable appointment at 3 Mil. I looked forward to every day in case news arrived. Mrs. Dreyer in the sickbay became tired of me calling her to enquire after news.

"Don't you worry, I will call you the moment I hear," she assured me, but October had already passed and I felt as if my life itself was slipping away with every passing day.

Sean's court case in Kimberley had resulted in a suspended sentence as he was serving in the army and would be tried by a military court in November. The consensus was that he would have to serve six months in detention barracks, the customary sentence for first time possession of cannabis. If he was terrified by this prospect, as I surely would have been, he didn't show it. His main concern was whether he would be able to score some good grass whilst in detention barracks. Ironically, we both received the news we had been waiting for on the same day. Sean was to travel to Pretoria to face a military court and I was to travel to Bloemfontein to face the long awaited medical, this time with renewed hope that it would lead to a tribunal hearing and reclassification.

Ward 5

Early in the morning of 15th November 1979, I set off again for Bloemfontein's 3 Military Hospital with grim determination, focused on the task in hand as if my life depended on it, which in some ways it did. I had spent hours preparing the presentation I would deliver in the event that I had the opportunity to address the medical board. I made lists of possible questions they might ask and prepared a variety of answers to cover every eventuality. I took the additional precaution of examining the contents of my medical file, handed to me in an oddly familiar sealed envelope for delivery to the doctor in Bloemfontein in case there might be some entry that would prejudice my chances. After I was given the envelope along with the route pass and train ticket, I made straight for the bookstore where I had prepared a duplicate envelope and had the 11 Kommando seal at the ready. For the second time it was the work of moments to access and read through the contents of my file. I had already removed the most damaging note, the report by Muller from my previous visit. This time I removed the 'Notification of Hospital Discharge' document that a Dr. Visagie had signed returning me to active duty. My file now contained no reference to any previous visit to 3 Mil. There was one note by the camp doctor in Afrikaans referring to the suspicious nature of nine separate occasions requiring sick notes for a variety of maladies that suggested a pattern. This note included the word 'gyppo' which I knew could never be a good thing. The note was withdrawn from the file and added to the stash of documents that I hoped would one day serve as contemporaneous notes should I survive to write about the experience.

Secure in the knowledge that the file was now clear of any information that might prejudice my position, I sealed it in the new envelope and prepared for the journey. One precaution I took with me into the unknown was a stamped passbook. Standard issue military passbooks were authenticated by the stamps of the various units to which the carrier belonged. I stamped a new passbook using the official 11 Kommando stamp, filling in my name but leaving the dates blank. A prescient foresight as events would soon reveal.

It was steaming hot when I arrived in Bloemfontein station. Calm and ready for the challenge ahead, I kept visualising my goal, a medical board hearing at which I spoke articulately and at a controlled pace, persuading them into support for my position and hearing them pronounce me medically unfit.

I checked into the hospital admin office where I was directed to a doctor's waiting room. There was no air conditioning and the heat was paralysing. An hour passed in a succession of cigarette breaks and then my name was called. The nurse told me I was to see Dr. Muller. I was stunned. In this huge hospital the odds against seeing the same doctor as the last time must be immense. "Surely the Gods would not throw me this curve ball now?" I thought, but they had. I recognised Dr. Muller straight away. He looked up at me, and a glimmer of vague recognition crossed his face.

"Haven't I seen you before?" he asked.

"No," I replied in the smallest voice I could muster.

Of course with an unusual Greek surname it was an impossibly distant hope that he might have forgotten our previous encounter, especially as we had conducted a conversation with medical school references. On the previous occasion, however, I was presenting a high-energy confident personality but not on this one. I tried to make myself as small as possible physically, hunching my back and keeping my voice quiet and slow. My subconscious mantra was: "My feet are broken. I can't walk properly. I am in pain. I can't wear boots. My feet are broken. I am in pain. I can't walk. I can't wear boots," and this kept playing in my head as the odious Dr. Muller spoke. On some level of telepathy I was trying to transmit the broken feet mantra to him. Although I knew he was sure that he knew me, there was also a measure of doubt. His thought processes were so clearly governed by conformity and reliance on the system that he would even override the obvious if the instruction to do so came his way.

"We'll soon see who's right," he said as he set about opening the sealed medical record on the desk in front of him. I felt a bead of sweat trickling down the back of my neck as I watched him scanning the file. His face seemed to darken as self-doubt took hold. He repeatedly flicked through the pages of the file as if searching for the document that he knew should have been there but clearly was not. He rose from his seat and walked over to the open window of his office while I sat in silence. Minutes passed while the cogs turned in his brain, until eventually he turned to face me.

"So. You have been recommended for a medical tribunal because you have flat feet. But the tribunal only sits on a Wednesday and you won't be able to go in for today's hearing because its too late to include you, so I will recommend you for observation for one week before the next tribunal and they can have a look at you then." He looked to me with the face of pure evil. I said nothing as he filled out a form.

"Take this to the nurse and she will show you to your bed. You will spend a week in Ward 5 and then we will assess you."

He handed me a form. I thanked him in a small voice and made my way to the duty nurse. She read the form I handed over and instructed me to follow her.

Ward 5 was some distance from the admin section. I had no inkling of how the various wards were laid out. I had seen a few injured looking soldiers walking around but I did not have any idea of the scale of operation that 3 Mil covered or indeed its long history dating back to the Boer War. The nurse delivered me to Ward 5 where another directed me to a bed. It was the middle of the day and it was sweltering inside the ward. There were many rows of beds, all occupied. My first indication that this was an unusual ward came when I noticed that some of the occupants appeared to be strapped down on their beds.

At first I remained in my sickly mantra state. I took off my clothes as directed, stored them in the provided drawer and put on the strange gown provided by the nurse. "Oh well," I thought. "I'll have a little nap and see what happens next." No sooner had I settled down in my bed than a man in a white coat with the appearance of a doctor, came over, shouting in a loud and angry manner.

"Out of bed. Inspection!" he bawled. He had a thoroughly sinister demeanor and bore little resemblance to any doctor I had seen before. I complied, getting out of the bed and standing next to it.

"Now make your bed!" he instructed. I set about this task with minimal enthusiasm. When the bed was made up, I stood next to it waiting for the next development. Around me I could see that all the beds had been vacated and the stoned looking inmates all seemed to be staring at the floor. After some 15 minutes had passed, the scabrous looking doctor returned.

"The next inspection is in one hour. Get some rest."

Before returning to bed I went to the toilet, where I struck up a conversation with a fellow patient standing next to me at the steel urinal.

"Have you been in here long?" I asked. He looked at me with a vacant expression. I was reminded of the Ken Kesey book, 'One Flew Over the Cuckoo's Nest', as he looked like one of the stoned out mental patients described in that book.

"Yes," he eventually replied.

In that moment it became clear to me that Ward 5 was no place to be. Something there was not right. Immediately following this realisation came the awareness that I was not going to survive one week in Ward 5 without shipping some serious blows to the side of the head. The adrenaline that had driven me onwards after waking up in Kimberley that morning on my mission to conquer Bloemfontein was replaced by deep fatigue. I just could not see myself standing around in this terrible place for a moment longer. Without pausing to consider my actions I went directly to the dressing area where my clothes were stored. There was no one around. I changed into my browns as quickly as possible, picked up my rucksack and walked purposefully straight out of Ward 5. The adrenaline was kicking in again. No one on the staff turned their head as I passed through and headed directly for the toilets in the admin section that I had visited earlier. Once inside, I locked myself in a cubicle. I needed a moment of calm to gather my thoughts.

Tucked inside the rucksack was the passbook that I had prepared in the bookstore, stamped with the 11 Kommando authority. Because of this bit of foresight all that remained now was to use the passbook to forge a pass. I filled in that day's date, with a return on the following Wednesday, the day of the tribunal. Within a minute I had a seven-day pass 'signed' in the authorising officer's signature space by 'Lt. Whiteley' whose scribble I approximated from memory. Thus prepared, I took several deep breaths of hot dry Bloemfontein air, unlocked the cubicle and, with due consideration for the appropriate houding, I set off for home.

I knew that I was technically AWOL and that in a time of war, as was the case in 1979, the maximum penalty was too grim to ponder. With every step I took, I knew that any passing officer might spot my lack of correct houding, the inadequately militarised spring in my step being easily recognisable to the trained eye of an officer. The sidewalk under my feet might as well have been an electric eel making every step a monumental challenge requiring concentrated effort. I approached the guards at the hospital gate, my passbook at the ready. A bored looking guard looked up at my approach. I adopted my most dispassionate expression and held out the passbook. He looked over the detail. In Afrikaans he asked me:

"You're from Kimberley. Why are you leaving from here?"

"Medics maak kak (Medics causing shit)," I mumbled, trying to imitate a hard Afrikaans accent. He said nothing, looking down at the passbook and then looking straight at me. I held my breath, willing the most expressionless feature I could muster. He handed back the passbook without saying anything. I took it, betraying no sign of the tingling nervousness that consumed me. "Dankie," I said and walked through the gate and into the street outside. My heart was racing. I had no idea where I was but I knew I had to get out of Bloemfontein as quickly as possible since every passing moment presented a new opportunity for being caught. There seemed to be military personnel everywhere. Every time I walked past an officer, the protocol required a salute. My saluting technique was something of a give-away as, in keeping with my overall lack of houding, I had never mustered the appropriate stiffness that a proper salute requires. Despite this, I survived several saluting encounters before I saw a signpost saying 'Johannesburg 400 kilometres'. The adrenaline overload made me feel quite capable of walking the entire distance.

Eventually after half an hour of pavement pounding I reached the outskirts of the city. There was no more pedestrian traffic and there were fewer military vehicles on the road. I decided to chance hitching a ride, hopeful that whoever stopped would not be an officer. As was common in my hitch-hiking experience, virtually the first vehicle to pass stopped for me and soon I was comfortably dozing in the front seat of a Chrysler Valiant as the afternoon sun settled on the horizon. I had time in these few hours to gather my thoughts. I would have a whole week away from the army nightmare, something I would never have predicted when I woke up in Kimberley that morning.

On weekend passes I always returned to my home in Bryanston where my time was usually spent looking up old friends from school and university. As time passed, the distance between my position and that of my civilian friends who were still maintaining a student lifestyle made these meetings less and less interesting. The occasions when I felt comfortable socialising with others tended to be with friends who were also in the military. At least they had an insight into the horrors of military service that separated us from the rest, although even within the context of socialising with fellow conscripts I still felt alienated, perhaps because no one else seemed to share the same approach to national service.

This difference was best illustrated by an interpretation of what success means. For many youngsters, going into the army was approached as a challenge with success measured by progress within the structure of the military. For many, this meant applying to train as officers and taking tremendous pride in their success within this endeavor. My understanding of success in the challenge of two years in the military was quite different, being the exact opposite of the majority view. Because I believed strongly that conscription was wrong and offensive, I resolved not to compromise my position by allowing myself to excel in any area that might demonstrate personal advancement in the guise of demonstrating support. My goal from very early in my conscription was to be the worst soldier possible. The worse my achievements in the military, I thought, the greater the measure of my success as a national serviceman would be. This approach was not one that I found reflected in many of my peers and so, almost without exception, I kept my views to myself and pursued detachment from the national service experience and those sharing it with me.

While I was home on this stolen week-long break, my longest running friend, Craig de Villiers, who I had known virtually since birth, also in his first year of national service, was home on leave from border duty. This gave us the opportunity to spend some time together catching up on events in our lives. Following his conscription, Craig, who was a keen motorcyclist, had applied for a newly formed army unit, the 'Bike Squad', formed to explore the possibilities of using off-road motorbikes to move gunmen around quickly in bush war situations, giving them an advantage over foot soldiers. Craig had eventually been posted to Potchefstroom for training before serving a six-month stint on the border with the Bike Squad. His tales of the border were pure black comedy.

Craig was blessed with a natural ability to laugh off the unpleasant elements of reality and replace these with the bits he decided would be important, a survival instinct that served him well in the madness of the bush war. He explained how the bike squad commanders tackled the challenge of mounting a rifle on a motorbike. To be able to fire an automatic rifle whilst riding a bike at high speed over rough terrain clearly requires special skills. It also presents a few logistical challenges. Military intelligence came up with the idea of fixing an R4 automatic rifle onto the handlebars of the bike, to be triggered with the left hand as the right hand would be needed to keep the accelerator going. The first squad to find themselves in a firefight using these fixed position weapons soon discovered the logical flaw in a system that required them to ride directly at their targets since they could only aim straight ahead, giving them virtually no hope of hitting any target. It was not an ideal solution and was indicative of a shallow level of intelligence all too commonly given rein in the military.

Eventually, Craig explained, they realised that bikes were not effective as a strike force. Their only value lay in scaring the enemy and so the average attack would involve Bike Squad riders shouting at the top of their voices whilst firing an R4 automatic rifle with very little accuracy while steering the bike one handed over bush-veldt - a challenging skill to master, especially with someone firing back at you with an AK47.

For Craig, the success in getting into Bike Squad and developing his riding skills, plus the adrenaline rush of motorcycle firefights, provided him with some degree of reward with which to interpret the experience. My attitude to firing a weapon was quite different from Craig's. On the occasions when shooting practice was called, I simply avoided appearing at the shooting range. This was easy to do as shooting was viewed as one of the good things that every young man enjoyed doing and so there was no system in place to catch out those dodging shooting practice. I had been a keen target marksman before going into the army and always enjoyed the process of squeezing off a round or ten, but somehow the thought of doing it in a military uniform at the behest of an instructor for the purpose of refining a technique for killing other humans was something to be avoided. By allowing myself to enjoy this opportunity, I would be compromising my resolve to do as little as possible towards becoming a trained soldier.

"But wait," said the faint inner voice of temptation. "You get to go to a professional shooting range, using a professional automatic rifle and unlimited ammunition with which to develop your skills as a marksman." I resisted. By my measure of success, I could not have done any better than to become the only G1 K1 troop that I knew who never fired a single shot in two years of military service.

This one week unscheduled sabbatical from the army was not without its own stress. Never far from the surface was the fact that I was AWOL, which gave me a new insight into living outside the law. Despite this stress, there is no doubt that I was better off in Bryanston for that week than in Ward 5 of 3 Mil, being zonked out by medication and subjected to psychiatric evaluation by people to whom the word 'sinister' would have been a compliment.

The medical board

As the seven days passed, I felt much restored physically and emotionally by regular diet and regular sleep and once I was feeling suitably re-humanised, the stress of my experience in 3 Mil had, by and large, dissipated as I prepared to return. As an added precaution for my return, I decided to catch a train rather than risk hitch-hiking to Bloemfontein with a forged passbook and so, late that Tuesday night, I found myself once again stepping onto the platform of Bloemfontein station. I walked to 3 Mil, straight past the sleepy guards and into Ward 5. I had learned by now that Ward 5 was in fact a psychiatric ward and that the energy vacuum in there was horrific. No one noticed my arrival. I saw the bed I had been checked into six nights before was empty and without further ado, still in my clothes, I slid under the covers of the bed. I was woken by a nurse at 5.30am the following morning and in the general hullabaloo of starting the day in a psychiatric ward it was not difficult to make my way from the ward to the waiting room in the visiting area outside the doctors' offices, the one location inside 3 Mil with which I was familiar. From there I enquired from a random passing nurse as to the location of the medical board hearing. Not for the first time that day, luck was with me and she directed me to a waiting room where the day's intake for the medical tribunal was to gather. I established that my name was on the day's list before settling in for a long wait. It was still only 8am and I was the sole occupant in the room. Before long the door opened and a nurse showed in a troop. She looked at me and said, "You're not dressed correctly". I was still in browns. She showed me to a changing area and provided me with a hospital gown, conspicuously open at the back. I changed and returned to the waiting room feeling somewhat wrong footed by the fact that I was wearing a gown that had no way of closing up at the rear.

Back in the waiting area things were getting livelier as the room filled with troops all hoping for military reclassification. One of them entered the room, picked up a magazine from the table in the middle of the room and sat down against a wall, seemingly to read the magazine. Instead, he slowly and with marked precision, tore off a page. Next he tore off a neat section of the page, taking his time to be certain the proportions were just as he intended, before he crunched this piece of paper into a round ball. He put the paper ball into his mouth with evident relish and slowly started chewing, with a contended look in his eye. "I guess he's trying for the crazy option," I thought to myself.

I recognised one of the troops, Richard van Lijr, from the original intake at the shooting range. He recognised me too and we started to chat. He had been classified G2 K2 as his vision was poor. When the January intake had transferred to Walvis Bay, Richard had been assigned to Jan Kemp Dorp ammunition dump as a guard. He was a keen pot smoker who started each day with a good pipe. Perhaps the long-term effect of this lifestyle choice had impaired his rational thought to some degree. I asked him why he was going in front of the medical board.

"I want a discharge from the army," he replied. Apparently, Richard had found the endless guard-duty at Jan Kemp more than he could stand. I could relate to him in the sense that he too recognised a 'life or death' gamble in forcing a decision by the tribunal. In his case, the gamble with his life had involved a neatly thought out suicide attempt.

One evening while on guard-duty as was usual on these occasions, he started his stint in the guard tower by preparing to smoke a pipe with his fellow guard. They fashioned a bottleneck pipe in the traditional manner, by heating the neck of a Coke bottle head with a lighter and then dipping it in cold water to snap the glass. All was progressing normally as the two guards inhaled and passed the pipe to each other, until Richard took the pipe for the last hit. Sucking in a huge lungful of smoke, he pressed the sharp end of the glass pipe against the vein on his left wrist and sliced open the artery in one swift movement. My first thought was for the blood-sprayed guard who witnessed this, having just got extremely stoned only to see his buddy hack open an artery before announcing, "I think you better call the guardroom," as his blood spurted in pulsing waves from his wrist.

In the intervening month since that incident the wound to his wrist had healed and Richard seemed quietly confident that this would be the day when his gamble paid off. I wished him luck and returned to my own nervous thoughts. The mantra, "Please, dear God, let this work for me" repeated as a loop inside my head.

Every so often a nurse would open the door and call out a name and one of our number would be led away down a corridor to face the medical board. During this wait I struck up conversation with the troop seated next to me who seemed quite well centred and spoke English with a smart accent. Although I had not seen him since the first week, I recognised him as Grant Enfield who had been in the same intake as I was at 11 Kommando. We exchanged pleasantries before I told him my flat foot saga. In return he told me the intriguing tale of how he managed to get this appointment with the medical board. Grant was clearly an intelligent individual who shared my resentment towards national service and had come up with a plan for getting discharged from the army. This stemmed from his discovery that in the army culpability is mitigated by a short period of time during which the individual cannot be held responsible for his actions, that brief moment during which an individual's actions are considered to be a reflex action and not a premeditated, considered act. He found a precedent in Military Law that demonstrated any action committed within a half-second of a trauma was exempt from liability on the grounds of being a motor reflex action.

Grant had worked out that the half-second defining the difference between a reflex action and a culpable bad choice would provide the opportunity he sought. He waited until bayonet practice where he contrived to persistently irritate the junior lieutenant carrying out the training. At the opportune moment he engineered such extreme provocation of the young officer that it resulted in the delivery of a slap to the side of the head whereupon Grant turned, quite deliberately and in one movement thrust the bayonet into the young lieutenant's shoulder, executing a perfect 'twist and extract' that belied his previous seeming inability to master this technique. I was reminded of the effect the barbed fish hook arrangement on the bayonets base had on the sack I had performed this manoeuvre on in training.

In the subsequent report of the incident, it was clear that the troop had been struck by an officer and had reacted inside the period of time that constitutes a reflex action. Though the court martial he faced had found him not guilty, he was, however, considered unsuitable for continuing national service and was ordered to appear before the medical board for their estimation of his psychological condition following the month he had just spent in Ward 5.

I was to meet with him again, back at 11 Kommando when he arrived at the bookstore on his way to clear out, having achieved his 'discharge from national service'. Not long after that I read that the bayonet was no longer to be included as standard issue, perhaps because the SADF had been forced to recognise the possibility of an officer being killed by one of their own troops. Grant's was one of the most ingenious and effective plans for escaping the army that I had heard. I have often wondered since then what became of Grant Enfield, then a teenager capable of executing such a remarkable plan as well as surviving a month in Ward 5.

Finally, my name was called. This was it. I followed the nurse down a corridor and into a large room in which five people were seated in a half circle facing me. In the centre I recognised the rank of brigadier and the purple colouring of medical insignia. On either side were four lesser officers, two majors, a captain and a second lieutenant. The brigadier was in the chair. He had my file on his desk. I had the impression that they had discussed my file before I entered. For a few minutes not a word was spoken. They looked at me, and I looked back, trying not to appear afraid or overwhelmed.

"So, you have flat feet," said the brigadier.

"Yes," I replied.

"How does this affect you?" asked one of the majors.

"Putting weight onto either foot causes pain. Walking causes pain, which increases in direct proportion to the amount of walking I do."

"What kind of pain?"

"Pain in the arch of my foot that feels like it's being burned and cut at the same time. A debilitating, crippling pain."

For some 10 minutes they fired questions at me and I replied directly, and concisely. The questions seemed part of a strategy, coming in all directions, and varying subject matter quite dramatically.

"Where are you from?"

"Johannesburg."

"Were you born in this country?"

"Yes."

"Where did you go to school?"

"Bryanston, then Damelin then Wits Medical School."

"Are you enjoying national service?"

"I would enjoy it a lot more if I could walk properly."

"Have you had problems with your feet before?"

"Yes."

I answered every question evenly without once showing any emotion until eventually they excused me. My intention had been to appear terminally depressed and I hoped I had conveyed that impression, not that it was a million miles from the truth. The nurse returned me to the waiting room where I had time to consider the experience. I was in no doubt that the firing of questions from all directions would have met with a very different response had I come into that situation after being softened up beforehand by a week in a military psychiatric ward. After an hour's wait I was summoned to the admin section of the hospital and given a route form and ticket back to Kimberley. I asked a nurse what the outcome of the medical board had been.

"They will reach a decision and prepare a report and that can take a week or two. You will be notified when you are back in your camp," came the reply.

As I sat on the train going back to Kimberley that evening I did not allow myself to feel confident or otherwise in the matter of the decision. I had had enough experience of bitter disappointment by then to recognise the value of detachment.

In no time at all, I was back in the Kimberley routine. The band had two bookings that weekend, one of them another Friday night dance in the hall at Jan Kemp, when during one of the breaks I was able to chat with one of the guards who knew Richard van Lijr. I asked if he had succeeded with being discharged from the army.

"Well, he's out of here now, but not out of the army. They charged him with damage to government property. They sentenced him to two years in Detention Barracks."

I was stunned by the news, as well as the information that our status was 'government property'. This explained why the soldiers in the war are called 'GI's', short for 'Government Issue'. I couldn't see Richard coping with two years in Detention Barracks so this was more or less a death sentence. I never heard anything more of Richard van Lijr, another casualty of conscription.

The Kimberley Hotel

The following night we were booked to play at a dinner dance in the Kimberley Hotel, a part of the prestigious new Southern Sun Hotel group. This was the smartest gig in town. The guests were suited and booted and mostly English speaking. As usual, we wore our regulation 'step-outs'. It was a typical four-hour night consisting of four 45 minute sets broken by 15 minute cigarette breaks, or in my case, joint breaks. I had found through a process of trial and error that the best way to have a smoke during these long working nights was to pre-roll a 'two-toke'. This involved squeezing the end of a cigarette to release some of the tobacco without crushing the delicate paper and then filling this one-inch space with enough cannabis for two good hits, enough to keep one pleasantly stoned throughout the evening. A number of these two-tokes were pre-prepared in the Bedford on the way to the gigs and stored behind the silver paper lining inside a cigarette packet.

The ideal repertoire for the stoned guitar player frequently draws from the work of JJ Cale and we would invariably start the sets with Cale tunes that tended to go on for some time with the now customarily lengthy guitar solos. 'Cocaine', 'Cry Sister Cry' and 'I'll make love to you anytime' were our three standard post-joint filler songs.

The minor pentatonic scale became a fixture of every one of our gigs.

Close encounters of the worst kind

Back in camp on Monday morning, as soon as sickbay opened I was there to enquire after news from the medical board. Nothing had arrived yet. This was a difficult start to the week. No news at all and with the eleventh month of the year almost over, keeping my spirits up was becoming a daily struggle. The prospect of starting the second year of national service in Kimberley was unbearable. That night, made less cautious by the weight of depression, I returned to the bookstore after band practice to read a book and possibly sleep over if the signs were right. At around 10.30 I decided to step outside for a two-toke. I lit the twisted end of the cigarette and inhaled deeply, enjoying the balmy warmth of the summer's evening when an unexpected scurrying movement in the shadows of the building ahead of me caught my eye. I heard the sound of shuffling feet and immediately assumed the worst. In an instant I crushed the end of the cigarette between my fingers and walked on as if unaware that someone was approaching me from behind. I knew as soon as the two red arm-banded military policemen appeared that it was a stake out. I also knew that the stench of marijuana was a dead give away, but more importantly I knew that there was no remaining evidence of possession. I had crushed the lit end of the Camel cigarette between my fingers, and removed any trace of the cannabis, leaving only tobacco and a filter.

The two Afrikaans-speaking military policemen were over the moon. I still held the remainder of the extinguished cigarette in my hand. One of them grabbed it from me. I watched him place it inside a plastic packet. They had come prepared.

"Nou ons het jou!" they beamed in joyful unison. "Now we've got you."

They led me to the guardroom, attached to which were several cells complete with heavy barred gates. As they marched me in, the duty officer, a young military police lieutenant who I had never seen before looked me over. The two arresting officers energetically detailed their bust to their commander.

"We have caught him red-handed smoking dagga and we have the dagga joint!" they enthused, handing him the evidence which was the plastic bag containing the Camel butt with about a quarter inch of tobacco attached to the filter.

Although only minutes before I had inhaled a hit of cannabis, I was entirely sober. I waited in silence to see what would happen, thinking the more time that passed the better so that any lingering smell of cannabis could dissipate completely.

After some whispering in Afrikaans, the lieutenant turned to me and said "Follow me."

He led me into a small room behind the desk. There was a map of the local area on one wall. A naked light bulb hung in the centre of the room, beaming harsh bright whiteness. There was an amateur element present in the process that I found most reassuring, like being in a scene from a particularly low budget movie. I was thinking that their dilemma would be to decide which one gets to be the good cop. The clarity with which I viewed my predicament made me feel confident enough to want to burst out laughing. The Koosie and Frikkie show, dumb and dumber still. One of the two MPs stayed in the room with the lieutenant, who sat down opposite me at a small table.

"Where did you get the dagga from?" he asked me.

"I don't know what you're talking about. I don't have any dagga," I replied.

He drew a breath, clenched his jaw and tried again.

"Where did you get the dagga from?" he repeated.

"I don't know what you're talking about. I don't have any dagga," I repeated in a deliberately semi-moronic monotone. He sat up rigidly.

"Where did you get the dagga from?" this time delivered with more menace.

"I don't know what you're talking about. I don't have any dagga," I said, matching the phrasing and timing of his previous delivery as best I could.

By now I felt no fear at all since their buffoonery had convincingly eroded any possibility of my taking them seriously. I felt almost excited by the entertainment value of having some fellows to play with on an otherwise boring Monday evening.

"Where did you get the dagga from?" he started again.

"I don't know what you're talking about. I don't have any dagga," I replied, this time in a softer more accommodating voice.

The 'good guy' MP tired of waiting for his cue.

"Look, you had better tell him what he wants to know or we will be here a very long time."

"I understand," I replied. The lieutenant returned to his theme.

"Where did you get the dagga from?"

"I don't know what you're talking about. I don't have any dagga."

His voice rose in level and pitch.

"Where did you get the dagga from?"

"I don't know what you're talking about. I don't have any dagga," I replied, softer than before.

"Now look here. You were caught smoking dagga. We have the joint you were smoking. You had better start talking or you will be spending a long time in jail."

"I was smoking a cigarette when your two MPs grabbed me. If

you look at the evidence, you will see a Camel cigarette," I said in a firm evenly paced voice.

The MP interrupted.

"We could smell the dagga. It was dagga, not a cigarette."

All eyes turned to the evidence on the table where a solitary Camel cigarette butt mocked them from inside a plastic packet.

"Yes, Camel cigarettes do smell like dagga but I can assure you this is a Camel cigarette and not a dagga joint. You have made a mistake."

The atmosphere was now becoming infused with a new element: embarrassment. The officer looked at the MP with an angry expression and both exited the room. I wondered what they would do next, fairly certain that they would not accept defeat so readily. They returned five minutes later and resumed their positions. The lieutenant faced me and started speaking.

"Where did you get the dagga from?" he asked, looking straight at me.

"Is there a problem with your hearing? I told you, I do not have any dagga," I replied but before I had finished what I was intending to say the MP leaned over me and said:

"What's this in your pocket?"

With a triumphant flourish he produced a plastic bag of what appeared to be cannabis. As far as planting evidence goes this was such a poor attempt that my first instinct was to laugh rather than react in horror but things were becoming tiresome and it was definitely time to nip this deviance in the bud. I stood up and raising my voice so as to speak as authoritatively as possible I said in a tone reserved for directing morons:

"Are you a complete moron? Attempting to plant drugs is a criminal offence. Not only are you second rate soldiers bringing disgrace to the uniform, you are acting like common criminals. You are in possession of drugs, in a packet that has your fingerprints on it, but most certainly not mine, and you have just attempted to plant drugs on somebody to cover up the fact that you have made a mistake. I am going to have you both in court for this and I will make sure you spend a good and long time inside."

They were stopped in their tracks, dumbfounded by this entirely unexpected turn of events. Both stared at me open mouthed and uncertain.

"You have no idea who I am, do you?" I continued. "I work with Major Van Der Riet. I report to him on the conduct of troops in 11 Kommando. The next thing that is going to happen will be me telling him how you go about your business. Get me a phone line. Now!" I pointed at the phone on the desk.

"You can ask him who I am and you can also explain to him why you have a bag of dagga in your possession."

My reaction was so far removed from their experience that they needed time to retreat to work out an appropriate response. They both went silent and left the guardroom without saying a word, leaving me alone beneath the glaring Nazi-era light-bulb. Five minutes passed before the officer returned, looking a lot less confident than when I had first arrived.

"I have tried calling Major Van Der Riet, but there is no reply," he said, almost apologetically. "I'll have to wait until the senior officer comes back to see what he wants to do and I'm sorry but you'll have to wait too. Please wait in here." With that, he opened the door to the one cell facing the room and directed me to enter. I walked into the cell and he closed the door behind me. The heavy door clanked shut with a jarring thud. I had never been locked in a cell before. The clanking sound stirred some deep inner claustrophobic terror. I felt myself having a panic attack. The MP had not even made it back to the desk before I started yelling.

"You can't lock me in here. Open this door immediately. Major Van Der Riet is going to be furious about this. I want to talk to him right now. Get him on the phone immediately. Open this door, right now!" I started pounding on the lock with the side of my fist, generating an impressive noise that was magnified by the stone floor and the reflective wall surfaces. The MP was by now quite unsure of himself and came back to the door.

"I'll unlock the door, but please just wait here until I get the major on the phone."

I felt a wave of wondrous relief as the door opened. I made an immediate mental footnote to be sure to never get locked in a cell ever again. The MP tried calling the major's number but still there was no reply. Evidently he was out for the evening. Ten minutes passed. He tried again. The duty lieutenant and the other MP were still nowhere to be seen and the atmosphere was now beyond uncomfortable. I decided the time was right to leave. I opened the cell door fully and walked out into the duty room hallway towards the watching MP.

"I can't wait any longer for this. I am leaving now. If you need to talk to me again you know where I am. I will decide what to do about this after I have spoken to Major Van Der Riet."

Without waiting for his reply, I strode out of the guardroom and headed back towards the barracks, fuming with anger mostly towards myself for being so stupid as to come that close to getting caught but at the same time elated by the rush of having turned the tables so convincingly and with such apparent ease on two military policemen.

I didn't sleep much that night, lying in my bed awash with thoughts of my powerlessness to change my situation. Almost a year had passed since I arrived in Kimberley. Much had happened during this time, but, crucially, I was still in the place where I had started. If I did not succeed in moving soon I could see that any chance I had of getting to the Entertainment Corps would recede with the amount of time I had left in the military.

After the recent stress, the weekend gigs provided welcome relief. The first Saturday of December, found us at Copperton Mine performing a four-hour outdoor set for several hundred people. The discipline of performing provided a restorative effect and although many of the songs were of no interest musically and the crowd consisted of religious Afrikaners and permanent force soldiers, playing guitar and singing with a reasonably well-grooved band in support was a path leading to a pool of wellness.

Don't give up the fight

By December 1979 I had grown so accustomed to smoking two-toke spliffs during the breaks that performing stoned no longer presented any challenge and made the time pass more agreeably by making the music more interesting. On bigger gigs such as this, when the moment seemed appropriate, I would play the Bob Marley song, 'Get Up Stand Up', to see if anyone would react. I must have played this song fifteen times in this way, to right wing Afrikaner/military audiences without ever once being questioned as to the lyrical content. Somehow I concluded that even the Afrikaners would have related to the idea of 'Stand up for your rights' as if they were the downtrodden.

Now you see the light. Stand up for your rights.'

On one occasion, a suspicious Van Vuuren, with a quizzical expression on his face, approached me in the break to ask, "That song, stand up for your rights. What's that about?"

"Corporal, its called "Get Up Stand Up", written by a Christian songwriter, name of Bob Marley. Apparently, he wrote it because his father, who was in the war, was injured and he didn't get a very good pension from the army. Also, the medical care was bad. So he wrote this song to try and get other ex-soldiers to stand up for their rights. Better pension plan and better medical too. I think its also a bit of a gospel song because he does talk about God, which is obviously important."

"Hell that's a good song," said Van Vuuren, knowingly.

After the show, the organiser gave us each an envelope with 17 Rand in it, a useful sum considering that a bank bag of prime quality cannabis buds cost 10 Rand and would last for several months.

As had become the norm since my return from Bloemfontein, Monday morning found me heading for sickbay to enquire after news. I was approaching the entrance when I saw RSM 'Blikkies' Blignaut coming towards me. All my concentration went into assuming the correct posture and preparing for the salutation.

Non-commissioned officers such as a sergeant major, required a 'strek' which is basically standing to attention whilst walking. commissioned officers, (second lieutenants upwards), were to be saluted with the right hand. At no time had I invested any proper effort towards mastering either of these salutations. More often than not, an improper strek would result in some form of punishment so with total concentration I pulled off a semi-passable impression of the strek and made it past Blignaut without being accosted, surmising that he must have been on an important errand to have missed an opportunity to have a go at me.

Buoyed by this minor success, I detoured to the Post Office room for coffee with Sean, who was in. A mug of Nescafe with an Ouma Rusk doubled as breakfast and was taken at a leisurely pace whilst chatting about one of the two subjects that dominated our every conversation: music and cannabis. After coffee, I set off back to the bookstore to start another day as a clerk. The store was already open and Dobson was seated at his desk, drinking tea and smoking a cigarette.

"Someone came in looking for you," he said. "They left something on your desk."

I made my way across and looked down at a scrap of paper. It read:

'Medical Report received.'

Status confirmed: G4 K3. Geen wag staan nie.

The rhyme seemed ironic. As I repeated the words in my head I remembered one of the questions at the medical board relating to guard-duty. I had said that the inflammation in my knee was caused by standing while on guard-duty. I felt overwhelmed by the magnitude of the moment. After so many months of determined and sometimes heartbreaking effort visited so frequently by bitter failure, persistence had finally been rewarded.

I made a celebratory cup of tea for Dobson and myself, relishing the feeling of the new set of options now available to me. I felt like a lottery winner taking in the enormity of good now available for the first time. I would never need a sick note again since I now had a permanent one. I could never be threatened with punishment drills or guard-duty ever again. This was a sweet feeling and one that drew me towards a new understanding of the meaning of gratitude towards whatever mysterious forces had come into play. I could not stop repeating the phrase G4 K3.

Going, going...

My first call with the happy news of my reclassification was to Major Hayden's Entertainment Corps number and was pleasantly relieved when he took my call. I explained the circumstances of the reclassification and reminded him of our meeting at my audition.

"Oh yes, the bouzouki player," he commented. "I'll send the transfer request to your camp and let's see what happens." And so another cycle of waiting began although this time it was made far more bearable by the immunity document my new classification represented. Having G4 K3 status was like carrying a laminated get-out-of-jail and access-all-areas pass. Any enthusiastic officer suggesting to me that I should run around a tree or similar was rendered powerless and speechless by my new standard reply.

"Gee, officer, I would like to help you out here. Honestly, I would. There's really nothing I would like more than to listen to you speak. But, sadly, I can't. Unfortunately, I am G4 K3. I can barely walk without catching my breath. Maybe if I'm feeling better later I can come back to you and see if we can arrange something for then, but right now, as you can see, regrettably, its just impossible."

Never before and perhaps never since have four characters meant as much to me as G4 K3 did then.

My days of waiting for transfer news were spent in the usual blur of bookstore activity, memorising song lyrics, writing thousands of words a day in the form of diary entries, song lyrics and letters. I was also practising the guitar and learning new songs to try out with the band during evening rehearsals. After a week had passed since my call to Major Hayden without any news, I went to Whiteley's office to enquire. Our mutual dislike was at an all time high. I recognised the familiar look of real hatred in his eyes when he spoke to me. He was infuriated by my reclassification and appeared to take this news as a personal insult. I think if circumstances had found us meeting in the war zone and out on an operation, he would happily have waited for an appropriate opportunity to shoot me. However, this was no time to stand on pleasantries. I was anxious to leave and was not short of confidence in my position.

"I have been told by Major Hayden that the transfer request has been sent to this office, and I will be grateful if you would confirm when I can go."

"Wait here," he said in Afrikaans. He left the office and I saw him knock and enter the Kommandant's office. Some ten minutes later he returned, addressing me once more in Afrikaans.

"The Kommandant wants to see you. Follow me."

I was ushered in the Kommandant's office. The look in his eye was similar to that in Whiteley's. He addressed me in English.

"I have received a transfer request from the Entertainment Corps for you. I have decided to decline this request on the basis that you are needed at this camp. You will therefore return to your duties and that is now the end of this matter."

I experienced a surge of incandescent rage. For a moment, I felt surrounded by a flash of white energy that scorched my very being. It soon passed, though, and I felt a calmness born of certainty. Without saying a word, I retreated from his office, leaving the Kommandant seated at his desk and Whiteley standing next to it, staring at me with his baleful expression. I did not salute. I had made the acquaintance of a new emotion, burning hatred, and the experience was disquieting.

I returned to the bookstore, which took around three minutes at a furious pace. In this time I had transformed the anger into a clearly defined next step. I knew from my dinner meeting with General Steenkamp that he was stationed in Pretoria in the 'Electronics' sector of the army. Now was the time to call in any favours possible. I phoned my mother in Bryanston and asked her for the general's number in Pretoria and, with this information, I called the number which was his direct personal line. No more than 10 minutes since the Kommandant had told me that I was not leaving Kimberley, I was speaking directly to a general in Pretoria on a first name basis.

I explained my predicament in measured terms, being careful not to go too far in vilifying the Kommandant. Such caution proved unnecessary. General Steenkamp seemed more than willing to take up my corner.

"You just leave this Kommandant to me," he said. "I'll call him right now."

The next fifteen minutes passed in a haze of accelerated excitement that comes from close association to perceived power. The chain-smoking and endless cups of coffee meant I was as wired as can be, thinking that it's not every day a troop can author the disciplining of his camp commander.

"Ja Kommandant, sien jy daar boom. Nou gaan jy kak," was the Afrikaans phrase that kept repeating in my head. And then the phone rang. It was the general.

"I have had a good talk with your Kommandant. It seems he is correct in military protocol in denying you the transfer to Entertainment Corps. As your commanding officer, he has first call on your placement. Your Entertainment Corps request comes from a major and as a Kommandant he outranks that request. So we will have to approach it in a different way. First we need to get you out of there because he is not going to look after you. What I will do now is put in an emergency request for your services to be transferred into my unit here. As I outrank him, my request will go through and that will get you out of his control. Once you are here in Pretoria, I will release you to the Entertainment Corps. It will take a week or two more but it's the best I can do. Now all you have to do is wait. I think you must be quite good at that by now. You should get a call from your Kommandant before the end of the day."

It was Friday, 7th December 1979. I waited in the bookstore within grabbing distance of the phone, chain-smoking Camel cigarettes and drinking endless cups of Five Roses tea. My kidneys ached from the caffeine excess. Finally at four o'clock the phone rang. I was summoned to the Kommandant's office and minutes later I found myself standing in exactly the same place as I had stood earlier that day to be told that I was not leaving 11 Kommando.

"It seems you have powerful friends," said the Kommandant in a rasping hiss, waving a document at me.

"This is your transfer to Pretoria." He was the embodiment of undiluted disgust. If looks had the power to chill, I would have been flash frozen.

"Take this to the adjutant," he said, thrusting the document in my direction. I took the papers from him then turned and left the room without looking backwards. No salute. What was he going to do about it. Not until that moment had I ever entered Whiteley's office with a joyful feeling - first the reclassification and now this. I handed him the documents with a blank expression, sending him a mental message of "You're an arsehole. You. Are. An. Arsehole. Youranarsehole," repeated at a confident, measured pace.

Silently he filled out a form, making no eye contact with me until his task was complete. He handed me a signed and stamped set of forms, which I took from him. Not a word was spoken. I didn't salute or acknowledge him on leaving the room.

Once back in the bookstore, I read through the documents. I was to 'uitklaar', 'clear out', the following Wednesday and travel to Pretoria on the Thursday. In a week's time, I would be out of Kimberley. Or so I thought.

The following night we had a gig booked and I set off for it in unusually good cheer. It was supposedly my last gig in Kimberley, at the Kimberley Cellars restaurant located in the town centre. We were booked from 8pm till 12 for a dinner dance. This was not a military event and so I was moved to ask the manager how he had booked us. He told me he had heard there was a great band in the army camp, so he had phoned the camp, been referred to the

Kommandant and had booked us that way. It turned out he had paid the Kommandant 300 Rand for the band's services, of which we received nothing.

The night went unusually well. The band was right in the groove and the sound in the room was great, so much so that the manager approached me after the last song and asked if we would do another hour for 50 Rand, this time payable directly to me. Songs in our set that night were 'JJ Cale's', 'Cocaine', 'Don't cry sister cry' and 'City Girls', Eric Clapton's 'Wonderful tonight', Gloria Gaynor's 'I will survive' and a lengthy Rolling Stones medley including 'Jumping Jack Flash', 'Satisfaction' and 'Honky Tonk Woman'.

After returning from the gig and unpacking the gear, Sean and I stayed on in the band room smoking tobacco-rich spliffs and chatting about our impending visits to Pretoria. Sean's sentencing was due the following week and he had been advised to expect six months in the Detention Barracks in Voortrekkerhoogte, the military camp in Pretoria. "At least I'll be closer to home," he remarked optimistically.

Faced with the prospect of leaving Kimberley, the place where I had now spent an entire year of my teenage life, I could not think of one thing about it that I would miss. Kimberley to me was the byword for 'your worst nightmare' or as Sean remarked 'the pimple on the asshole of the world.'

One last thing...

Bright and early on Wednesday I packed all my belongings in their appropriate order. Clothing items were to travel with me to Pretoria but all the hardware was to be returned to Inventory: the kas, the trommel and so on. I was driven to the Quartermaster's Office and worked my way through the list as the duty staff sergeant ticked off each returned item from a list on his clipboard. We arrived at item 27, one R1 rifle. I placed my R1 on the counter.

"Read me the serial number," he instructed. As I reached the last digit, he looked up at me.

"Let me see that," he asked, taking the rifle across the counter and reading the serial number.

"This is not your weapon."

"That's impossible," I replied. "It's the only weapon I have."

"The serial number on this weapon does not match the number you were issued. This is not your weapon."

This was a calamity beyond imagining. I soon became aware that losing one's weapon is a court martial offence, with a maximum tariff of many years incarceration. I set about trying to figure what had happened. My first thought was that somehow the Kommandant or Whiteley or both in collusion had somehow switched my rifle for another. As I had never fired this rifle and had no relationship with it in any meaningful way, I was unlikely to ever see the difference between one black R1 and any one of the many thousands that all appeared identical. In reality, however, this imagined switch was unlikely, the most probable explanation being that on the single occasion when I stood guard-duty I had placed my rifle in the rack and when I retrieved it I had accidentally taken the wrong one.

It became obvious that neither the staff sergeant nor myself were likely to find a solution to this obstacle to my clearing out at that time and so after agreeing that the matter would need further consideration, I headed back to the bookstore, leaving the rifle I had thought was mine with the quartermaster. As I made my way back the reality dawned on me that I was technically a soldier in an army fighting a war who had lost a rifle and that I was in deep trouble. My first call was to General Steenkamp. I explained the circumstances to him and he told me he would call me back once he had the opportunity to take advice. When he called back the news was not good. Losing one's weapon was a court martial offence. Without a weapon to hand back, I could not complete my 'clear out' and complete the transfer to Pretoria. The only way forward was to be court-martialled. I was told that the minimum penalty was repayment of the cost of the rifle and was advised that this sum was 427 Rand. The general told me the best case was to go to the Kommandant, explain what had happened and ask him to schedule a court martial as quickly as possible. This was heart-sinking news. I knew that this provided the Kommandant with every opportunity to seek more than the minimum tariff and the general's assurance that he would keep an eye on proceedings did not convince me that the Kommandant would be sufficiently deterred. Here was his revenge, served up on a plate.

My next call was to my mother in Bryanston. Fortunately, she was in and I explained the urgency with which I needed 427 Rand. She assured me that she would transfer the money to the Kimberley Post Office immediately, to reach me by the following day. Finally, after several fortifying cups of tea and having considered every possible option, I made my way to the HQ and to the Kommandant's office. It was almost five o'clock by this time, the end of the working day for the admin staff. I was shown in to the Kommandant's office almost immediately. As I told him the story, his face lit up in a broad grin.

"You won't be leaving us for some time then, it would appear." He looked at his diary before continuing.

"We have to schedule a court martial for you, but we have our Christmas break starting tomorrow. I will not be back for two weeks, by which time it will be Christmas. I think we will have to look at a suitable date for the New Year. I will schedule it when I return in January. In the meanwhile, you can carry on as normal." With that I was dismissed. It was past five o'clock by then. That morning I had envisaged myself at the end of this day packing my few belongings in readiness for my last night in Kimberley but instead I faced this eleventh hour hiccup. Wednesday night was a long and miserable affair, but not without hope.

I awoke with the dawn on Thursday feeling charged with energy, sensing that this was to be an important day. I had the outline of a plan and the will to force events to suit my purpose. A few phone calls from the bookstore to Dino in the law office confirmed that the Kommandant was indeed away for a fortnight, as was Whiteley. The highest-ranking officer left in HQ was a young captain, Captain

McCauley. I had never seen him before. Dino could provide no additional information, beyond the fact that he "just arrived in the HQ last week, he is English and he looks young." With this as my cue and, fortified by a morning coffee, I presented myself at the HQ at five o'clock, where Dino escorted me to Captain McCauley's office. He knocked on the door before opening it to usher me in.

"Captain, there's a troop here to see you on urgent business," he said. My first sight of the slightly startled young officer left me feeling confident that things would work out. He was English-speaking with a gentle voice. I was armed with my transfer documents, which served as props for the story I presented him with.

"Captain, I am so pleased that you are here. I have recently been transferred to Pretoria. Here are the transfer papers signed personally by General Steenkamp, who has requested this transfer. I was supposed to leave today, however there is a problem. I have switched rifles with someone else, we can't locate the other person who has my rifle and so without a rifle I can't uitklaar. I have been told that the only way for me to uitklaar is to have a court martial. I have also been told that I must uitklaar today. This means that I have to be court-martialled today. Unfortunately, the Kommandant is away on holiday and you are the most senior officer in the camp and, as you are the senior officer in the camp, you will have to complete the procedure."

Captain McCauley looked horrified.

"But I don't know how to do a court martial. We will have to wait for the Kommandant."

"That is not an option. I have been ordered by a general in Pretoria to complete a task today and I don't think I want to be the one to tell him that he will have to wait." Warming to the moment, I was surprised by how easy the process was.

"Look Captain, don't worry about a thing. It's like anything in the army, there's a form for it. We get the form, we fill it out together and we'll find me guilty and sentence me to pay the fine for the replacement cost of an R1, which incidentally is 427 Rand. Then we simply stamp the form with an official stamp, I give you the money for the rifle and that's that. Job done. The general is happy and we can all get on with our day."

The next hour passed in a blur of activity. I went with Dino to the law office where we located the appropriate court martial form, filled in the relevant detail, before returning to Captain McCauley's office with the paperwork completed. Clearly no procedure in Officer's training school had prepared Captain McCauley for this moment. He was entirely bemused. Respect for superior rank was ingrained in the average officer and the constant reminder that he was being instructed by a general, albeit indirectly and by a troop, reduced him to a state of unsteady compliance. I revelled in the moment. This, I convinced myself, was the last of the chess moves with the Kommandant and Whiteley and one of such tactical significance that surely they would not now be able to reply.

The final detail in completing the court martial procedure was getting the money for the fine from Kimberley Post Office. I issued myself a route form and had Captain McCauley sign it, authorising me to use the duty driver. Armed with this document I set off for the Duty Room to locate a driver to take me to Kimberley Post Office. While sitting in the passenger seat of the Land Rover on the road to Kimberley, I envisaged the return of the Kommandant, refreshed after his two-week summer holiday, looking forward to his moment in the sun with me. I imagined the look on his face at being told that I was long gone. Light had prevailed and darkness had been vanquished.

I returned from Kimberley with the cash withdrawal in my wallet, feeling elated. Nothing could stop me now. I returned to the HQ to finalise the details of my court martial. Reading from the manual Dino had provided, I guided McCauley through the procedure, line by line. A formally executed court martial within the protocols specified in Military Law.

"The charge is losing your weapon. Now you say to me, how do you plead?" I directed him.

"Umm. How do you plead?" he repeated.

"I plead guilty. Now, we are at the sentencing section. You accept my guilty plea and sentence me to the minimum tariff, a fine of 427 Rand. You fill in the sentence here, saying that a fine of 427 Rand is imposed."

I handed over the envelope containing 427 Rand. McCauley carefully counted out the notes. The form was duly signed and stamped, the court martial was concluded and I was free to leave. As I left his office, the exhilarating thought occurred to me that I was probably the first person in any army to effectively court martial himself.

With this detail resolved I could now conclude the check out procedure. I showed the quartermaster staff-sergeant my court martial document which concluded the missing rifle aspect and he completed my uitklaar documentation. By mid-afternoon I found myself sitting in the bookstore for what I believed must surely be the last time. I resolved to leave immediately and packed the contents of my drawer, my song-writing book, a paperback novel and a few cassettes, into my rucksack.

I didn't call General Steenkamp to confirm that I had successfully cleared out of Kimberley. I decided instead to treat myself to a long weekend pass and then call in the following week, to make it appear as if I was transferring directly to Pretoria from Kimberley. Issuing the weekend pass was easier than it should have been. I had the official stamp to use and forging the signature of the duty officer in the passbook could not have been simpler. Before I left I made a point of taking whatever documents I felt might be helpful at some future point. This included issuing myself a Military Heavy Duty Driver's licence enabling me to drive armoured vehicles. I experienced a tremendous feeling of joyfulness at receiving my heavy-duty vehicle licence only three minutes after deciding to apply for one. Luckily, there were no CCTV lenses inside the bookstore at that time, as I started laughing uncontrollably and talking to myself, saying, "Andrew, I would like to congratulate you on passing your SADF Heavy Vehicle Licence test."

With all my remaining belongings squashed into a rucksack

and with my guitar in its case I was ready to hit the road to Johannesburg. I deliberated over saying goodbye to the few people in camp that I felt bonded with but decided against it, thinking that since technically I was setting off on an AWOL weekend without a legal route form, the fewer people who knew my business the better. Further to that, any news of my departure was best kept secret in case somehow the Kommandant was informed at his holiday location by someone like Van Vuuren.

Although there were people there with whom I had spent the best part of a year, I felt no ongoing empathy with anyone except for Sean. I called him from the bookstore phone to say goodbye and reassured him that since I would also be in Pretoria I would do my best to visit him in the Detention Barracks. It was a stiff farewell.

Following that final call, I made my way to the guardroom. My loyal friend, George, had offered to drive me to the outskirts of Kimberley to a good hitch-hiking point and so, at five in the afternoon on a day where I had court-martialled myself and cleared out of 11 Kommando after 11 months of trying, I was finally able to watch the sun setting over Kimberley in the wing mirror. I felt ablaze with a new and wonder-filled sensation that I came to understand as personal achievement.

I made it back to Johannesburg in good time. As usual the drive took three or four stops, with plenty of time on the journey to bask in the wondrous thought that I would never have to see Kimberley again. One should never think that.

During this unexpected weekend pass, I attended a Folk club meeting in Braamfontein where I bumped into a school chum from Bryanston, Anthony Kiennis. This meeting was made more interesting because Anthony was also in the military. Anthony had signed a contract with the permanent force. By signing up for a four-year air force training program which provided training for a diploma in electronics as well as a monthly pay cheque he was excused national service. I could never understand why anyone would even consider voluntarily joining the military but with this reservation notwithstanding, Anthony, like myself had completed his first year in the services and we had this common ground on which to compare experiences.

Anthony had recently completed a three-month stint on the border and he had interesting tales of the war and its progress. News of the war was not easy to come by unless received first-hand and even then first-hand information on the war originating from some Afrikaner zombie who was fighting for the Fatherland had to be taken in context. The opportunity to hear first hand accounts of the various goings on from an informed objective source was of great interest to me. On subsequent nights out with Anthony we would smoke joints and he would relay the details of his experiences on the border.

The backdrop to these social weekend pass outings was the emerging alternative sub culture blossoming in Johannesburg around this time, played out in live-music bars and clubs dotted around the Johannesburg suburbs where arty types conglomerated to smoke pot and debate the issues of the day. For the first time, I felt I was meeting people with some capacity for independent thought, living to the tune of their own morality and not cowed by the dictate of the state and these settings provided my first opportunities to discuss my thoughts without fear of being summarily assaulted. My favourite theme was the tremendous wastefulness that war represented.

The Entertainment Corps, Voortrekkerhoogte

All too soon, the extra long weekend pass that I had written for myself came to an end and I faced up to the new chapter in my life that would be starting in Pretoria. On Monday morning, I phoned General Steenkamp to confirm that I had completed my transfer and would be able to travel to Pretoria. He advised me on the procedure for checking in, providing me with an address in Pretoria for this purpose. My understanding was that I would check into his unit, the 'Tiffies'. Once there I should contact Major Hayden at

Entertainment Corps asking him to make a transfer request for my services. Once this request was received the General would rubber stamp it and I would be on my way to the Entertainment Corps.

It took two weeks, during which time I was given accommodation in Pretoria in the Tiffies' dormitory and my instructions consisted of two daily requirements; I had to attend check-in parade at 8am every morning and then check-out parade at 5pm in the afternoon. In between, I spent most of the day lying on the bunk in the dormitory reading and smoking, leaving in the middle of the day for lunch at a nearby burger joint.

Every evening after the 5pm roll call, I drove back to Bryanston. By then I had taken over the green 1969 Peugeot 404 Sedan that my mother had been driving for the past 10 years. Underpowered though the 1600 cc engine was, the car was reliable enough as a means of commuting between Bryanston and Pretoria, a journey of no more than 30 minutes via the back roads.

Christmas meant additional days off and more nights spent in the music clubs. The biggest hits of the day were 'Message in a bottle' by The Police and 'Another brick in the wall' by Pink Floyd.

It was, as usual for December, a hot dry season. The temperature during midsummer in Johannesburg reached well into the thirties and the days were characterised by spectacular electric thunderstorms. Within minutes of the pressure dropping, the clear skies would darken as thick black edged cloud swept overhead, swirling in ever darkening waves. Whiplash thunder cracks of jagged silver lightning would explode in deafening crescendos through the blackened cloud and then torrential rain would come sheeting down, often accompanied by hailstones that could dent the bodywork of a car. Ten minutes after the explosion of electric energy, steam would be rising off the ground into a clear blue sun-lit sky. The thunderstorms were among the most exhilarating aspects of growing up in Johannesburg, along with the immediate access to abundant nature. These provided some form of redressing balance to the dark energies affecting my prospects as a uniformed soldier.

Soon the Christmas break would be over and my year at the Entertainment Corps would begin.

Bandsman

Finally, on Wednesday 11th January 1980, my transfer became official. It was a steaming hot morning as I drove the green Peugeot from the Tiffies building where I had completed my uitklaar, through the winding streets of Voortrekkerhoogte and into the sandy parking area of the Entertainment Corps lot. I locked the car and set off towards the admin area, noticing as I walked across the courtyard a group of musicians standing chatting and smoking on the porch. One looked over as I approached. He stepped forward with a smile to say hello and offer a welcoming handshake, almost as if he was expecting me. I felt an immediate connection with this fellow who I recognised as the first soldier whose lack of houding was a match for mine, a remarkable achievement and one I predicted would make us great friends. He introduced himself as Pete Sklair. His beret had no line to its fold and his boots had clearly not seen polish or brush for some time. The first word that came to mind was 'snap'.

Major Hayden welcomed me with a warm handshake, rather than the more traditional salute. He walked me around the unit making introductions along the way. The Entertainment Corps, he explained, existed to provide the military hierarchy and high government office with two professional bands to attend their requirements.

The main band, the George Hayden Big Band, performed in the style of Glen Miller and was made up of around 30 permanent force members. The second band was a smaller 'functions' band made up largely of national servicemen who would be chosen from the small pool of national servicemen at the unit. It was immediately apparent that that no one here had much houding. Most of the permanent force troops had hair way beyond the regulation army length and none displayed the proper carriage of a soldier. Best of all, this wonderful set up was located right in the heart of the defence force headquarters.

The 'Big Band' musicians were mostly recruited from the South African professional music circuit and appeared to be players beyond the age when they could hope for big success in the music industry. Using the double lure of a regular wage and a pension plan, George Hayden had assembled a remarkable collection of musicians whose performances of big band standards like 'In the Mood' or 'Tuxedo Junction' were of an extremely high standard.

The 'functions' band was drawn from a pool of around fifteen national servicemen but, being the end of the year, most of the band members had come to the end of their two-year service and had cleared out. My first day was the prelude to meeting and playing with the various band members in the functions-band room in a selection process that would determine the line up of the functions band for 1980.

The Entertainments Corps building was located in a converted house with a corrugated iron roof inside Voortrekkerhoogte, the sprawling military base formerly known as Roberts Heights that was established in about 1905. In 1939, a time of growing Afrikaner nationalism, the construction of the nearby Voortrekker monument began and Roberts Heights was renamed Voortrekkerhoogte (Voortrekker Heights).

The building used by the Entertainment Corps had probably been a residential unit, now modified into an L shaped arrangement to provide two main band rooms, an admin section, some lesser offices and a row of smaller rehearsal rooms. The first room as you approached the building was the functions-band room and the second much larger room housed the Big Band.

As a part of the checking in process I was issued with the pale blue beret of the Entertainment Corps, which bore the insignia designed around a harp. Like all new berets, this one had no shape. During basic training, the shaping of the beret formed a useful opportunity for instructors to belittle troops. It had to be folded at a certain angle until a crease was formed, giving the beret an edge that provided the particular angle required to avoid punishment for the wearer. Achieving a suitably impressive fold in the beret might take many hours of determined endeavour. You could immediately identify those troops who took their training seriously in the houding displayed by the condition of their beret. My green 11 Kommando beret had only acquired a barely passable crease because I had paid someone to do it for me. As the owner of this new blue beret I realised that it could be worn in its natural baggy condition without fear of being screeched at by an obese moustachioed Afrikaner sergeant major. The issue of the beret was an apt metaphor for the change in my circumstances. My rank too had changed from RFN (Rifleman, the lowest rank in Infantry) to BDM or Bandsman, a pleasing step in the right direction. During the course of the first day, I heard the sound of music from the big-band room and went to the front door, kept open for fresh air on a hot summer's day. Standing in the doorway listening to the horns blowing in beautiful unison just a few feet away, I realised that I had after all found my way to the best possible place in the army. Any school leaver's dreams I may have had of attending a prestigious music college in America may have been dashed on the jagged rocks of economic reality but this was the next best thing. Here were real musicians reading from charts and being instructed by a world-class arranger and conductor. I couldn't wait to get started.

George Hayden had not forgotten the bouzouki reference in my application and neither had I. Suspecting that this would be raised, I had spent whatever available time I had in acquiring some skills on the bouzouki. Two obstacles soon became apparent. My bouzouki, a souvenir-quality gift from my Aunt Eftihia, was not a professional standard instrument which made tuning it something of an ongoing challenge and secondly, I was unlikely to raise my bouzouki playing skill levels to a professional level within a few short weeks. Instead, I came up with a workable alternative by developing a rolling-plectrum style on the guitar that eventually sounded not dissimilar to a bouzouki. By turning up the chorus pedal I was even able to emulate the jangling string tone of the bouzouki. As a party piece, I learned the only Greek style song I had any chance of playing convincingly, which was 'Never on a Sunday':

'Oh you can kiss me on a Monday, A Tuesday, A Wednesday...'

During the afternoon of my first day, I was finally called by George Hayden and led into the functions-band room. I had already spoken with a few of the other musicians and got to know a little bit about them. This audition was with a drummer and bass player as accompaniment. The drummer, who had an impressive looking Tama Kit that seemed to fill half the room, was Lloyd Martin from Cape Town, a flamboyant player overflowing with confidence in his extravagant skills. Whereas Toby the drummer in the Kimberley band had learned to play with an economy of rhythm best suited to keeping perfect time, often meaning little more than a very basic bass drum snare drum marking the beat, Lloyd's approach involved a complexity that filled every available space.

The bass player was Pete Sklair, the first person I had met on my arrival. With these two musicians providing a rhythm section, I was to perform a few standards for Major Hayden to evaluate my suitability for the functions band. The adrenaline rush that accompanied playing with such competent musicians eradicated any nervousness I may have felt. Up until that time, I had never played in a line-up where everyone could play to a high standard and this was an exciting feeling. We were directed through a few standards, which I played and sang on and then came the bouzouki emergency.

"Andrew, have you brought your bouzouki?" asked the major.

"I'm afraid not, Major, because the bouzouki is such a fragile instrument and I didn't really want to risk bringing mine in for day-to-day use. However, I do have a Greek song that I can do as a bouzouki sound-alike."

"And what is that, then?" he asked.

"'Never on a Sunday,' in the key of C."

It was my great good fortune that the musicians playing along were so good that the piece sounded entirely believable. I had not learned the lyric in Greek but was able to improvise some Greek words to fit the rhythmic meter. I banked on the high probability that no one present spoke Greek well enough to spot any anomalies in the lyrics. By the time the song ended everyone in the room had a smile on their face and Major Hayden wore the widest smile of all. It had worked out so convincingly I had surprised myself. Quite clearly, when it came down to emergency bouzouki playing, I was a born natural.

During the first day, the expectations of my new role were explained. Eventually I would be part of a band that would be available to perform at functions when required. This would include tours requiring that we be away from home, possibly for lengthy periods. The touring schedule would include a morale boosting tour of the border during which, it was said, we would accompany 'top stars'. When the band was not performing locally or touring, we would be expected to rehearse every day, starting at 8am and finishing by 1pm. I couldn't believe my luck. I faced a 30-minute drive from home in the morning and would have the afternoons and weekends to myself. This new freedom was a wonderful opportunity to set about rebuilding my hopes and to work through the trauma of my year in Kimberley. The therapy was to be music, pursued with a consuming passion. I was obsessively committed to improving as a musician, practising for hours on end, often managing four hours a day of scales and other routines.

Along with the physical improvement of skills resulting from my obsessive attention, I found a growing insight into spirituality through music. After a few hours of playing scales on the guitar, with the pain barrier that this endeavor involves and the monotonous repetition of the same passages, I experienced many of the benefits that come from meditations that rely on a disciplined repetition to shut down a part of the conscious brain and allow the subconscious to prevail. Through this raised awareness becoming available to me, my understanding of the individual's connection to the grand scheme of things grew appreciably. Music translated the lessons of life for me, informing me consistently and reliably as to my place in the grand scheme of the universe. It was never anything less than a beautiful relationship. When I wasn't playing, I listened to music of all styles, with the sole criteria that it be 'good' music.

Within days of my arrival at Entertainments, George Hayden announced the line up of the functions band at the morning parade. The bass player, Pete Sklair, was the most competent musician in our group and certainly the most accomplished musician I had met up until that point. Pete was from a musical family. His father, Sam Sklair, was a well-known bandleader, arranger and film composer and his older brother, Josh, was a jazz guitarist, a graduate of Berklee Music College who lived and worked in Los Angeles. In many ways, the level of Pete's skills vindicated my obsessive determination to get into the Entertainment Corps.

Pete also seemed to mirror many of my own reactions to the experience of being drafted. He too had adopted a disdainful attitude to the army, pointedly avoiding the acquisition of any militaristic demeanour while distancing himself from the darker extremes of the call-up experience. Another similarity was a shared interest in taking our musical education further. I think he also felt he would have benefitted far more by spending these two years of national service at a music college rather than in the uniform of a system against which we both felt the same revulsion.

As Lloyd Martin, the flashiest drummer in the unit, was due to complete his national service in June, he was not able to remain as the band drummer but would fill in that role until his permanent replacement arrived. This was to be Al Debbo Junior, the son of the famous 'rubber faced' Afrikaans comedian, singer and veteran film actor, Al Debbo. Al Junior had a pleasing air of confidence that was perhaps the result of growing up in a successful showbusiness family. Taking over the drum stool vacated by Lloyd would put Al's skills very firmly in the spotlight and it would be fair to say that though he was not as accomplished technically or as flamboyant as Lloyd, he was not bad either. He had a happy and endearing willingness to please that was attractive and made him an easier player to work with than the departing self-proclaimed virtuoso. An aura of congeniality surrounded him, in stark contrast to Lloyd's willingness to remind anyone listening of his musical superiority.

The singer was Gerald Sharpe, a Capetonian who, having already completed his university studies before commencing his national service, was the oldest member of the band. Gerald was a reasonably good singer in the conventional sense with good pitch, a good range and a reasonable delivery but from the beginning I recognised an arrogance in his vocal delivery that I felt would impose a time limitation on his prospects for a singing career, a patronising over-confidence that consistently made him sound unconvincing and to my ear, slightly ridiculous. I was not at all sure of Gerald whose swaggering salesman's persona had managed to raise my hackles the first time we met. He was the diametric opposite of Pete, reminding me of John Coltrane's observation that: *'How you are as a person is how you are as a musician.'* When he sang, I didn't believe him.

The keyboard player, by way of contrast, was a gentle introspective fellow who ironically had also just arrived from Kimberley. Tony Drake, a serious young man with a conscientious approach to practice and technique, was clearly looking to make a career as a musician. Despite his plentiful abilities, however, Tony seemed under-confident to the point where he made a compliant foil for Gerald's overbearing ego.

The final member of the band was Nick Paton, who played saxophone and guitar. Nick was from Parktown North, another of Johannesburg's more affluent northern suburbs. He was the grandson of the esteemed South African writer and liberal intellectual, Alan Paton, whose classic novel, 'Cry the Beloved Country', was one of the literary set pieces during my school years. Like Tony, Nick seemed to prefer a quiet approach, both of them being more comfortable listening than speaking.

With the sextet lined up, the business of developing the band into a working unit began in earnest. We were supplied with amplification and guitars. Although I chose to use my own instrument, I also used the army-supplied amplifier, a Fender Twin Reverb Combo, the reliable old workhorse of the gigging guitar player.

In rehearsal, the character of the band became apparent. Pete and I represented one side, charged with anti-establishment attitude, left wing liberal leanings and musical assertion, and we directed the proceedings in terms of repertoire and musical leadership. Gerald, Tony and Nick on the other side completed a tidy quartet of smoking abstinence with Jesus, the invisible but ever present arbiter of their performance.

Somewhere in the middle was Al, a 20-year old Afrikaner, already married and occupying something of an honorary role in our midst. On the very first day that we convened for band practice, Gerald tried to assume a leadership role by establishing each one of our positions with regard to Jesus. Nick and Tony safely identified themselves as believers. When it came to my turn, Gerald chose a discreet moment during a break to approach me while I was having a cigarette and a contemplative moment in the parking lot.

"I see you are wearing the cross. Do you know what that means?" Gerald was pointing at the small gold cross I wore on a neck chain, a gift from my aunt when I set off to the army. Its significance was aesthetic and sentimental, not a symbol of Jesus' love, a commemoration of the crucifixion or a defensive shield against Satan and his minions. I knew exactly where the conversation was heading and I tried to discourage the conversation as politely as possible.

"Yes Gerald, I do know the symbolism the cross represents, thanks for asking."

"I am pleased to see you are a Christian," he replied.

"Actually, it's not an advertisement of Christian belief. It's just a gift from my aunt."

"Well surely you must have some idea about why we wear the

cross or don't you have any interest in the spiritual world?" he sneered.

I looked at him.

"I'm very interested in exploring the spiritual dimension to life, but, and this is only my personal view, Jesus is not the way that works for me. It's not that I haven't invested considerable effort into exploring the merits of Christianity. It's because I simply have my own views on what goes where and I generally find it's best to not get into any discussion about Jesus or my thoughts on the subject with strongly opinionated believers."

I might just as well have suggested his mother was a wharfside whore and his father a venereally diseased sailor with a spare dime on a Saturday night. Gerald appeared incensed by my lack of belief in Jesus.

"And what is the considerable effort you have put into understanding Jesus?" he scoffed, his voice rising in both pitch and volume.

"Gerald, honestly, this really is a no-win for either of us. Let's talk about something else," I tried one last time.

"No. I am really interested. You have explored the merits of Christianity and I want to know what that means." It was clear Gerald was not going to let me go without establishing a position and so I started out tentatively with a hopeful explanation.

"My relationship with Jesus started at an early age. From as far back as I can remember, I guess around three years of age, I was taken to the Greek Orthodox Church near Johannesburg city centre every Sunday. My mum would dress me in a suit and I would sit in that suit silently for hours on end listening to sermons conducted in ancient Greek that would go on and on. This gave me lots of time to think about God and Jesus and the idea of a higher power. I am not saying it was all bad. Actually, there was much about the experience that I enjoyed."

"Like what?" asked Gerald, evidently keen to get to the point about Jesus. I thought about this for a moment. What had I taken away from that experience that I had treasured later?

"The exotic smells. They burn frankincense in Greek services and this was the first time I got to smell incense. Then there are the icons. Orthodox history has a strong icon legacy and I grew to love the Byzantine iconography on display. In Greek culture the men kiss, so I would kiss the cheeks of a lot of bearded men, a tactile sensation I would not otherwise have experienced but for church visits. I especially enjoyed hearing the choir singing ancient Byzantine hymns with their haunting melodic timelessness that resonated with such astounding clarity inside the stone walled church. There was a 'taste' element as well, where during the Easter services they would provide delicious bread that represented the body of Christ, and we had to drink sips of wine that represented the blood of Christ. There's no doubt that on some level the experience addressed every one of the senses. As an experience and as an education in the significance of a church-driven organisation to bond a community, my early insight into the Greek Orthodox Church was wonderful."

I paused to light another cigarette. Gerald waited politely, hoping no doubt for an opening into which he might insinuate the Jesus wedge.

"The Orthodox Church is Christian, so if you have been so many times how can you not understand about Jesus and the sacrifices he made for us?" he asked.

"Well Gerald, the things I found most interesting about visiting Church decreased in direct proportion to the number of times I visited. Something happened to me that changed everything."

I paused for another draw on the Camel, feeling the hot glare of his hostile gaze.

"I turned seven and my vocabulary grew, which enabled me to ask questions. It was Jonah and the whale that did it for me. The idea that a man could stay alive inside a whale's belly started me questioning all the stories. The more questions I asked, the more the answers came back to the same point. Don't think; just believe what you're told. Remember that ignorance is bliss. For the next many years I was forced to go to church which, I guess you can understand, gave me quite an evolved insight into the less attractive qualities of a church visiting experience."

"It may have been a little uncomfortable for you to visit a church, but how uncomfortable do you think it was for Jesus up there on the cross, bleeding from the nails driven through his hands and feet, hanging there hour after hour, for one reason. Do you know the reason he went through all that?"

Gerald's eyes were ablaze with righteous indignation. With fortuitous timing the bell clanged marking the end of break time and we had to return to rehearsals. Gerald's news of the painful sacrifices Jesus made on my behalf would have to wait. I knew with a weighty sense of foreboding that this was only a temporary reprieve.

Any argument on the merits of religion could not in my mind outweigh the reality that religion is a divisive doctrine, polarising into opposing camps individuals who, if sufficiently primed, will continue as they have done throughout history which has been to destroy each other. My familiarity with the subject, along with considerable experience of zealots having targeted me for conversion to the flock in the past, meant that I was painfully aware of the potential for confrontation with Gerald and resolved to make every attempt to not be drawn.

It became apparent that when Gerald looked at me, or at Pete for that matter, he saw us less as people than as a threat to his belief system and one that must, at any cost, be vanquished. On the next occasion where he sought to corner me during a break for a 'little chat', I asked him why he couldn't just avoid the subject in the same way as I was.

"Can't we just agree to differ?" I asked him. "Let's be Bob Dylan about this. You go your way and I'll go mine."

"That's not how it works," he explained dismissively. "As a Christian, it is my duty to save the lost. On judgment day, heathens will suffer the worst agonies imaginable, an eternity in hell with non-stop suffering for the rest of time." He paused. "If I can save you from that, what kind of Christian would I be if I just turned my back on you and left you at Satan's mercy?"

Ordinarily I expect Gerald had a high success rate with his conversions. He was a fairly handsome, tall, well-spoken fellow, evidently from a well-to-do background. His confident presentation had all the qualities to suggest a good future beckoning in the sales department. My first thought was that the bedding section in a major department store would be one possible avenue for his future after the army. There was an unusually sleepy quality to his look that bode well for this prospect of directing lucrative sales programs in the luxury bedding sector.

With Gerald as an ever-present reminder of the pressure to conform to religious subjugation, I worked steadily towards my own spiritual understanding as if it were the most important aspect of my day. The uncertainty that accompanied being an insignificant speck in an infinite universe could not be addressed by the simple salve of blind faith and the benevolence of an imaginary friend, but that did not mean there was no higher level in which life and the universe did not resonate. Life must have a reason and that, I believed, must include a journey toward a period of bliss, at least in aspirational terms. All the struggles that I was encountering must be a part of a plan and the measure of my success would be determined by how I dealt with the obstacles in my path. I equated conforming to what I considered the iniquitous ways that surrounded me with cowardly surrender, an unspiritual eventuality if ever I knew one.

Although I had no absolute picture of where I wanted to be, I was developing a more detailed insight into knowing what I did not want to be. In the person of Gerald I had been confronted with the embodiment of the least attractive qualities of human nature, including what appeared as reliance on the need to project his own personal failures onto others in order to validate them. To my mind, instead of representing spiritual confidence, Gerald's attitude just screamed mindless blind deluded arrogance.

During the Christmas break I had met up with Julian Gallow, a band mate from 'Hobo', my first band during school days. Julian had gone into the army six months ahead of me and we had not seen each other for some time. During our reunion, he shared with me the joy he had found in being 'born again'. His enthusiasm was immense as he described the miracles that accompanied the experience and had opened up a whole new world for him. He eulogised in glowing terms about his church, where the congregation offered concrete proof of God's existence via what he described as 'the miracle of talking in tongues'. Such was his determination not to let me miss out on this exciting discovery that I realised that to ignore his invitation to visit his church would be construed as a personal slight and would not reflect well on my own belief that almost everything should be tried once, two notable exceptions being suicide and heroin.

On a Sunday evening in January, I found myself accompanying Julian to a church hall in Bryanston to join a congregation of some 200 'born-again' Christians. A minister led prayers and then what could have been taken for 'speaking in tongues' commenced. The experience was a lot like looking at some pitiful attention starved young man muttering gibberish that increased in direct proportion to the number of "Hallelujah's" being directed his way. I watched in stunned disbelief, thinking this was less the promised proof of God's existence than disturbing evidence of mankind's idiotic inclination to believe anything that might delay the onset of self-awareness.

I stayed for as long as I could bear it, which was no more than a few minutes, but it was clear to me that the only answer I was likely to find in this room was the answer to the question: "How desperate do you need to be to believe in something that relies on blind faith?"

My position in respect of a practical spiritually sound code by which to live was, as with so many aspects of my development, encapsulated in the words of a song, in this case, 'Try a little kindness.' It worked well for me.

Music and cannabis

By the end of my first year of military service I had developed strong views on drugs, following on from my introduction to the subject at medical school, especially as cannabis played such a significant role in my experience in Kimberley. The factual medical insights gleaned from my year at medical school, where I had been fortunate to experience the lecturing wisdom of Dr. Sylvan de Miranda, in respect of the physical and psychological consequences and benefits of smoking cannabis supplemented by the past year's experience of cannabis usage left me feeling bemused by the disparity between my understanding of the subject and the prevailing legal status of cannabis.

Cannabis was widely used by the majority of my peer group. As it was illegal, anyone who smoked cannabis was breaking the law yet based on my own calculations more than 50 per cent of my peer group had smoked it and were thus criminals in the eyes of the Establishment. I could think of no other law that affected the majority of citizens in a similar way. In the meanwhile, prescription drugs capable of causing damage far beyond the effects of the naturally occurring cannabis plant continued to generate vast profits for pharmaceutical company shareholders.

My primary objection to the point of criminalising drugs lay in the aspect of choice. Those who chose to smoke smoked whether it was legal or not. Those who chose not to smoke did not abstain because of the law. They simply chose not to smoke and this meant the theoretically deterrent aspect of the law was irrelevant.

Regardless of the law, the supply and distribution of cannabis funded an underworld sector that engaged negative as well as positive forces. Away from Kimberley, where Sean or George the Driver could always be relied on to supply the best of whatever was around, I now had to find my own sources in Johannesburg. On occasions where we went to 'score' some grass, I would find myself in surroundings that I would never ordinarily have seen and encountered people that I would never ordinarily have come across. It was immediately evident to me that this opportunity for a criminal underworld to interact with ordinary non-criminals provided a rich seam for increasing the criminal population, one that would not occur were drugs to be supplied legally within an officially registered legal distribution network. Quite obviously the use of cannabis had benefits as well as potentially unfortunate consequences but the idea that making cannabis illegal would stop anyone taking it was plainly unworkable. It was clear to me that the profits generated by these illegal sales may well add up to a considerable amount for a dealer, providing a motive to encourage wider drug use outside of individual choice as well as placing vast amounts of money and the power that represents in the hands of amoral drug dealers whose motive to widen the spread of drug use is obvious. This aspect alone laid a fertile ground for grievous social consequences arising from the illegality of drugs, creating as it did many billionaire drug lords able to exert their malign influence in proportion to their extraordinary economic power.

I became particularly fascinated with Bob Marley, not just because of his musical accomplishments but more because his open stance in promoting the use of cannabis was at such extreme odds with my own position in trying to keep it as secret as possible. In that Rastafarianism required that its followers remain constantly stoned, Marley had even contrived to twist a religious endorsement into pot smoking. It struck me that just as there was a powerful lesson in the way the Afrikaners found a passage in the Bible to legitimise their racism, the Rastafarians had also found one in the Book of Psalms to justify pot smoking which is:

"He causeth the grass to grow for the cattle, and herb for the service of man." (Psalm 104:14)

What a different world Bob Marley occupied from the world of the freshly laundered white youngsters in Johannesburg's northern suburbs. Marley was able to stand up and proclaim his beliefs when all around me people cowered in fear at the consequences arising from expressing the same sentiments. Bob Marley was a pioneer in the battle to hammer down the walls of delusion behind which the prejudiced and small-minded sought to maintain a punitive resistance to evolutionary growth. 'Tuff Gong', as the diminutive Marley was known in Kingston, had learned to fight for the right to be heard. A keen reader of the Bible, Bob Marley demonstrated that somewhere in the Bible there is a line than can be interpreted to suit any purpose.

Back in the rehearsal room we faced the challenge of finding a name for our band, a process resulting in the eventual choice of Ad Lib. The six of us were playing as much as possible so as to get the band up to speed as a working unit.

The drive from Bryanston to the Entertainments building in Voortrekkerhoogte took around 30 minutes and on most afternoons I would return with Pete either to my home or to his in Orange Grove where we would work on new songs in preparation for the following morning's rehearsal, writing out lyrics and preparing basic chord charts for the rest of the band.

Each working morning consisted of two two-hour sessions of playing through the songs. Before long the band started to sound really good to the people in it. The habit of playing for four hours a day was uplifting and spurred us on towards improving our skills. Whatever spare time came my way would be spent in practising scales and chord progressions on the guitar, including my recent discovery of the diminished minor ninth.

The discipline involved in obsessive practising presented an unexpected spiritual dimension. Sitting alone and summoning the motivation to play finger-numbing scales for hours on end is not something that happens without commitment. After five minutes of 'do-rey-mi-fa-so-la-ti-do' at ever increasing speeds and incorporating ever more diverse intervals, the interest factor is exhausted and all that remains is a test of stamina. But, much as with a mantra, the repetition of the same exercise starts to produce a relaxing and releasing effect under which the physical process eventually separates from the mental concentration, resulting in a calm and detached state.

It became clear to me why the disciples of Jazz so commonly

used strong drugs to shut out the world and make it possible to focus on and accentuate the importance of musical discipline. John Coltrane, it is said, used copious amounts of heroin in order to control and shut out every non-contributing influence and enable the elevation of his already immense musical skills. Use of heroin is a common element in many of the most accomplished musicians of the modern era.

In my studious pursuit of the recorded works of great players like Buddy Guy, John Coltrane, Miles Davis, Thelonius Monk, Wes Montgomery and Keith Jarrett I came across a recording of Joe Pass which was to have a significant effect on my approach to music as a career. Here was a guitarist playing an independent bass line whilst simultaneously executing complex harmonic and melodic parts. I was totally knocked out when I first heard his playing. In attempting to emulate his style I realised it would take many years of total commitment to doing nothing else to even come close to matching this man's achievements with six strings, but then what? Where had this tremendous sacrifice led him?

My understanding of his towering musical innovations increased when I learned that Joe was arrested on charges related to heroin use and incarcerated for nine years, cruel treatment for a great musician that served as a warning by showing that to obsessively pursue musical greatness without balancing the other elements essential to life is to invite failure or, at worst, catastrophe. There is no doubt that Joe Pass was a spectacular success in his chosen field. As a guitarist his achievements were so far-reaching that anyone seeking to learn the instrument must pay homage to the magnitude of his accomplishments, especially in view of the period during which he was working.

My understanding of the Joe Pass story was to have a bearing on my concept of success. If submission to musical excellence takes over your life to the point where you become dysfunctional in most other areas then what sort of success is that? Joe Pass may have been a genius on the guitar but his obsessive pursuit of virtuosity unbalanced the other aspects of his life. Once he put his instrument down, his life stank. Outside the musical world he was in the conventional view a helpless drug addict, an ex-convict who lived most of his life in poverty-riddled misery. The temptation to pursue Joe Pass' level of virtuosity was affected by this thought and did not represent any type of success that I could imagine. This insight refined my musical goals towards living according to a musical philosophy, intuitively translating the essence of music into the value system of my life. I began to identify the light-headed thrill that came from hours of obsessive practice as something unhealthy and my interest in pushing those boundaries toward a virtuoso excellence was balanced by the idea that as soon as something no longer felt like fun, it was time to stop.

One square at a time

Sometime in March, I was driving home after the morning's rehearsal when I decided to experiment with a different route out of Voortrekkerhoogte in the hope of finding a shortcut. Vootrekkerhoogte was a maze of little dirt tracks that led off the main through-road, any one of which might have shaved a few more minutes from my daily journey. This detour led me down a bumpy side road where I passed an imposing brown brick building with enormous gates that seemed to be glaring down at me. I slowed to look more closely at the sign which read 'Voortrekkerhoogte Detention Barracks'. I decided this was an omen telling me to call and see if Sean was there and the following morning I located the phone number for the Detention Barracks. Subsequent enquiries with the admin there confirmed that Sean was an inmate and I was able to make an appointment to visit the following day. Evidently, he did not receive many visitors and so his quota was not used up. I parked in the visitor's parking area and made my way through the ominously forbidding gates into the Detention Barracks' perimeter. The guard at the entrance showed me into a waiting area.

"Just wait a few minutes and we will bring him to you here," he said, whilst a sour-faced, red arm-banded military policeman went to summon Sean.

There was a wooden bench for visitors but I felt too nervous to sit down, preferring to pace the waiting hall instead. There was a glass fronted display case on one wall presenting a number of items evidently chosen for the amusement of waiting visitors. I looked in at an open Bible with the pages inside cut away to form a bottle-sized cavity, ideal for smuggling in a half litre brandy bottle. The most prominent display item was a revolver, which I recognised it as a Webley .38. On closer inspection it became apparent that this weapon was constructed entirely of soap and ink. There was something disquieting about so much effort and skill being invested in such a pursuit. My cigarette had burned close to the filter and, with no sign of any activity, I lit another off the glowing butt whilst mulling over the meaning of this soap gun. Did the maker of the soap gun ever get to use it for its intended purpose? If he had managed to use it to stage an escape, how come the gun was still there? Was it just found in his cell before he had the chance to use it? I noticed how phenomenally clean the floors were, mirror clean. The whole place had an air of cleanliness about it that suggested much misery for many unfortunate knees. In the dry heat, the smell of disinfectant hung in the air making me reflect that not even the dirtiest germ infected fruit fly would choose to land in this location.

Eventually the red arm-banded military policeman reappeared, leading Sean out from the bowels of the building into the visiting area. His face lit up when he saw me. We shook hands. He couldn't stop smiling. Although he looked reassuringly well, I felt sick to my stomach from a combination of empathy with the sheer horror of what Sean must be going through and my own horror at being inside this horrendous place. This felt like somewhere that the light had not shone for a very long time. Having gone to the trouble of arranging this meeting, I now couldn't wait to leave. I felt a terrifying panic urging me to get out. I became increasingly aware that we were both constrained in that area and that while I was there I was as much a prisoner as he was. We couldn't just go for a walk or sit in the Peugeot for a cigarette. Waves of claustrophobia reminded me of the occasion in Kimberley when the guards had locked me in the cell. Every passing moment inside those dark walls seemed like a hypodermic needle stabbed into my soul, draining the very life essence from me and the draining effort at keeping up a positive outlook for Sean's benefit was a huge challenge. Though I was overcome by the urge to get out of there as quickly as possible, I somehow sensed in that moment that I would never see him again. As dictated by the circumstances, our conversation was stilted and awkward.

"They only give you seven squares of toilet paper every day," he said. "Every morning they issue you toilet paper and the guy counts out seven squares for each inmate. Can you figure that one out? And the weird thing is no one in here ever gets the shits."

Though this seemed a uniquely bizarre treatment of the inmates, despite this one exception, Sean seemed otherwise stoical in dealing with the experience.

"When I get out I am going to make the biggest spliff ever," he said. Clearly the punishment for smoking spliffs had no deterrent effect.

And then my stomach started to go. The walls were quite literally closing in. I felt like vomiting and I was struggling to breathe. I had exhausted all the energy I had available to me to give some form of friendly sustenance to a friend in diminished circumstance. I had to get out of there as quickly as I could. I left with as much dignity as I could muster, which amounted to very little. Voortrekkerhoogte Detention Barracks was the darkest place I had ever visited in my life, worse than the military hospital in Bloemfontein. It was a factory designed for the deliberate manufacture of nightmares built to last a lifetime or, in some cases, to shorten it. For days afterwards, I berated myself for having been such an ineffective friend. Instead of offering Sean some reassurance or comfort during the living hell of his prison days, I had leeched off his hard-won positive energy whilst there and had run for the hills at the first opportunity.

As I made my unsettled way from the prison building back towards my parked car, I noticed a troop of boys in blue overalls walking under guard across an adjoining field. I paused to look at a sight that remains one of the most chilling of my life so far. The boys in blue overalls being shepherded by a brown-uniformed junior officer were Jehovah's Witnesses, serving their six years in detention barracks rather than performing two years of national service. Having faced the issue of conscientious objection I felt somehow encouraged by the choice I had made. I was proving by my own example that objection to a system does not need to be registered with that system in order to be a conscientious objection. It has always seemed pointless to me to announce your intentions to your enemy.

The religious irony that the God of the brown-suited guards had determined that the blue-suited prisoners serve six years in jail for believing in their God was another in the long list of things about God belief that made perfect nonsense. Six years in prison for young men, most entering as 18 year olds, whose parents were Jehovah's Witnesses was seen as God's will and, on the surface at any rate, the young men accepted it.

Durban by the sea

2nd April, 1980, a Saturday night saw our first official engagement as Ad Lib. We drove down to Durban in a military combi on the Friday to perform for an Officers' Ball on the Saturday night, a journey of around five hours of mostly motorway driving. Our designated driver was Gerald who had a military licence and possibly enjoyed the metaphor of shepherding his flock down the highway. The show was a dinner dance in Durban City Hall for army officers and their wives, an audience of older, less worldly people whose look was familiar from the Kimberley experience. This was quite clearly a show demanding more of a 'standards' repertoire than the contemporary hits that our band had worked so hard to perfect. Though the nature of this gig was obvious from the outset, my suggestion that we drop our modern repertoire and stick to known standards was not well received, particularly not by Lloyd or Gerald and we set off with an unchanged set list.

In terms of delivering the right performance for that gig, the band was absolutely terrible. It was Lloyd Martin's first and only gig with the band as the drummer. Having performed many gigs of this type with the Kimberley band, I could see quite clearly that this band, with Gerald at the fore of attempting the band-leader role was overlooking a crucial element for any gig which is the need to please the audience.

The contrast between this gig which was my first with the Entertainment Corps and the last time I had played in the Kimberley band could not have been more glaring. Compared to the seasoned professionalism that the Kimberley band had developed after playing together so many times, this line up lacked both the experience in dealing with the bottom-layer of entertaining an audience as well as the will to perform well. Drummer Lloyd was clearly not interested in putting any effort into working the gig and his technical approach of 'Why play one beat when seventy two will do' ensured the reliable absence of a groove the rest of the band could slot into and start to contribute, demanding instead that we all worked frantically to accompany the drummer.

Gerald appeared equally uncommitted. He was sticking to his set list come hell or high water. The people in this audience were beneath him and he made sure they knew it. We had rehearsed the Christopher Cross song, 'Ride like the wind,' which was a new hit at that time and for which both Gerald and Lloyd had their parts down, which was perhaps why they were especially keen to play it despite the fact that it was music of no relevance to the audience.

"I was born the son of a lawless man, always spoke my mind with a gun in my hand," sang Gerald, while I played along with a sense of disbelieving horror. What were these guys thinking?

All things considered, the performance that night was a complete disaster. I felt that only Pete and I managed to demonstrate any semblance of professional effort despite the unhappy cacophony emanating from the stage. That night, Ad Lib never managed to be anything more than out of time and out of tune, both in terms of pitch as well as in the appreciation of the audience's interest. I was aching with self-consciousness from the first song until the last until eventually the show finished to a smattering of grudging applause before we hurriedly left the stage. Seething with indignation at having been compromised in this way, Pete and I set off to make the most of the weekend by heading for the beach with a portable cassette player, where we stayed up most of the night listening to the newly released and much anticipated Donald Fagan album 'Nightfly', smoking and picking at the bones of our disastrous first gig which had me ruminating over the irony of my efforts to get to Entertainments to work with great players only to find myself performing with a band immeasurably less capable than the one I left behind in - of all places - Diskobolos.

  It was over a month before the band performed again, the time between being filled with intensive rehearsal. Our second gig came as a private booking. The Entertainment Corps enjoyed a reputation as a sourcing ground for musical talent and occasionally agents would call up to enquire after bands for private functions. We were offered a wedding gig at Megawatt Park, near Pretoria, on 17th May, a gig that paid 410 Rand after the agent's commission. Pete and I were keen to do it, the rest of the band less so. Gerald wanted to take a weekend pass back to Cape Town and Lloyd said he was 'not interested' which left us without a lead vocalist or a drummer. Pete had a circle of musical friends from the Yeoville jazz club scene and he proposed two of these as stand-ins for the gig, Mario Cappazario as the singer and a drummer I remember only as David. Both fitted in successfully and the gig went fantastically well on the levels of repertoire, sound, pace, performance and crowd-pleasing entertainment value.

  By the time midnight arrived, we had packed up the equipment, paid the rest of the band and Pete and I headed off to Rockey Street for the post gig debrief that was to become traditional.

Remembering the Durban City Hall fiasco, we were euphoric especially as it was clear that our combined energies represented something capable of providing considerable rewards. Earning money for playing music had a stimulating effect on both of us, along with the confirmation that we were able to direct musicians towards a common end. Replacing two band members with stand-ins was the challenge we had faced from the outset and one we had addressed successfully.

The following week saw the arrival of our new drummer, Alvin 'Al' Debbo, who, in glaring contrast to Lloyd's attitude, approached the job with huge enthusiasm. The rehearsals immediately reflected this improvement. Our next gig was announced as an Officers' Ball at Waterkloof Air Force Base, a four-hour affair requiring four sets of around 45 minutes with a 15-minute break between each set. Gerald sang for most of the night although I sang a few songs in each set, far less than I had done in Kimberley.

When we had packed up after the gig, Pete and I drove back to Jo'burg in the Peugeot and headed for Rumours, our favourite late night haunt in Rockey Street where we would stay up until the early hours drinking coffee, listening to music and talking endlessly about life and the universe. Although we were never far from any reminder that we were conscripts in the military, this was about as close to normal life as we might have hoped for under the circumstances. I was very aware of my tremendous good fortune in finding such a similarly minded friend with which to interpret the harrowing experience of conscription. Chatting with Pete in a trendy coffee shop, I was moved to remark how much more enjoyable it was to discuss the lyrical intention in Donald Fagen's writing than listening to Johannes van Staden talk about tractors in Bethlehem, which might so easily, there but for a turn of fortune's dice, have been my position on this night.

The bookings started to come in at an increasing rate. Our next gig was a Navy Officers' Ball held in the Union Hotel in Pretoria. Now that we had a more committed drummer, Ad Lib was working well as a band. Al had settled into the drum chair and our core repertoire of around 40 songs was well established. If there was one ongoing hiccup, it was to be found in what Pete labelled 'the broken nail syndrome'. This condition arose on those occasions where Gerald was denied his particular whim, be it a simple cup of coffee or a conversion to his Jesus club membership. The consequences of the broken nail syndrome would involve the depositing of a job lot of bile on everyone within earshot, an 'unpleasantly characteristic need to diminish those around to make oneself feel better' as Pete and I had concluded in a rare moment of clarity.

I think Pete was largely excused the worst of Gerald's zealotry by virtue of his Jewish background but Gerald never missed any opportunity to remind me of how much closer to eternal and all-consuming damnation my every move led me.

Despite Gerald's hiccupping interest, the Union Hotel gig was our best to date. It was hardly like a military gig at all. Although we still wore military step-outs for the performance, by and large we might just as well have been a civilian band showing up for a performance. There was no element of military supervision in the experience and the set list was drawn up by Pete and myself and accepted without any arguments. Every band member played their parts proficiently and the overall effect was, to my ear at least, wonderfully proficient. On the drive home I reflected that this experience was exactly what I had hoped it would be when struggling to make the move to Entertainments.

Because the lifestyle at Entertainments was so far removed from the hierarchical military way, incidents of conflicting wills were always a possibility. In my case, this happened in the week following the Union Hotel gig, when I was required to go into Pretoria for administrative stamping of some documentation. I drove into the town centre, parked on the side of the road and was strolling determinedly down the sidewalk towards the office when I was confronted by an angry-looking Major. He started bawling at me in Afrikaans, the gist of which was that my houding was not right, my hair was too long, my beret was a 'fokken' disgrace and that I was now in big trouble, a jarring reminder that I was still a troop in a man's army. My mind immediately reeled back to the horrors of Kimberley.

As the Major kept up his yelling I imagined myself inside a cocoon of white light. When it became apparent that his tirade had ended and a reply was expected, I looked at him and found myself at a loss. There was nothing I could say. I had no words to offer towards the malice I saw in the glaring steel blue eyes. It was obvious that any conversation between us could have no possible up-side for me, especially as I would not speak Afrikaans and I felt certain that the sound of an English voice might tip him over the edge into violence. Weighing up the available options, I opted simply to walk away.

With an expressionless look directly into his eyes, in which I tried to telepathically transmit the message, "You can fuck off now, you fuckpig," I turned on my heel and walked away from him. A further torrent of Afrikaans rage began as he appeared to follow behind me for a minute or two, bellowing at full volume, but I kept walking and soon the sound faded before disappearing completely. I like to think my telepathic transmission had been a success.

When I got back to the unit I felt sufficiently disturbed by the incident and its possible ramifications as to speak to Major Hayden. The offended officer had already called in a complaint. My blue Entertainments beret had identified my unit and he had immediately called in to complain about the 'outrage'. Major Hayden was entirely supportive of my position and agreed that my silent approach was the best way forward in that situation. I thought it prudent to avoid any mention of the telepathy. As a result of that incident we were all issued with official looking cards that read:

'The carrier of this card is a member of the Entertainments Unit and is not to be detained. Any enquiries regarding the carrier to be directed to Major G. Hayden, Entertainment Corps.'

"Next time that happens, don't say anything," the Major announced. "Just present this card."

This document, along with the G4 K3 stamped in my ID book, meant I could feel reasonably confident should my by now legendary lack of houding attract further military attention.

Never on a Saturday Night

On 7th June 1980, we were booked to perform a cocktail party at which the Argentine Polo team and assorted Argentine government guests evidently of high rank were to be entertained by their South African hosts, including Prime Minister P.W. Botha and Minister of Defence Magnus Malan. Major Hayden explained to us that this was an especially prestigious gig booked directly from the Prime Minister's office.

Providing musical entertainment at official government functions was one of the reasons why the Entertainment Corps had been formed and allowed to continue. It provided government offices with on-call professional entertainment to use as they required it. Emboldened by my recent dabbling in happy experiences, I viewed this occasion with a ghastly clarity as I looked out on that night's audience. P.W. Botha, known as the Big Crocodile or something similar, perhaps because of his thick skin, was revolting to me. I knew him as a member of the pro-Nazi Afrikaner Nationalist Ossewabrandwag, whose mother had been interned in a British concentration camp during the Anglo-Boer War. P.W. Botha, another of whose nicknames was 'Piet Wapen' (Piet Weapon), was known to support all out war on the Communist blacks by directing the country's resources toward increasing military strength to the maximum extent including the rumoured commission and testing of a nuclear arsenal. P.W. Botha was largely responsible for the policy of recruiting young white males to ever increasing periods of so-called national service and on many levels, not the least of which was his physical appearance, P.W. Botha was completely disgusting to me and to countless thousands of young South Africans from all cultures.

Having invested so much effort in opposing the military system and not becoming an asset to it, suddenly here I was performing exactly as was expected of me and being that cog in the machine that kept the system ticking over. The rebellion in my ways seemed suddenly to have been doused by the contented waves of opportunity that had transformed me into an 'army asset'. Something seemed terribly wrong with this picture and I pondered whether I had become the 'Universal soldier who really is to blame'.

During the first set of well chosen light cocktail jazz standards, as I crooned away on 'Girl from Ipanema', I looked out at the sea of faces in front of me and the room started to spin. "Tall and tanned and young and lovely..." I sang as I saw the Minister of Defence and Chief of the Army dancing past with the wife of one of the Argentine ministers. I could hardly believe what I was seeing. She was dressed in an ornate ball gown and stiletto heels and he was wearing veldskoene. Most of the guests were in impeccable evening dress with the appropriate black leather footwear and there, gliding across the dance floor in a pair of farmer's shoes, was the Minister of Defence. I started to believe that I could see an aura surrounding this man, a hazy shimmering veil of serpentine blackness outlining his ample frame. The more I looked around the room, the more uncomfortable I became. These were the leaders of the system that had incarcerated me and who represented values that offended me on a deep level. For all I knew, Jimmy Kruger, Minister of Justice, was also in the room, the man who effectively murdered Steve Biko and greeted news of Biko's death in his custody with the press release of: "It leaves me cold". Not only was the worst type of South African present but the Argentines too seemed a pretty dodgy bunch as well. And there I was playing 'Girl from Ipanema' for them to dance away their cares. I felt sick to my stomach, worsening with every smile of acknowledgement directed my way.

Our first break arrived after 45 minutes. I had a pre-prepared 'two-toke' inside my Camel cigarette pack. Although the area was seething with security operatives and military policemen due to the high profile of the guests, Pete and I managed to find an open space to walk across, each having a good toke on the modified Camel cigarette whilst keeping a vigilant eye open for any military policeman showing undue interest in our walk. I was beginning to feel slightly hysterical with the stress of the moment. Our conversation became increasingly surreal.

"This is a severely weird gig. These guys suck real bad," I remarked to Pete. "What the fuck are we doing here playing Uncle Tom to these munts?"

"Ya, their bums stink," said Pete. "You can see the stink haze from their stench bums."

As a result of the weird combination between the cannabis and the high tension in the air, this juvenile thought started us both sniggering.

"These guys' bums stink so bad they have to refer to it in a code. They nod to each other knowingly and murmur "Bim Schtunk," I continued, warming to the theme.

"Yes," he agreed. "That's what the problem is here. They have the dreaded curse of chronic Bim Schtunk." A minor gale of laughter accompanied this ridiculous word play.

"Perhaps they need to find a treatment for it," I suggested helpfully. We pondered this conundrum.

"I have it," said Pete, "'In-and-Around', the new lotion for treating embarrassing Bim Schtunk." More stupid laughter followed.

"Soothes, heals and stops the schtunk. You could certainly make a fortune marketing 'In-and-Around' in and around this place," I observed. "A lot of demand for 'In-and-Around' around here." It was beginning to sound like a song. All too soon, the break was over and we were back on the stage, strapping on our instruments in between outbursts of giggling provoked by what we thought was our fabulous new joke.

"That guy could do with a jar of 'In-and-Around,'" said Pete in my ear, indicating an overweight Argentine minister who drifted past the stage. Once again, the dance floor filled with Argentine and South African government ministers and their wives, looking on expectantly as we tuned up for the second set.

Second up on the set list was 'Never on a Sunday', the emergency bouzouki song that was by now firmly established in the band's repertoire. I was singing the melody in my Greek wording when Pete leaned over in my ear as I reached the words on the chorus end 'On a Sunday' and in a happy falsetto a third above the melody sang "Yo Bim Schtunk".

Somehow I kept on singing into the microphone. At this precise moment, a dancing couple twirled in front of us and suddenly I was looking straight into the face of P. W. Botha, no more than a few feet away from me, who it must be said did not make an attractive sight with the lights reflecting an unfortunate glow off his shiny, bald head.

In the lightning clarity of that moment I suddenly found myself adapting the verse of 'Never on a Sunday' to incorporate the immortal line 'Yo Bim Schtunk'.

That night, the lyric to the tune of 'Never on a Sunday' as I sang looking right into the face of the big Crocodile, went:

'Ela kita pos
yo bim schtunk
yo bim schtunk
Yo bi i i im schtunk
Kai ela tho se mou to
Bim schtunk
Yo bim schtunk
Yo bi i im schtunk'

Charged with the exhilaration of recklessness, I heard Pete strike up a harmonious backing vocal. This was surely the most surreal moment in my life to date. Looking into the eyes of the Prime Minister, whilst the Minister of Defence looked on, telling him to his face that "YOUR BUM STINKS" while dressed in the uniform of a SADF soldier.

Before we had reached the end of the chorus, an angry-looking officer stormed onto the stage and escorted me physically off the stage area, almost lifting me off my feet and tearing the guitar cable out of the amplifier in the process. The band ground to an embarrassing halt as all eyes following my removal from the stage.

"What did you just say?" he hissed menacingly as the crowd in the room looked on in electrified silence.

"It's a Greek song. I am Greek and I am singing in Greek," I replied with a straight face, amazed by the calmness that I intuited would be my best hope of surviving the next three minutes without having my head knocked off, or sent to Jimmy Kruger's office for a personal interview. Stalemate. Once again the ability not to incriminate oneself in the face of the blindingly obvious had wrong footed the accuser. In the background, I heard Pete strike up the next song 'You are the sunshine of my life' and the band quickly fell in, returning the atmosphere to pleasant cocktail lounge mode. The eyes in the room switched from looking at me being harangued by the officer back to the dancing. It felt like a magic trick in progress.

"Excuse me" I said to the irate officer in his moment of indecision. "I have a job to do here," and made my return to the stage area to slide back into my anonymous guitar player's role from where I continued the night's performance under the laser glare of many steely eyes.

Later that night, safely seated in a side window in Rumours, Pete and I giggled like naughty children at what had happened. Passive resistance had been taken to a new level of absurdity.

"You just told P.W. Botha to his face that his bum stinks!' said Pete, at least a dozen times.

North of the Border

On Monday morning, Major Hayden came into the band room to announce that we were to go on our first border tour. This did not come as a complete surprise as rumours of a possible tour had been circulating for a while. The opportunity of a first-hand visit to a battlefield about which so much was spoken and so little known was exciting enough. We would be accompanying two well-known

Afrikaans music stars, Sias Reinecke and Mynie Grove, as their backing band. Unfamiliar as I was with Afrikaans music, I had not heard of either of them until then.

The shows would feature the artists each doing a 40-minute set for which we would provide the accompaniment. We would also be the opening act for each show, performing a 15-minute set of our own songs. We would be provided with musical charts for the two artists' sets. My immediate concern was over my sight-reading, as I had never bonded with the discipline of reading music, finding that when music was dominated by such closely controlled order the point in playing it was lost. I was drawn to the freedom of spontaneity rather than the discipline of diligent recreation.

The first rehearsal with Sias Reinecke quickly allayed my concerns over any reading inadequacy. The songs were basic three chord vamps, providing a gentle backing for his sentimental crooner style Afrikaans tunes. Mynie on the other hand had a lot more vim about her. She was a bubbly personality with a mane of curly blonde hair and she arrived with professionally scripted charts for each of the players. She conversed comfortably in either English or Afrikaans and made the effort to speak to each of us individually and to remember our names. Mynie's star quality was as impressive as it was agreeable. Included in her set was the Kim Carnes song, 'Bette Davis Eyes', as well as the Pretenders', 'Brass in pocket', two hits of the year which relied on fairly specific guitar parts, neither of which I knew. After the first rehearsal with Mynie, I spent much of my available time learning to play the guitar parts of the arrangements as accurately as I could and finding out as much as possible about our imminent border tour.

John Watson

The prospect of visiting the border was not without the particular interest arising from meeting troops returned from the war zone bearing visible scars of psychological damage. John Watson was a Bryanston resident whose younger sister was my age and was in the same class as a girlfriend of mine at Brescia House, the local Catholic girls' school. I had met John on a few occasions during school days, enough to be on first name terms but it was only now, in a bar on Rockey Street shortly before my departure for the border that I bumped into him again and we had the opportunity to talk at length.

John had completed his military service and was discharged back into civilian life. He looked a complete mess, his hair unwashed, his clothing filthy and smelling. He wore no shoes and his feet were black with ingrained dirt. He was chain-smoking plain Camel cigarettes as we spoke and he was agitated and anxious, exuding the sparking energy of a raw nerve. He seemed eager to talk and was enthusiastically interested in my musical progress. I accepted his invitation to go back to his flat in Hillbrow to smoke some of the 'prime weed' he claimed to have there and to chat about music. I mentioned that I was soon going to the border and this he took as an opportunity to tell me about his own experiences in the military. We went back to his dingy one bedroom flat and sat on the floor while he rolled a three-blader of grass taken from an enormous plastic bag. John started telling his tale.

"I went straight to the army after Matric. January call up, just after my eighteenth. I wanted to do well, actually I wanted to be the best, and so I volunteered for Recce's."

One Reconnaissance Battalion was the toughest unit in the South African Army, similar in approach and mentality to the British SAS. Any recruit to the SADF was aware of the reputation of the Recces. The opportunity to hear a first-hand story of one of them was irresistible. Even if John Watson appeared to be insane, I was riveted.

The 'First Reconnaissance Regiment' was founded as a small specialised SAS or Selous Scouts type unit capable of operating deep inside enemy territory to obtain valuable intelligence on enemy movements, positions and numbers. The Recce members were termed 'operators'. These men were trained to an extraordinary level, kept a low profile socially and were rarely filmed or photographed. A code of silence accompanied their achievements. Recce operator training was to enable optimal functionality in small units or individually, far in the field with little support primarily to gather strategic and tactical intelligence about the enemy from behind his lines. Stealth, stamina and the ability to blend into the surrounding bush were essential elements of the operator's skills repertoire.

The Recce's would also on occasions be used in aggressive operations behind enemy lines, destroying targets, harassing troops and causing smallscale havoc. Recce units usually operated in five or six man teams, though it is known that two man reconnaissance teams regularly operated inside Angola. Each team member was a specialist in a particular field such as navigation, tracking, demolition, medicine or signals, although all operators would be cross-trained to minimise dependence on any one specialist.

The Recces' training was hellish. Applicants were required to meet stringent standards and only men prepared to enlist for three years in the Permanent Force following national service were required. Applicants had to be between 18 and 35 years old and of demonstrably sound body and mind. They had to demonstrate appropriate military skills upon arrival and were required to be educated to at least Matric level, to be a South African citizen, have no criminal record and be fluent in both English and Afrikaans. They had to articulate willingness to serve the country in a special way, along with the wish to achieve an outstanding military career. Once accepted for the training phase the applicant would be aptitude-guided towards a specific area such as those mentioned above but including logistics, weapons, diving, boating, close combat, demolition or research and development.

Some 700 realistic prospects were put forward in every intake from all branches of the SADF of whom less than 50 would be accepted to start the training process. Only a minor percentage of those would eventually graduate as Recce operators. Training consisted of an initial three day pre-selection phase, then Special

Forces orientation, which took two weeks. Selection then took three days, followed by training for 42 weeks and, finally, specialisation.

The three-day pre-selection phase started with a day of psychological testing leading to a board interview to establish the psychological suitability of the applicant. If successful, an exacting one-day physical test followed, which would include a 30 kilometre march within 6 hours, in full kit including a rifle and carrying a 30 kilo sandbag. Then, an 8 kilometre run carrying all kit and rifle to be completed in under 45 minutes; 40 push-ups, 8 chin-ups, and 68 sit-ups in a tight time-limit; 40 shuttle runs of 7 metres each in 90 seconds and a sprint swim of 45 metres inside a specified time.

The third day included a stamina-testing route march. Once a candidate was deemed satisfactory following the pre-selection course, the special forces' orientation course began which entailed two weeks of advanced infantry skills and intense physical training including eight hours PT each day of. By this stage of the selection and training process the drop out rate usually stood at around 20 per cent.

The next step of the process included three days of survival training and bush orientation during which candidates were evaluated on their adaptability, discipline, navigation skills, fear of animals or situations, care of weapons and equipment, memory, powers of observation and their ability to move in the bush. Special watch was kept on the candidate to evaluate the ability to work successfully with other candidates under extreme stress.

The 42-week training course consisted of an individual phase; a basic parachuting course, training in minor tactics (foreign and platoon weapons instruction, survival, urban warfare and vehicle movement training), water orientation (small boat instruction, basic diving, swimming and survival), air orientation (static parachute jumping, rappelling, fast rope decent, forward air control and direction and helicopter drills), and basic demolitions and explosives training.

Extensive endurance and bodybuilding training was conducted

for ten 40-minute periods every day to ensure candidates would be in top physical condition and to evaluate their reactions to stressful influence when fatigued. Speed marches progressed from five kilometres to twenty-five kilometres with full kit, rifle, all timed and evaluated by instructors. By the end of this second phase, around 50 per cent of the class would have dropped out.

Several extreme tests followed, including a forced march of 38 kilometres. Well into the march the soldiers were allowed to fill water bottles with warm water while their instructors enticed them to quit by offering ice-cold drinks and food. When the men reach their destination they were presented with rations which they would then find were soaked in diesel oil to make them inedible, before being given a new marching order for a further 30 kilometres, without food or drink. Alternatively, they were presented with the opportunity to withdraw their Recce applications and enjoy the delicious meal and ice cold drink assortment shown to them, along with a ride back to camp. Instructors, monitored by medical staff would devise extremely cruel tortures to test the stamina and endurance of the applicants to the very edge of permanent damage.

Other common ordeals included being 'captured' and treated as a prisoner by the trainers dressed as terrorists, or having to solve mind-bending puzzles while exhausted and starved. Those who successfully completed this phase graduated as 'operators', while those that had failed at any point were sent to other SADF units, with no disgrace attached as even making it in to the training program represented a degree of achievement.

Though John Watson was speaking more freely and was more lucid than when we had met earlier in the evening, perhaps because we were by then well into the second three-blader, he displayed several disturbing indications of being unwell, including the uncontrollable shaking of his hands and a stutter that prevented him from completing certain syllables. His facial muscles contorted spasmodically until I could no longer contain the obvious question.

"John, I hope you don't mind me asking but... why are you looking so fucked?"

Having already rehashed the basics of Recce training, he then began to describe his experience as an operator.

"I spent a lot of time in Angola on special ops. When the terrs (terrorists) hit inside the border they would make a run back to their camps in Angola. Sometimes we would be brought into the hot pursuit, tracking them back into Angola. Running at a fast pace for mile after mile, hour after hour, in full readiness for ambush attack all the time. Often the spoor would lead to kraals in the bush. Our point man would go in while we followed in a straight line. This was the most vulnerable time because if you were going to set up an ambush, this would be the place to do it. They could be hidden anywhere. It wears your nerves down going in time after time. One day we were in pursuit. We had run at least 30 k's in the heat with full kit and ammo. The spoor led straight into a kraal. The point went in first and a little kid came out to greet him. We all stopped and watched as the kid went up to him, and then the kid, a little guy, just a small picannin, held up his arms as if to be picked up, when he just exploded. Our guy was killed outright. Hand grenade taped under the armpit. The next week we were on another pursuit and I was on point. The spoor led us to a kraal. It was like déjà vu. A little kid came running towards me. Everyone stopped, I could hear the clicking of safety switches from the guys behind me. I had less than a second to decide. The kid was looking straight at me less than 10 metres away and closing. I popped him in the head. Single shot. Brain splash. I braced myself for an explosion as he went down, but nothing happened. When we went to check the body he wasn't carrying any grenade or any explosive. A woman came running out from one of the mud huts, screaming hysterically at me. My buddies said I did the right thing, and we carried on through the kraal following the spoor for another 20 k's. That night I couldn't sleep and my hands started to shake. I couldn't lose the sound of the screaming woman's voice and the look on the kid's face as I popped him. Soon after we got back to camp the army sent me for counselling and then three months ago I was discharged. Now the army pay me a disability allowance."

I don't know whether the story he told me reflected his own life or someone else's. It may have been a well-rehearsed hard-luck story constructed from elements of his acquaintances' experiences but I don't think so. It was told with such conviction and with so much pain that even if it were not true, he certainly seemed to believe it. Whatever the case, his condition must surely have been the consequence of some terrible times.

I came across John Watson again a few years later, still alive though he looked like the haunted ghost of a 70 year-old. He had a sinister open wound on his forehead. I asked him what had happened.

"I was hitching up from Durban," he slurred pensively, "waiting on the side of the road. I waited four days and then the Devil appeared. Right there in front of me. He told me to mark myself, so I obeyed him."

Conscription and national service had done John Watson no favours. On the side of the highway between Durban and Johannesburg, in a distorted subconscious impersonation of Charles Manson he had carved a swastika into his forehead using a penknife.

Touring

I woke before the dawn on the 19th June 1980 to prepare for the border tour departure. It was a freezing mid-winter's morning as I drove to the Entertainments building for the seven o'clock collection. An air force Bedford truck was waiting to load our equipment and, along with the two stars of the tour, we were driven to Waterkloof Airbase in Pretoria.

Waterkloof was then the busiest Air Force base in Africa and, along with Swartkop airfield, it was the hub of all flying operations from Pretoria by the military. The ubiquitous C130 Hercules planes that landed every 30 minutes operated a shuttle service between

Waterkloof and Grootfontein in South West Africa, delivering personnel and supplies and returning with tired and broken troops on an airborne conveyor belt on a 30-minute rota.

We travelled in browns and in addition to our instruments we had to take the R1 rifles that were issued to us along with one magazine of live ammunition. Being in possession of an automatic weapon and 20 rounds of 7.62mm bullets was a first for me. The experience of holding a killing machine of such power was exciting despite my intellectual reservations over engaging in any way with the process I had previously distanced myself from with such success.

The bustle of a working military airport has an energy all of its own. We were guided to our plane, another Hercules C130, where, once aboard, we were seated on benches running along the side of the plane. It was unlike any commercial plane in that even inside the fuselage the noise of the propeller engines was deafening. The journey was approximately 820 miles, flying at a cruising speed of 370 miles per hour. Less than three hours after leaving Waterkloof we were close to the Northern border of South West Africa, approaching the Grootfontein airfield. As we came in to land I had a glimpse of the terrain and was struck by how brown everything looked. There was a lot of sand. We offloaded our gear into two long wheel base, brown Land Rovers that pulled alongside the plane on the runway. Mynie and Sias travelled in one vehicle along with Gerald and Nick whilst Pete, Tony, Al and I travelled in the second. Our destination was Chetto camp. The journey took several hours, travelling North East from Grootfontein along sand roads that changed with surprising speed from desert terrain into a lush jungle-like landscape. Our driver, a national service first lieutenant, explained that we were heading for the Caprivi strip which we would join at Rundu before making our way east towards Chetto, the base securing the eastern perimeter of the South African front line.

The officer driving the Land Rover was a gold mine of local information and his guided tour through the war zone felt like a privilege. Until then, my only vivid frame of reference regarding modern warfare had been the most recent comparable conflict, the Vietnam War. My impressions of a war zone had come from movies, books and songs. My senses were heightened by the opportunity to see this incredible scenario unfolding before me in real time.

"In simple terms," our driver explained, "this road is the front line. To the north is Angola. The terrs have their camps there and every so often they come over the border to attack us. To do so they have to cross this sandy road, so we have camps every 50 k's or so along the strip. Every night at sundown we send out Land Rovers between the camps dragging branches behind them to sweep the road smooth. Then, at first light, we send a Land Rover with a bushman tracker, perched on a special seat on the front bumper, to examine the road. If the tracker spots a spoor, he can tell with tremendous accuracy the nature of its cause - how many people crossed, when they crossed, how much weight they are carrying and in which direction they are heading. This info goes by radio straight back to the nearest camp. There the commander uses map references to calculate the maximum radius that the terrs could have covered. Remember they are always on foot, so there's a maximum speed they can travel. If there's a gunship about, that gets sent up to search. They circle the area until they spot the terrs. Usually that's the signal to call in the nearest ground troops and with any luck we finish them off in a fire-fight. Other times they come in overnight, plant mines and then run back to their camps inside Angola. We are not supposed to cross into Angola to chase them, but when we have to we do."

The scenery as we approached Chetto had changed to sub-tropical jungle, reminding me of terrain I had only seen in movies of Vietnam. Unbeknown to any of the members of the touring party at that time, the fighting was at an all time high. Whilst we were there, a major offensive, known as Operation Sceptic, was underway. This was a lightning attack on a SWAPO base in South Angola that developed into an extended operation as more and more SWAPO caches were discovered in the territory. Operation Sceptic also saw the first serious clashes between the SADF and the Angolan forces (FAPLA). This operation in which 380 of their fighters were killed cost SWAPO its forward base facilities. Seventeen members of the South African force were killed but several hundred tons of equipment and supplies and many vehicles were captured by the security forces. This battle was raging more or less as we were making our way along the Caprivi Strip towards the first gig of our border tour. Many of the audience members in the Chetto show would have participated in this engagement, many having experienced the loss of a friend or the killing of a stranger. From a performer's point of view this would present a unique audience.

The last light of the day was fading as we arrived at Chetto Camp. First, we were shown to our accommodation, which consisted of bunk beds in a tented area, then we were invited to join the Kommandant for a braai dinner in the boma-style dining area they called the 'officers' mess'. For most of the young men stationed in the camp the sight of an attractive blonde made a huge impression and Mynie was a sensational hit even before she had sung a single note. Pete and I stood to one side watching the drooling fawning reaction of the young men who queued up to speak with Mynie or just bask in her radiant blondness. Mynie was loving every moment and certainly justified her description as a morale boosting visitor to the soldiers. I felt a new respect for Mynie in seeing the obvious joy she brought to the troops and I was amazed at the non-sexual aspect of these interactions. Mynie seemed to have some aura of untouchability around her that kept the troops at a respectful distance even as the drool accumulated on the sides of their mouths. She had a determined professionalism that was impressive along with a great ability to generate a good feeling amongst her visitors. It cannot have been easy for any woman on her own in a war zone surrounded by thousands of fighting men pressing for her attention to keep a constant, happy smiling face without once becoming moody. Watching Mynie perform for her all male audience quickly became my favourite distraction. "Not a sight you see very often," I reminded myself on more than one occasion.

Back in the boma with the officers after enjoying barbecued

meat, boerewors and chicken and the bread rolls that were the enduring legacy of the now departed Portuguese colonists, Pete and I decided to explore the camp and see if we could find a spliff.

We made our excuses to our hosts and fellow band-members and set off outside the safe confines of the officers' mess into the row of tents and wooden frame buildings that made up the camp. We approached some troops who were milling about and smoking and struck up a conversation. They seemed only too glad for the opportunity to speak.

One lad seemed disturbed by our presence, making agitated sounds in our direction, clicking his tongue and jabbering unintelligible words while hopping about on tip toes and flapping his arms before he scuttled off.

"Don't worry about him," said one of the smoking troops. "He's bosbefok." This was the first time I had heard this expression of which bossies was the more formal version. 'Bush-fucked' is the literal translation, an unsurprising consequence of putting 18 year-old boys into a tropical jungle dense with malarial mosquitos, armed with automatic weapons and sent out to kill other 18 year-olds for reasons not of their own choosing or understanding. Our new self-appointed local guide explained bosbefok to us as meaning 'his nerves are gone'.

The conversation soon came round to smoking marijuana. "Do you guys have any zol?" I asked, using one of the South African nicknames for cannabis.

"Of course," came the reply and we were invited to join them for a skyf in a secluded section of the camp, where we found ourselves seated in a small circle of half a dozen young soldiers dressed in brown fatigues. Our host, an English-speaking troop of a similar age to ours, put his hand in his pocket and produced a handsome black leather drawstring pouch with a shoe-lace threaded through the opening edge. He untied the lace, opened the bag and took out a bud of fine looking cannabis, which he proceeded to crush in the palm of his hand and stuff into the neck of the clay chillum he produced from another pocket of his browns. I was struck by the unusual nature of his dope bag.

"Nice pouch," I said, admiring the soft black leather.

"Made it myself," he replied.

"Really?"

"Yes. Terrorist's balls. Shot the fucker through the head and then cut off his ball sack. Dried it out on a broom handle and threaded a shoelace through the top. Presto."

As he said that, I experienced an almost paranormal transportation to the journey I had made to Sfakia as a 10-year old when my uncle Elias told me the story of the skinning alive of the resistance fighter. Remembering what the Nazis had done to one of my kinsmen I looked at the soldier who had made the pouch but instead of seeing a Nazi officer with a razor in one hand I saw a sweet-faced, English-speaking teenager in a South African army uniform holding a ganja pipe without any sense of wrongdoing. I turned away, thinking that the training of 18 year-old boys to do that to each other could never be justified. The culpability for this debasement lay firmly with the Christian controllers, those deluded Afrikaners and their fear based ignorance, the masters of war.

There but for fortune

Our first show was in Chetto Camp the following evening. We started and finished early to fit in with the routine in the camp. The show started with a 15 minute set of our four best tracks, in this case, 'Babe' by Styx, 'You may be right' by Billy Joel, 'Fly too High' by Janis Ian and 'Hot stuff' by Donna Summer, followed by 45 minutes of Sias doing his Afrikaans songs.

After a short break, enough time for a quick cigarette behind the stage, Mynie performed her mixture of English and Afrikaans songs to tumultuous applause. Mynie was spectacular and the reception she received from the predominantly teenaged soldiers was rapturous. I may have been having a bad time in the army but when I saw how much the performance meant to them I felt an overwhelming sorrow for the boys in the audience who were fighting a war that was not of their own making. I kept thinking about how desperate my position would have been if I were on the other side of that stage.

After the show we retired to the officers' mess. The atmosphere was very different from my experience of SADF military conduct in 11 Kommando. In this situation of real war, the real thing as opposed to the preparation for it, the pettiness that was the hallmark of the training in Diskobolos was absent. Mostly the troops I spoke to were locked inside their own personal relationship with the moment, each one dealing with the situation in their own way. All were highly conscious of the fact that they were in the front line of a war, making me aware that, for the first time, I was seeing a group of people entirely free from any delusion, every one of them familiar with the thought that this day might be their last. Every youngster we met seemed desperate to talk. One of them asked me if I'd ever eaten snake.

"We shot a puff adder the other day and braai'd it," he said. "It tasted like chicken."

The following morning we breakfasted with the officers before loading up the Land Rovers that would transport us to the next camp. Our destination was Omega Base, home of the legendary '31 Battalion' also known as the 'Bushmen Battalion' which consisted primarily of Bushman soldiers from the Mbarakwengo and the Vasquela tribes of Namibia. These soldiers had legendary tracking and bushcraft abilities and were organised by white commanders into a specialised and highly effective counter-insurgency unit which provided a uniquely African illustration of how white command allied to black manpower can produce remarkable results.

The Omega Base was larger than Chetto and seemed to be peopled almost entirely by coloured troops. We had most of the day to loiter about, giving us the opportunity to talk to a few of the troops resting in the camp between operations. I heard the story of the well-publicised 'Operation Safraan' launched from Omega in the previous year.

Omega Base

The show was a tense affair. Omega Base was about as hard core a front line base as can be imagined. Most of the audience of about five hundred men in uniform had been on patrol all day and the contrast between killing to appreciating rock and roll must have been surreal. As usual, all eyes were on Mynie and her splendid blonde mane.

Before the show that night, we accepted an invitation to go for a smoke with some troops who had recently returned to camp. An excited young troop with deep black dilated pupils approached us with an offer.

"We've got something really lekker that you can look at."

"What is it?" I asked.

"Two dead terrs, from the contact today. They're in there," he said pointing to a tent. "They are very young. You can see them if you want."

"Not just at the moment, thanks. Maybe later," I replied before disappearing as quickly as possible.

After the show, the band were invited to join the officers for drinks with the commanding officer in the officers' mess. Whilst standing in another boma-style thatched roofed bar drinking a bottle of cold Castle beer I heard the distant sound of voices in song carried on the evening breeze, a choral harmony of such striking beauty that it took all my attention, not least because it was so unexpected. I was immediately transported to the Sundays during my youth when I had heard the black Christian choirs singing near my home. I would creep up close to their gathering in the veldt to listen. This music that hung in the African night had the same enticing effect. I asked an officer what the singing was.

"Oh don't worry about that" he replied. "There's a Bushman camp nearby and they sing every night."

"Would it be possible for me to go and listen to them?" I asked. He looked at me as if I was insane.

"Why would you want to do that?" he asked, with a bemused expression.

"I am a musician and I am interested in singing. That's a very interesting choir there, and I would love to hear it if that's possible."

The officer said: "I will ask the Kommandant for you." Moments later, I was summoned to where the Kommandant was seated.

"So you want to hear our Bushmen singing, do you?" he asked with a jovial smile.

"Okay. Why not? They're not dangerous. Just make sure you take your rifle with you."

Pete was similarly interested and together we prepared by donning our army hats and taking up our rifles as instructed. We left the camp after explaining our purpose to the gate guards and made our way towards the sound of the voices in the distance. About a kilometre away we could see the flames of an open fire. As we approached we saw a few mud huts in a cluster next to which a collection of some 40 people sat or squatted around the glowing wood fire. To one side a man sat astride a long log with a skin pulled tightly over its hollowed end. He beat this natural drum to a booming rhythm, singing a call out phrase the length of a short sentence in a language I had not heard before. When this line was completed the entire group sang a reply in the most harmonious and haunting conformation of notes I had ever heard. Experiencing the power of this mesmerising chorus was akin to undergoing a spiritual experience. We stopped some 20 metres away from the group, thinking that if we went any closer the sight of two armed soldiers might frighten them into silence. A few faces turned towards us, but the singing continued. Despite being in a war zone, at no time as we approached a black settlement with loaded rifles in the uniform of the oppressor did I feel any menace or threat.

"Let's go in and sit with them," I urged Pete.

"Okay," he agreed, "but we can't take our guns in. We can leave them here against a tree. No one will take them."

We leaned or R1s against a tree trunk and walked slowly towards the group. Curiously the thought that I had already been court-martialled for losing one R1 never entered my mind. A small child separated from the group and came towards us, gazing open-eyed as if he had never seen a white face before, which was almost certainly the case. There was no hint of menace in the child's curious expression. I thought of John Watson.

If it's true that 80 per cent of what we communicate is non-verbal information, then that might explain why we simply walked into the group, seated ourselves close to the edge and no one blinked an eyelid. I think that these Bush people, unaffected by formal education and city ways, remain in touch with their natural instinct of being able to sense danger more reliably than we would.

The singing continued as if we were invisible guests. Although I was not familiar with the music or its lyrical content, I formed the impression that the lead singer was relaying some aspect of the day's news to which the body of the choir was joining in a response. It seemed like a form of mellifluous nightly telegraph providing each individual with a say in the day's events. To some lead lines they sang with more gusto and to others with more softness, which I interpreted as a subtle measure of their reaction to the message being presented. Intoxicated by the moment we stayed for about half an hour, during which time I heard the most spiritually connected singing I have ever heard. When it seemed appropriate to take our leave we stood and bowed toward the headman who acknowledged with the slightest tilt of the head and walked slowly back to where we had left our rifles. They were still there.

As I dozed off that night the thought occurred to me that my visit to Omega was most likely a very different experience from that of most other visitors. Once more we slept on military bunks in a tent, followed by an early rise and load-up in preparation for transportation to our next destination about one hundred kilometres westwards.

Bagani, 23rd June, 1980

The military camp at Bagani was located on a hillside near the road. A typical military camp much like the others on the Caprivi Strip, this one was made memorable by its bar. Located to one side of the camp, the bar overlooked a fast flowing river far below from its spectacular location on the edge of a gorge. It was decorated with memorabilia such as rugby shirts and foreign banknotes pinned to the walls in much the same style as you would expect to find in any popular country bar. The occupants of the bar were unusual because they were 'campers'. The 'camp' system required national servicemen who had completed their term to return the following year for a one-month tour of duty then again in the second year for a three-month tour. With this cycle repeating for the next ten years, it meant that an average of two months every year would be spent as a 'camper'. We were welcomed warmly into this bar and offered a drink. As usual, the soldiers were keen to talk to us but this lot were different from the others we had met in that they appeared to be loving every minute. They were there by choice.

"We come here every year at the same time," said one. 'It's fantastic. We get three months' paid leave from our usual jobs and we get to hang out together. We did our service here six years ago and we all loved it so much we come back every year. We have a ski boat down there on the river and here beer and cigarettes are subsidised. A beer costs 20 cents and a pack of cigs is 30 cents. Every night we have a lekker braai with fresh meat that we shoot ourselves. And look at our view!" he said as he waved his arms expansively over the spectacular landscape beneath us. "Africa at its most spectacular!"

There was not a lot I could say to any of this. Clearly my blanket dismissal of all things military was in need of revision. If an army was a necessity, then it should only be populated by this kind of person. The people we were talking with were happy to be part of an institution like the South African army and were able to turn it into a rewarding personal experience. And if they had to shoot a few 'terrs' along the way, well, that was the nature of the game.

The show that night was especially successful. Our featured songs at the start were 'Sometimes a fantasy' and 'Fly too high'. The crowd loved it and we went off the stage feeling elated. We returned to the bar overlooking the Okavango River below. It was hard to imagine sitting there that war and death were competing for prominence just a few miles away. The impression of a postponed reality was unavoidable.

The following morning we set off once more, heading further west down the corrugated sand road that led to Rundu.

Rundu, 24th June, 1980

Rundu was the capital of the Kavango region. As we turned off into the camp the Angolan town of Calai was visible, literally a stone's throw away across the Okavango River. It was the closest I had ever been to Angola. The camp at Rundu was bigger than the others we had visited and the atmosphere was tense as there had been a contact that day and several troops had been wounded. We went about our pre-gig set up and with that out of the way I found myself with a few hours to spare. Pete and I went in search of some food in the mess tent and whilst there I saw my old school friend from Bryanston, Anthony Kieniss, stocking up his metal tray with the day's offerings. Anthony was in his second year of Air Force training, having signed a four-year Permanent Force training option. He was now completing a three-month border stint at the nearby airfield where he worked as a radio operator. He had almost completed his task and was looking forward to going back to 'the States', as home was known. After the initial pleasantries of a chance reunion we set off for a quiet corner with our food to chat.

"What's it been like?" I asked him.

"Not a problem, really. I'm with the Air Force so I don't go out in the field. It's just a radio job for eight hours every day and then I am off. I feel sorry for some of these troops though. There's a lot of shit going on."

"So I've heard," I said. "Have you been in any fighting yourself?"

"No, I'm based in the camp and our camp is supposedly secure but I get a lot of calls on the radio and I often have to direct follow-up ops to radio calls."

"How do you mean?"

"Well, if the terrs cross over and a spotter tracks them they call in the co-ordinates, and I relay the message to the nearest reaction unit."

I asked him if he knew much about the contact earlier in the day.

"That's why I am here," he said. "I was on radio this morning and a call came in. Terrs crossed over 10 k's from here sometime before dawn so a patrol went out only it was an ambush. The terrs are getting clever now. They disguised their spoor to make it look like 12 guys had crossed, but when the troops got to them it was more like one hundred and they had set an ambush. Our guys were outnumbered. They took some bad hits and called in for help on the radio 'Surrounded by hostiles', 'low on ammo', 'taking casualties' and messages like that. It was bad. I tried to raise a chopper to go extract them but there was no one near enough. The only chopper remotely close enough was 4,000 feet up, shipping six SWAPO prisoners to Grootfontein."

He paused to take a long slurp on his tea.

"I gave the pilot the co-ordinates of the ambush. He said he could get there in five minutes, but he wouldn't have time to land and offload the prisoners."

"So what did he do?"

"The only thing he could do. Our guys in the chopper tossed the SWAPOs out at 4,000 feet and then went straight to the scene. Terrs ran when the chopper arrived. We had three dead and a dozen wounded, but it would have been a lot worse otherwise."

I was left speechless, wondering, how do you toss men out of a helicopter at 4,000 feet? Surely they would resist with all their strength, even if they were handcuffed and tied. Surely they would have screamed and surely those screams would never be forgotten? Although Anthony seemed strangely detached from the incident I couldn't help thinking that it would come back to haunt the participants.

It was only after the war had ended that I heard the story of the shooting down by the SAAF of a Mig fighter over southern Angola, after which it was revealed to almost universal amazement that the pilot of the downed aircraft had been an 18 year-old Cuban girl. I wondered how many of the 19 year-old South African Mirage pilots had any idea at the time of just who they were fighting against. Cold War politics at its most cynical, placing teenagers from Cuba in Russian planes in a life or death struggle against teenagers from South Africa in French planes above Angola, where none had any business being in the first place.

Our show in Rundu that night was more sombre than was the norm and afterwards we went to bed early. During the night I heard the sound of distant gunfire.

The week had passed rapidly and now we were back in Grootfontein getting ready to board a Hercules back to 'the States'. The plane ride out was very different from the one going in. One side of the plane was lined with casualties, wounded boys being evacuated to the hospital in Pretoria. The first time I heard the word 'Casevac', short for 'Casualty Evacuation'. They were lying on wheeled stretchers surrounded by an eerie stillness. Not a single cry or moan came from the drip fed casualties throughout the entire journey. "Flow morphia, slow," I thought to myself.

We were in no mood for conversation, my main concern being that despite having been told that it was strictly forbidden I had sneaked a small camera along and was hoping that we were not going to be too well searched on our return. I had also stashed a couple of rounds of ammunition as souvenirs. I was uneasy about this too as it might well have become problematic. The C130 landed safely at Waterkloof and we went through the gates without a hiccup. With my camera and rounds of ammunition stashed in the speaker cabinet of my amplifier, I was more than happy to turn out the contents of my toiletries bag for the inspecting officer at the gate. Before long we were delivered back to the Entertainments building and the trusty green Peugeot that was to carry me back to Bryanston and another night of troubled sleep.

After the border tour we were given a long weekend off which coincidentally marked the three quarter point of my two years' service. Although my anti-military predisposition was pronounced and enhanced by what I had just experienced, I also found a morbid fascination with the striking ways in which some men find their true vocation during warfare. Having visited SADF operational bases and encountered some of the personnel, no single story illustrated this better than that of 32 Battalion, a legendary clandestine outfit also known as 'The Buffalo Battalion' which achieved the highest number of kills in the Border War.

The Crowbar

Another unit that became a folklore favourite wherever tales of the Border War were told was known as 'Koevoet', the Afrikaans word for a crowbar. Koevoet was a police counter-insurgency unit famous for its astonishingly high kill rate of 25:1, much higher than the 11:1 SADF average of the Border War. That is a staggering statistic, the enormity of which it took me some time to comprehend properly: for every single fatality they suffered, they would kill 25 of the enemy. It took 25 violent deaths to bring down one Koevoet soldier.

Koevoet members were mostly black Namibians commanded by white South African officers, reflecting the equivalent ethnic ratio and structure to that in 32 Battalion. Their success can largely be ascribed to the extraordinary skills of the Ovambo trackers deployed to find and follow the spoor of insurgents and by using the Casspir mine-protected vehicles with solid rubber wheels capable of bundu-bashing through most obstacles while keeping their occupants safe even from anti-tank landmines while following the directions of the trackers.

One of the longest 'escape and evade' actions by a SWAPO freedom fighter was recorded by a Koevoet unit and serves as a reminder that when the circumstances of war place individuals in life threatening situations, remarkable feats of endurance result.

It began when Koevoet pursuers, travelling in a Casspir, picked up the spoor of two guerrillas north of the cutline near Handabo in Angola. They tracked them southwards over the cutline until the guerrillas split up, one turning north back into Angola and the other continuing south. The Koevoet unit stayed with him but every day he succeeded in putting considerable distance between himself and the pursuing Casspir despite being on foot and pursued by a state of the art off-road vehicle. The Koevoet unit chased him for five days, calling in helicopter gunship support in the afternoons as the trackers could detect from the spoor that he was nearby. Their quarry managed to remain undetected and the trackers found no signs of his sleeping places. It appears he kept going for five days virtually without sleep, running, concealing his tracks and navigating an evasive course. Discarded hypodermic syringes found at regular intervals on his tracks suggesting he stayed awake by injecting himself with Benzedrine or a similar amphetamine. Markings were found where he had collapsed from exhaustion. He appeared to have dragged himself up towards a tree to rest before pulling himself up for whatever sleep he could snatch. Eventually his spoor evaporated on the Chandelier Road where, it was suspected, he was picked up by a car.

The Koevoet unit had tracked him unsuccessfully for 368 kilometres over five days, during which time he had no proper food or sleep. If true, this probably rates as one of the longest successful evasive actions in military history.

Koevoet's counter-insurgency role would often result in the capture of prisoners. Intelligence extracted from those prisoners was of great value and in the unregulated wilds of South West Africa where the interrogations took place it is not surprising that the conduct of the participants reflected the dehumanising nature of warfare upon even the more moderate among them. I had a friend whose brother was a doctor, who while serving a border tour found himself at the call of a Koevoet unit, the officers of which were torturing a captured SWAPO fighter by burying him in the sand in an attempt to extract information. Eventually the prisoner was completely submerged and became unconscious. The officers dug him out and the doctor, being outranked, was compromised into reviving the prisoner in order that the torture could continue. His opportunity for revenge came later in the same week. The Koevoet soldiers were playing a macho game of dare with tigerfish in a nearby river, a test of courage that involved putting one arm in the water and waiting until the carnivorous fish attacked before pulling it out. For an ill-starred lieutenant named Kobus van Jaarsveld, the game went badly wrong when a split second's delay allowed a particularly vicious tigerfish to latch onto his hand. In the process of yanking his arm out of the water and trying to dislodge the firmly attached fish, its razor sharp teeth tore the tendons in his hand to shreds. Van Jaarsveld was rushed to the doctor who took one look at the damage to the soldier's hand and realised that amputation was the only option.

"Kobus, I see you are Koevoet," he said to the grimacing soldier.

"Ja, man," confirmed Lieutenant van Jaarsveld.

"Well, then. You're a real hard man, so you won't be needing anaesthetic for this," replied the doctor.

Van Jaarsveld nodded.

The doctor removed the young man's hand without administering any pain relief.

Back to the band

In June 1980, during our rest break from the border tour, the band played at a 21st birthday party in Randburg. I was finding it increasingly difficult to communicate civilly with Gerald and when he said he was not available for the gig an opportunity arose for our enthusiastic stand-in singer, Mario Capazzario, to acquire more experience.

After the secondary role that we had played on the tour supporting Sias and Mynie it was enjoyable to have the freedom to play the songs of our own choice and the performance went well. By now the thrill of earning money by playing music was a firmly established part of my life, suggesting as it did that there was a possibility of a career to be fashioned out of playing the guitar.

The new band configuration with Mario as the singer in Gerald's place was far more congenial and resulted in a far more creative ambience.

Touring with Mynie and Sias and working off sheet music had made it clear that becoming a sight reading player was not for me. The aspect of guitar playing that thrilled me most was arriving without thought at harmonious note arrangements. The rigid process of repeating the same structure time after time where the measure of success is conformity to the written notes reminded me of monkey tricks. Even a monkey, I thought, could eventually be taught this discipline. The ability to read music may be invaluable during the process of learning a piece but to me performing via reading the notes removed the magical spark of creativity that had attracted me to the instrument in the first place. I determined to ignore the necessity of relying on pieces of paper in order to hear, play or feel a piece of music.

With my musical progress came a growing interest in Jazz. I became increasingly interested in more technically advanced music. Fusion style 'Jazz/Rock' was in its hey-day in 1980. Pete had introduced the Steve Khan track 'Some Punk Funk' into the band's repertoire and I had the guitar part down. The occasions when we made it through the piece from beginning to end without any glaring errors were euphoric though I was invariably left with the feeling that I had just taken an exam.

Midwinter's day, 21st June, had come and gone. I was into the final quarter of national service and a new set of considerations was emerging. What would life after the army hold during the final phase of my conscription?

On 3rd July we played the Officers' Ball at Pretoria's Services School and on the following night at a dinner dance at 61 Base Workshops in Voortrekkerhoogte. On the next night we played in a show put on by the army for the public at the Sanlam Centre in Pretoria.

At many of the less interesting bookings where we were cast in a background role we would use the opportunity to switch instruments. The piano player would go for a drink, Pete would move to the piano and I would move to the bass, or, if I could get Al to move over, my favourite diversion was playing the drums. Some of our bookings involved playing for four hours, often to a roomful of drunks who would not know a virtuoso from a vegetable so it seemed appropriate to seize the opportunity to improve on other instruments.

With the finishing line of my two years now forming a moving blip on the distant horizon, for the first time I had to consider seriously what to do when I returned to real life. I had gone into the army with some skills as a guitar player and though these skills had been developed to some extent, my interest in becoming a guitar player was moderated by my insights onto what that life entailed. Joe Pass was already way better than I could ever hope to be without a lifetime's commitment to nothing else and look what happened to him. Gradually, I arrived at the conclusion that the guitar was the means to an end, the canvas but not the creation. I knew that my life would be dedicated to music but not the specific detail of how I might develop that into a remunerative position. Increasingly, I had become attracted to the idea of being able to perform alone as the wearying effects of working with band members and the quirks and foibles they brought into play diminished my interest in being part of a band. This meant improving my singing skills. I had never seriously considered myself a singer and had only ever sung when it represented the only way forward. Although I played electric guitar with the band and the skills I had developed were very much in a band accompaniment context, I started to assemble and rehearse a set of acoustic songs with a view to being able to put on a professional solo show.

Occasionally I would visit a Folk club in Braamfontein and perform a few Folk songs on a borrowed acoustic guitar. My solo set started with songs I had written myself, supplemented by Folk style standards like 'The Streets of London', 'Don't think twice, it's all right' and 'Danny's song'. Something was emerging from this vision of musical independence, but the light at the end of that tunnel had not yet shone through.

The 14th July saw Ad Lib booked for the 14 Field Regiment's Dinner Dance in Potchefstroom, an Afrikaner heartland town located some 160 kilometres from Pretoria and not an attractive destination though it remains memorable for me because of the far-reaching effects of the day's events. While we were preparing to leave for the gig, Gerald was at his zealous worst, eventually approaching me with another of his forceful reminders that unless I accepted Jesus forthwith, there was very little he would be able to do on my behalf when the time came. As usual I thanked him for his concern and continued my packing requirements, thinking no more of the matter after seeing him walk away. Several minutes passed before Gerald returned, apoplectic and radiating manic barely containable rage. He approached with such anger my immediate thought was that he was about to throw a right hook in my direction. He was beside himself as he strode forward pointing a finger at me, his face a mask of dark and distorted bitterness, declaring, "I know who you are!" Without so much as a beat's pause for comic timing he announced, "You're the Devil!"

This proclamation made, without waiting for a reply, Gerald turned on his heel and stormed out of the room, leaving a somewhat strained atmosphere during the subsequent drive to Potchefstroom. The weighty silence during that drive provided a few hours of calm to consider my thoughts, the first of which was how to address the bad manners directed towards me. I felt offended by having been called the 'devil' not because I cared what Gerald thought or said, but because he had not given me any opportunity to reply. I made two mental notes before we arrived in Potchefstroom, one of which was to bide my time waiting for the appropriate moment to reply to Gerald and the other was to improve my solo entertainer skills so I would not have to rely on band members in the future who might turn out to be as comprehensively unpleasant as Gerald.

Rockey Street

During one of many visits at that time to Yeoville, questionably regarded at that time by the more bohemian and left-leaning sector of white society as the cultural and musical epicentre of Johannesburg, I came across the Green Oasis, a restaurant with a bar and a stage for live folk music. I introduced myself to the owner, resulting in a booking for the 29th July, a Thursday night. It was my first professional solo folk gig. Step one on my journey towards becoming a solo entertainer. I borrowed the army's Shure vocal master PA for the occasion and, filled with trepidation, arrived at the Green Oasis an hour before starting time.

Because the venue was new, attendance was modest. There was a couple canoodling in the corner and three single people looking at me with varying degrees of curiosity who had the good grace to clap after each song. I played two sets on my Ibanez guitar plugged directly into the PA and was paid 12 Rand for the evening. (In 1980 that was £6.)

My repertoire consisted mainly of original songs that were unfamiliar to the audience. The band repertoire was largely unsuitable for this purpose as guitar arrangements for a quartet were very different from the requirements for solo presentation. I realised I would need to learn more songs that would work with just one instrument, such as those in my set list drawn from the songbooks of guitar based singer-songwriters like: Bob Dylan – 'Tomorrow is a long time', James Taylor – 'You've got a friend', Phil Ochs – 'There but for fortune', Jim Croce – 'Have to say I love you in a song', The Rodriguez songs – 'I wonder - Rich folks hoax - Forget it', Neil Young – 'Heart of gold', and Cat Stevens – 'Wild World', all of which were staples of the Johannesburg solo-guitar entertainment world at that time.

Despite the sparse turnout, the management seemed impressed with my performance and I was re-booked for the following Sunday night when, the manager assured me, a bigger crowd would show up. I was offered 60 Rand for the gig, an irresistible sum. Nervous at the prospect, I decided to take some insurance in the form of a keyboard player and so I asked the Ad Lib keyboard player Tony Drake along. We spent a few hours in the rehearsal room preparing two sets in advance. The gig went well and Tony and I were given dinner and paid 30 Rand each, about the same amount that a domestic servant would earn for a month's labour.

Between the army gigs, I was booking an increasing number of paid private shows, either as a solo performer or with the band. Since I couldn't afford to buy my own, having the opportunity to 'borrow' the army's equipment for these gigs was helpful to say the least.

The only thing missing was the sound track

Back in Entertainments the following week, I was left a note telling me to collect a form from the admin office. During our first break I walked over to the admin office to collect the form. The office was located on the far side of the building to our rehearsal room, in an isolated part of the building accessed by walking through a long hallway. It was next to Major Hayden's office. When I got there the office was empty. I looked around on either side. There was no one there. I called out to see if anyone was in earshot. Still no sign of anybody. It dawned on me that I was alone in a supposedly secure part of the building that was supposed always to be kept locked when there was nobody in the offices. I knew this was where our personal records were stored and in an impulsive decision consistent with the mind set of an anarchically inclined teenager I decided to look at my military file. I located the filing cabinet containing the member's personal files and soon located mine. I had seen this file before. When I was on the train returning from my first visit to Tempe Hospital in Bloemfontein, I had removed documents from the same file, but I had not seen it since my medical reclassification. I scanned the contents rapidly but having already removed any compromising documents on my previous visit to this file it contained nothing of any unusual interest although I was finally able to read the notice from the medical tribunal stating that I should be recommended for reclassification on the grounds of the collapsed arches in my feet and that I should not stand guard-duty. I hastily returned the file to its position in the B section of the filing cabinet and went back to wait in the doorway. No one had returned to the office. I thought I would look a little further. One of my precursors as a guitarist in the Entertainment's National Servicemen's Band was Trevor Rabin who had gone on to become one of the best known pop stars in South Africa with his band 'Rabbit'. I had read somewhere that Trevor had done his military service in the Entertainment Corps and since it was that memory which had informed me of the existence of the Entertainment Corps, leading to my presence there, I thought I would see if I could pay my respects to him by performing a similar editing job on his military file.

It was the work of a few moments to locate his file, in which there was an AWOL charge sheet. Seemingly, he had taken a day off without proper clearance and had been charged. Thinking that this might be used in some way against him if he ever came back to the army for camps I removed that page, along with several others that may have been unhelpful, folding them in half and concealing them in my shirt pocket, resolving that if our paths ever crossed I would present him with the papers from his file as a subversive souvenir of what I'm sure was a trying time for him as well. There was still no one around as I left the admin area to return to the band room feeling that I had struck another small blow against the evil empire.

White fright

August was the busiest month to date with 14 gigs booked for Ad Lib, one of which was the 'Pretoria Show' on the 28th. This was an open-air show attended by many thousands of members of the public and Ad Lib was a prominent feature of the show. A large banner behind the stage proclaimed 'The Entertainment Corps Showband'. We opened with an enthusiastic version of 'On

Broadway' and as the song continued, so the crowd grew larger. Soon there were thousands of people enjoying the music, dancing enthusiastically and creating a lively and enjoyable atmosphere. This was as big a show as we had ever done and the band sounded, to me at least, absolutely brilliant. Suddenly an officer hurried onto the stage and told us to finish the song immediately, making cutthroat gestures with his right hand to indicate the extreme urgency of his intention. His frantic energy made me assume there must have been some security crisis, perhaps a bomb threat or public violence elsewhere in the showgrounds. We went into a quick end routine and I announced to the crowd: "We will be taking a short break".

In the confusion that followed I asked the officer what the problem was.

"Look around you. Are you blind?" he replied in Afrikaans.

I looked around and it took me some moments to realise the basis for his concern before it struck me, the crowd was almost entirely made up of black faces, not what the army had in mind for their open-air show in Pretoria. We were told to wait for an hour before starting again. With Pete in tow, simmering with rage, I packed my gear and headed for the green Peugeot, wordless in the face of the questioning stares from the black faces.

A date in Heidelberg (with Al Debbo)

Things were to become even more bizarre. In the week following the Pretoria show we had a famous visitor to our band room, none other than our drummer's father Al Debbo, the veteran entertainer and major star in the Afrikaans community. I had never seen or heard any of his work, representing as it did an area far beyond my own interest. Al was described on his publicity material as 'the rubber faced comedian' and on meeting him it was immediately apparent why. He could scrunch up his face in a freakish way that he had exploited in the guise of becoming a comedy act. He had come to audition us at the suggestion of his son, who had proposed to him that we would be the perfect band to back him on tour. When the idea was first discussed my immediate reaction had been emphatic rejection. It was a horrific prospect. Though he sang as part of his act, Al Debbo Senior was not what we considered a real musician and therefore Ad Lib and he had no common ground, besides which he was Afrikaans and his large and loyal audiences were drawn from the lowest common denominator. Although he seemed a nice enough fellow, my every instinct was to discourage the progression of this arrangement. We watched as he disappeared into Major Hayden's office.

Some time later, the major approached us. He was almost apologetic. "Al wants you guys for one gig," he said. "It's in Heidelberg." Somebody groaned. "I know you're not thrilled about it, I understand he's not a musician, so to make it a little bit more worth your while, I will give you two days off after the gig and Al will make sure you all make a little something for your efforts."

And so we found ourselves in Heidelberg, a small Afrikaner town some 60 kilometres distant, playing three-chord comedy songs behind an Afrikaans singer making funny faces to emphasise the lyrics. The only amusement for me was when I realised that Al did a version of 'Suikerbossie' in his set, the one and only boere-musiek tune I picked up during my Kimberley stint, which enabled me to surprise everybody by stepping forward to execute an authentic sounding part to the song. The band had never heard me play this piece before and the merriment that resulted buoyed our spirits during the surreal event.

Heidelburg was a typical Afrikaner stronghold where time seemed to stand still though appearances can be deceptive. Little did we know then that Heidelberg had recently been the cradle of the neo-Nazi AWB, formed in a garage by a handful of diehards including the silver-bearded Eugène Terre'Blanche. The group of young Afrikaans girls waiting for us backstage after the show asking for autographs heightened the twilight-zone feeling. I thought they were joking. We were dressed in military clothing having just performed a severely unchallenging sequence of three-chord arrangements behind a man whose claim to singing fame was primarily based on facial contortions and whose comic timing had all the merits of a slug dozing off in the afternoon sunshine. Who in their right mind, I wondered, would want the autograph of a soldier in these circumstances? It seemed that those girls knew something we didn't. Shortly after returning to camp the following week, Major Hayden came to the band room to announce that due to our outstanding performance with Al, word of mouth had spread and there was demand for a tour with Al Debbo, starting the following week.

   I shuddered down to my very core at the prospect.

Vrystaat!

Our foray across the cultural divide started on the 15th September at eight o'clock in the morning when we convened at the band room in readiness for the load-up. This time Al Debbo was to be supported by two other acts, Norman Scott, an elderly fellow of unmemorable talent who would do a 10-minute opening act involving a plastic rabbit and a top hat, and a lady called Sue who was there to sing a few liedjies in Afrikaans to warm up the crowd for Al's tumultuous arrival, although it became clear that her reasons for being on the tour were not reliant on her skills as a public entertainer.

   We travelled 300 southwards kilometres in a long wheel base van through the Boerewors Curtain into the heart of the Orange Free State. Our first stop was Bethlehem, a predictably little town where clearly not much had happened before the advent of Al Debbo, the biggest news for a long time. Posters of his rubbery face adorned many of Bethlehem's lampposts, announcing his show in the City Hall for Monday night. We went straight to the Hall to set up and once the equipment was in place and the band had checked the sound we were shown to our accommodation in a basic hotel near the Town Hall. Show time was at seven o'clock. The audience was about 500 strong and they appeared to be having a great time, laughing uproariously at everything Al said, did or (if that's the word) sang. Once again we experienced a flock of young girls asking for autographs and after the show Pete and I went for a stroll around the town. It was 9.30 in the evening and there was not a soul to be seen on the streets.

Realisation

The following morning we drove to the small town called Marquard for an almost identical replay of the night before with the same sized crowd in a lookalike town hall, the same young girls in the same flowery frocks speaking in the same high-pitched, nervy-little-girl voices, even the same show by Al with the same ad-libs in the same places. The Free State was the home of conformity and even the hotel seemed to be the same as the one in Bethlehem, the sole difference being the writing in a black marker in the date slot on the street light posters announcing 'Al Debbo Town Hall – Tuesday Night'. The following day, we travelled to Winburg for the third show. We set up and sound checked in the Town Hall and seeing that it was still only two o'clock, we had a few hours to kill before show time. Standing at the burger joint near the Town Hall, I noticed what appeared to be a park in the centre of the town.

We ambled across the main road into the park, awash in bright early summer light. It was not a park at all, but a cemetery. On one side stood a line of marble headstones set in carefully manicured lawns and adorned with flowers. On the other, the grass had been allowed to grow over into chaotic and unsightly scrub surrounding rusting metal crosses, some at crazy angles. I walked first to the unkempt side. The crosses were all-identical and carried the same message: 'For King and Country'. I walked over to the other side of the graveyard and read the inscription on the first marble headstone, the largest headstone I had ever seen. It was in Afrikaans, and translated as:

'Here lies Auntie Sannie and her seven children, murdered by the British on this place, 1902.'

I felt a curious sensation unlike any I had experienced before. I knew a little bit about the Boer War since it was taught in the schools at the time but this experience was very different from reading facts of South African history from a book. I walked on through the towering headstones. Each one was a variation on the same theme:

'Here lies Auntie Justine and her twelve children, murdered by the British on this site, 1902.'

'They are not buried here; they are planted. And they will for ever be growing in the hearts of the Boer people.'

It suddenly struck me that I was in a monument to something truly dreadful. I felt as if I was standing at a crime scene. Despite my previous resistance to their culture and their politics I resolved to find out more about the Boer War and its long-term consequences for the Afrikaners.

The scorched earth and concentration camp tactics used by the British Army in the latter stages of the second Anglo-Boer war to counter the guerrilla tactics of the Boer Kommandos ultimately prevailed. The Boers surrendered and Britain claimed victory. Estimates on Boer fighting losses range from three to six thousand while over 20,000 British troops were buried in South Africa and another 22,829 were wounded. The majority of deaths were caused by disease. But mostly the legacy of that war lay in the tragedy of the concentration camps where the heart of the Afrikaner nation, some 25 per cent of the entire Boer population, around 27,000 women and children, of which some 22,000 were under the age of 16, died horrifically, with dramatic consequences for the survivors. **(See Note 7.)**

Winburg

The tiny dorp of Winburg produced two particularly famous Boers: Jacobus Herculaas de la Rey, better known as General 'Koos' De La Rey, a deeply religious, Bible-carrying father of 10 who was considered a brilliant leader. As the war progressed,

De La Rey conceived many elements that were to define the principles of guerrilla warfare. He also fought according to strict Christian principles. Towards the end of the conflict he famously captured General Lord Methuen along with several hundred of his men. Realising that the seriousness of Lord Methuen's leg injury was beyond the scope of the limited medical attention he could provide, De la Rey released him along with his troops because it was the Christian thing to do. The General's wife even provided them with food for their journey and the two men went on to become lifelong friends. Boer and Brit. De la Rey's Kommando of mounted militia was 500 strong, harassing and evading an army 40 times its size in the Western Transvaal. Included in De La Rey's Kommando was a brilliant young soldier destined to become a world influencing legend, Jan Christian Smuts. The insight and military wisdom that Smuts displayed in battles against the British earned him a growing reputation as a leader. At the war's conclusion, Smuts was instrumental in getting the Boers to agree to the terms of their surrender. Aware that more than 20,000 women and children had already died in the concentration camps, and despite Boer Nationalist elements wanting to continue the fight, he successfully argued for surrender and survival.

In the years following the Boer surrender, Smuts established himself as their brightest star, although his forward thinking was to make him unpopular with the more right wing circles of Afrikanerdom, especially the Dutch Reformed Church. As South Africa moved inexorably towards unification, Smuts was in favour of a unitary state with power centralised in Pretoria, with English as the official language and with a more inclusive electorate. Although his vision was negotiated downwards to some degree in 1909, the Smuts draft of the new South African constitution was ratified in London and the Union of South Africa was born. Just eight years after being a horse-mounted Kommando fighting against the British, Jan Smuts was now the most powerful man in South Africa. His distance from right wing Afrikaner nationalist elements increased to the point where civil war seemed inevitable, but Smut's political brilliance - allied to his willingness to use force ruthlessly - averted the rebellion that had threatened to erupt into a third Boer War.

During World War One, Jan Smuts played an important role, which included fighting in East Africa in the former German colony of Tanganyika and being instrumental in establishing the British air force as an entity that was independent of the army. The RAF would not have come about as it did but for Smuts' intervention. During this period, he founded the South African Defence Force. He was present in Versailles when the mandate for custodianship of South West Africa was ceded to South Africa and he enjoyed international celebrity for his remarkable intellect. As an academic, in 1926 he published 'Holism and Evolution', his philosophy based on the precept that 'small units develop into larger ones, and they in turn become still larger ones'. Advancement, said Smuts, lies in that path of events. The conclusion of this vision was that all the peoples on Earth will eventually be united in a common pursuit. His philosophy was to influence the formation of the League of Nations, and later the United Nations.

Smuts became a Field Marshal in the British Army in 1941 and served in the Imperial War Cabinet under Winston Churchill, a fellow Boer War participant. Smuts was the only person to sign the peace treaties ending both the First and Second World Wars and was especially interesting for his ability to fight against and for the British with equal efficiency. Obviously he was not motivated by blind loyalty. Smuts wrote the preamble to the United Nations Charter and was also the only person to sign the charters of both the League of Nations and the UN. He sought to redefine the relationship between the United Kingdom and her colonies by helping to establish the British Commonwealth.

His was a huge intellect, recognised by Albert Einstein, who described Smuts as one of only 11 men in the world who understood his theory of relativity. I cannot think of many Afrikaners who merited more global respect or left such a significant mark on the world in general. The boy from Winburg done good.

Unfortunately for South Africa, Jan Smuts was defeated in the 1948 election by D. F. Malan's nationalists and their apartheid policy that would dictate the status quo for the ensuing 46 years. How different South Africa might have been if Smuts had been shown greater recognition by his own people.

The other well-known son of Winburg is Martinus Theunis Steyn who became President of the Orange Free State and ran a government in hiding whilst the Free State was under British occupation, dispatching the ultimatum to the British that was to start the Boer War:

'I would rather lose the independence of the Free State with honour than retain it with dishonour.'

The show in the Winburg Town Hall that night had an unusual energy. I had been humbled by a sudden insight into South Africa's brutal, tragic past and had seen the root cause of events that affected me personally. I suspected that the occupants of the British graves I had looked over whilst eating my cheeseburger were most probably conscripts, just like myself, who had had the misfortune of lacking the means to avoid being shipped out to the darkest corners of Africa to die in the service of greed-driven fools. It was only partly surprising to learn later that although the British public's support for the war against the Boers was considerable there was also widespread embarrassment at the poor health of the volunteering British recruits, 40 per cent of whom were found to be unfit for military service. Most of the young men rejected by the military were suffering from poverty-related illnesses such as malnutrition, rickets or tuberculosis, reflecting the dire state of the health of the general populace of one of the richest and most powerful countries in the world. As ever, the poor were recruited to fight and die to protect the interests of the rich in the names of God, King and Country.

After the two-hour show came to its clamorous finale, we found our largest gathering to date of young Afrikaans girls lining up for autographs outside the stage door. And for the first time I felt I understood why. Locked as they were inside a present that could not escape its past, even a rubber faced comedian with a tuneless monotone and a bored army band were a source of much-needed relief.

Our mini tour of the Free State with Al Debbo had magnified my existing doubts for the future of South Africa. I knew with all certainty that South Africa and all it represented was something I wanted no part of. The more familiar I became with the South African character, the more European I felt. Although I had no experience of living in any other culture than South Africa, I felt certain that even the unknown would be preferable to the reality that I was experiencing. Although I sensed that I was different from every one around me, I did not feel that I was an outsider but that they had embraced a form of delusional denial that was inconsistent with my understanding of life, the universe and everything. I never felt the need to conform and very few of the people I came across had inspired me to want to be anything like them. Although on one level I considered how I might help uplift those I believed to be mired in hopeless ignorance, consistent with my belief in the 'Try a little kindness' approach, at no stage did I consider there might be a way forward in which I could be helpful towards my fellow countrymen for the simple reason that the gap between what I knew, or at least believed I knew, and the reality of the prevailing conformity meant that the challenge of encouraging change was hopeless, and if undertaken would mean no less than a death sentence. So, for me, every day was a countdown until the day I would be able to leave.

With the end of my military service within sight, I had to face the reality that for the first time in two years I would have the freedom of choice to decide what to do with my life. This started with the decision to leave the country as soon as I possibly could. First I would need to find the means to do so. From a 'living' point of view, I was holding my breath until that day would come. A life on hold.

Gerald's Birthday

On the 19th September we were booked to perform for a dinner dance in a place called Virginia. A two-hour drive there, four hours playing and two hours drive back. Pete had called in sick on the day of the gig, probably because he couldn't stomach another such low-brow engagement, so I agreed to play bass for the night, knowing it was going to be an unchallenging evening playing background music to drunk officers and thinking I might do a set on the drums. Such it proved to be, a mind-numbing occasion with no prospect of any musical dividend. Perhaps for this reason I had surplus energy and was looking for any distraction on offer.

It was also Gerald's 24th birthday. Since he had identified me as Lucifer, relations between us had not been repaired. I felt grateful toward Gerald though, for helping me advance my understanding of God. Prior to meeting Gerald I had thought of myself as an agnostic. It was only the prejudice of a true fundamentalist believer like Gerald that encouraged me to examine the issue of the Christian God more closely, if only to be in a position to defend myself against Gerald's constant and inflexible insistence that I accept that Jesus as the only true son of God, the son who died for the sins I was born with, in order that I could enjoy eternal life relaxing in God's bounteous and abundant Heavenly Kingdom rather than the certainty of an eternity spent suffering hideous deprivations in the flaming pits of Hades, which Gerald took pains in assuring me was the inevitable consequence of disagreeing with him.

Gerald's relentless persistence had proven to be a powerful motivator for my commitment to a more detailed examination of the finer points of Christian belief and on this day the twin aspects of my gratitude to Gerald for his help in advancing my religious awareness, along with the restless boredom arising from the long hours of playing three-chord ditties to drunken Afrikaners, instigated the moment when I would share my views with Gerald in a neutral environment in which he was something of a captive audience. He had enjoyed an open season in forcing his opinions on me and it was now no less than appropriate that he should enjoy the other side of a good hectoring. This, I decided, would be his day of reckoning for calling me names.

During our first break, under the guise of friendly banter, I suggested we take our drinks and adjourn to an outside table where we were less likely to be disturbed. I felt mischievously driven to make Gerald's birthday a memorable one.

"Gerald, I don't have a birthday present for you, but I have been thinking about Jesus and God so I can offer you my thoughts instead. A bit like a gift, but without wrapping paper."

His face lit up expectantly. For Gerald, there was never any doubt that everyone, eventually, would accept Jesus and salvation. There was no other possibility.

"I see why there is a need to have a God. I am familiar with the idea that if God didn't exist we would have to invent him. With so many big questions on life and death it's easy to see that a demand exists for a philosophy to address the unexplained. We all need a way of interpreting the big mysteries of life and death. And the needier we are, the greater the need for a belief that provides comfort. We all arrive one day at a place where we want to know what death is about and to make some sense of our own lifespan. Fear of the unknown is a natural reaction."

He nodded in accordance.

"We all start out the same. Little biological organisms that process food to grow into little human beings. Cells grow and multiply and we gradually develop motor skills. The right side of the brain starts to make synaptic connections enabling development of base functions, carrying intuitive messages, like when to poo and when to burp. Then one day the left side of the brain develops the basic ability to rationalise and we start to refine a capacity for considered action. Eventually this develops into the ability to form a code of ethical values that balance with our right-brain intuition to start us on the journey towards becoming considered human beings. From that point we begin to examine the issues that govern our existence, the two most dominant being death and sex. Coming to terms with the concept of death presents a challenge. The thought of death being the final event in life is difficult to accept. It generates a fear reaction. A life of poverty and hardship would be so much harder to accept if that's all there is. So many years back, early on in the evolution of mankind, we devised a coping mechanism. A one size fits all panacea for dealing with the fear and we called it God, an all-powerful all-seeing entity responsible for everything all the time. Over time we evolved our appreciation of this God to the level where we no longer had anything to consider for ourselves. God took on responsibility for everything. Where every speck of dust lands and where every raindrop falls. Where you go to the toilet and when, who you should sleep with and who you should hate. With God you don't need to wonder any more, to struggle in the maze of confusion towards establishing your own truth and learning how to take any of the big decisions. God exonerates us from any personal responsibility; our accountability for our actions is not ours any more. It's down to God, because accountability is something we need to steer well clear of. If we ourselves are responsible and accountable for what we do, then we have to learn how to make up our own minds and when that happens we don't need the idea of God anymore."

I paused for breath and saw, much to my surprise, that I still had Gerald's attention.

"Humour me for one minute. Let's take a look at some of the pillars that Christian belief relies on. Original sin. We are born guilty and so we need to earn forgiveness. You look at a little baby and label it a sinner. Mmmm. Can't say I think that makes a great deal of sense. Adam and Eve in the Garden of Eden. So their kids had sex with each other and then they had sex with their cousins. I mean it's a ridiculous notion. What do you do with your basic common sense when you look at that story? Oh yes! The magic of blind faith, the key to all God belief. Even the name gives it away. Who in their right mind would entrust the very essence of their spiritual existence to a concept relying on blind faith? A blind man perhaps. Perhaps in the dead of night it makes sense to follow a blind man, but how do you continue to do so when the sun comes up? Belief is a lot like that. When you are a little child, believing something in a dead-of-the-night moment of fear and weakness is one thing, but how can you justify it when you grow older and the light of basic common sense shines through? It's like babies and nappies. At first it makes good sense to use a nappy for baby. But as babies grow, they develop a greater capacity for self-awareness and taking personal responsibility and this translates in most cases to leaving the nappy behind and moving forward to a better system of self-accountable toilet decision-making. Religious belief is like a nappy for a young soul.

"Then there's the notion that we are created in the image of God. Can I ask you a yes or no question? Are we created in the image of God?"

"Yes. You know that we are," came the firm reply and before he had the chance to embellish, I was back in my stride, speaking at an ever-increasing pace as I knew Gerald's patience would expire the moment he determined the conversation was not going to lead to the glorious acceptance of Jesus.

"So God is almighty and the creator of everything and is responsible for the placement of everything in the celestial order. He made everything in existence. Little animals, birds, flowers, and all the people too. And he made cancer. He made the mosquito. Quadriplegics. Blind, deaf and dumb leukaemia suffering albino orphans. He made P. W. Botha's brain. He made mutating illnesses that paralyse and leave people howling in pain for years as they scream their way to sorry death without once ever understanding how a considerate all seeing celestial designer failed to spot the fatal disease that bled their life away. Every murderer, rapist and megalomaniac serial killer. The Lord God made them all. And what's more, after having made them, let's consider what he did next. We know God sees everything. He is all-powerful and all around all the time so when things happen it's never a secret. It's not as if anything slips past him. When his dreadful creations set about their ungodly business he watches benignly with a twiddle of the thumbs knowing his will is being done. It can't work one way and not the other. It is quite clear that this almighty God is responsible for a lot of nasty stuff. And because we are created in his image – all of us – rapists, murderers, poets, racist killers, politicians, homophobes. There is only one ineluctable conclusion. Our history of war and horrific barbarism demonstrates abundantly that we are mostly a sick bunch of nasty dumb fuckwits, so, if we are created in the image of God, then what does that make God?"

"You have it completely wrong," Gerald interjected. "All the bad stuff is Satan. God did not create all that disease and pestilence. If you think you know so much about religion how come you don't know that?"

"Ah yes. The Devil. Of course it is, Gerald. The Devil is the guy in black who does the bad stuff and God is the guy in white who makes it all better. This is a delusion a five year-old might enjoy in the guise of a fairy story, but holding onto this fall-over logic into adulthood is just plain laziness. Any informed debate looking to prove the mechanics of the 'Devil bad, God good' argument falls on its face trying. It's full of holes - from the Garden of Eden apple story, to the virgin birth, to the idea of original sin. These are fairy stories made up in desperate times to assuage fears and fuel ignorant superstitions. There simply is no Devil just as there clearly is no God. What does exist though are avenues of belief which convince individuals that God exists and that a Devil exists. This is a response to a need. It is not a logically realistic proposition."

"So now you think you can prove the devil doesn't exist?" spluttered Gerald.

"There is no need for any argument to prove something doesn't exist. That would be ridiculous. Proof of something's existence relies on proof that it exists. I can't say to you - there are 15 fairies at the bottom of my garden - and expect you to believe that, unless I can service the burden of proof. The onus is not on you to disprove the fairies in my garden. That would be ridiculous. If I make an assertion without a shred of even tangential evidence in support - then it is a delusion. I am attempting a deceit. I am trying to make you believe there are 15 fairies at the bottom of my garden and in so doing I am attempting to deceive you. It follows that if I am prepared to deceive you on this matter - I would attempt to deceive you on any other number of matters - because I rely on delusion to promote my belief. This is one of many dangerous elements that allowing blind faith to lead you to belief in an invisible God/Devil introduces. If you believe that delusion - you have agreed a process of acceptance of things based on deceit and this means you will believe more or less anything. It is dishonesty at its most cynical because it requires you to actually propagate the lie to make it work. Human nature and the workings of the brain encourage acceptance of that which we most need to believe. The process is driven by the need. We adopt a 'The truth is what I choose to believe' approach. And that becomes 'the truth'. So you believe a powerful omnipresent good god controls everything - and a bad equally powerful other lesser god - who is called the Devil - counteracts all the stuff the good one does. And that is your truth. But it is not a reliable truth, it's just one that you have elected, by reliance on blind faith, motivated by fear and need, to place your belief in. I know people who believe they have fairies living at the bottom of their garden. They believe. They truly believe. But that doesn't make it so. Truth does not follow belief. It's the other way round."

"The reality I see, the truth that I believe based on the facts presented to me and processed with the benefit of rational considered unprejudiced thought, is that God is your excuse for avoiding personal responsibility. God is the word you use to name the failure of your own accountability. God is the embodiment of your inability to accept the reality of your existence and the need to project an alternative that can be regulated and channelled. It is a lifestyle choice that relies entirely on delusion. Your belief is self-deceit and, with that deceit in place, your need to justify it requires that you use any means necessary to bludgeon those who don't buy into your movie with dreadful, cynical, malicious and abusive behaviour that is entirely at odds with the kindness, consideration and willingness to help others that forms the more reliable measure of spiritual development. You're not interested in the spiritual journey at all. You're just ticking boxes in a book of nonsense that tells you what you need to hear and you are in this position because you are just too lazy and to address the fear that drives your submission."

"Submission to what?" asked Gerald.

"Submission to God's will though fear. Fear of the unknown. Thousands of years ago the Roman Emperor Constantine, the power controller of the day, contrived a system for safeguarding the position of the elite by putting together a bunch of designer fairy tales based on a simple principle of generating fear and then offering protection from the horrors raised. The books purpose was to manipulate those frightened and foolish enough to suspend their critical judgment in the name of conformist compliance by threatening the most awful tortures ever conceived, like eternity in burning hell-fire. It's really simple in its cynical implementation. A ruling elite – the chosen empowered few – impose this doctrine of submission on a terrified majority, motivated entirely by their own self-interest. Dumb people down. Have them cowering in fear. Offer salvation at a price and Bob's your uncle. You have a winner. It's been easily achieved, because it exploits a basic aspect of human nature, which is fear, coupled with the need for protection. Just target children from the earliest age - before any logical development can allow personal choice - and then make sure that anyone criticising the good book's ways is persecuted horribly. You must be aware of the extent to which the Church has tortured and persecuted non-believers through the years.

"Religious submission to the One God is a belief system that turns minds so far from natural instinct that individuals will go out and kill people who don't agree with them in the belief that they are saving their victims from a life of sin and the certainty of eternity in hell. Their delusion is so complete that they describe their murdering criminal ways as a charitable Christian act."

Gerald had a glazed look in his eye, but I had suffered his odious efforts to enlighten me for many months and was not now to be denied my right of reply.

"Your use of God as an alternative to doing some proper thinking work is just laziness. People who choose God with all the ridiculous suppositions that process relies on are just plain lazy. Why invest all that hard thinking in a journey of spiritual growth towards finding your own truth when you can just hold your hands up at the outset and say, blind faith tells me Jesus is the son of God so I will do what they say and go to Heaven and if anyone disagrees I will hate them with a mighty vengeance? I can't think of a better word to describe this conclusion to a spiritual quest than - lazy. Because I reject your belief in almighty God does not imply I reject a spiritual consideration. Quite the contrary. I am always learning about the mysterious connection between events that I can't fully rationalise and that I can't give a set answer to. I am no different from you in facing many of the fears and uncertainties that living holds. My belief exists in a dynamic state evolving as and when information reaches me and that state develops from an ever-wider knowledge base. My belief does not rely on making you or anyone else bend to my will and agree with me.

"I am happy with my own relationship with spiritual growth. I have accepted a simple outlook. I try to be kind to everyone I come across. I try to help those less fortunate than myself. I listen to those who know more than I do and take those lessons on board. I try to share whatever lessons I have learned with those who have less. I don't steal. I don't kill. I don't wallow in the base emotions. I try and resonate at a positive frequency at all times and I do not allow negative thoughts into my life. And where I see injustice I rail against it with all the vigour at my muster. I decide for myself the best way forward in any situation and I take responsibility for my own decisions whether they turn out to be good or bad. I try to make the most out of every moment and every opportunity that comes my way and I try achieve this in consideration of what represents the highest good. I live in the hope that my success will be measured by how I leave the world when I go and by how much good I was able to do.

"Mine is not a belief whose success is measured in terms of how many converts are brought into my flock. I don't require that you agree with me to validate my belief. I don't say mine is the only way or that if you don't believe me you will be condemned to an eternity of the worst kind of pain ever visited on a sinning bastard. But that's what you bring to this argument. Yours is the only way. You are intolerant of any other views, meaning that, in your view, everyone else is wrong. Condemn and convert. That should be your mission statement. You polarise opinion on a right or wrong basis without a moment's pause to consider the consequences. What's worse is you don't even have the excuse of information not being available to inform you of the extent of this tremendous con."

In full flow, I was not to be put off by Gerald's lemon-lipped mask of disgust. I kept going, hoping to get in as much as possible before he either walked away or, as seemed increasingly more likely, punched me.

"Where has this intolerant and divisive faith system got us? Look at the damage the Bible has done. More people have died in Africa because of that book than from malaria and the hippopotamus put together. The slave traders that weren't reading the Bible as they traded human lives were reading the Quran, unphased by any conscience. In fact, those two books have killed more people than any other book ever written, including the AK47 operator's handbook. Look at how the Afrikaners found a piece in the Bible that shows how blacks are made to till the soil, which they turned into an argument for persecuting black people. Look at how many examples there are of people using the myth of God to get impressionable young people to commit horrendous atrocities all in the name of that God. I mean you're a singer, aren't you? Haven't you even listened to Bob Dylan's 'With God on our side'. Didn't your interest in God make you the slightest bit curious about what a great songwriter might have to say on the subject. It's not as if the information you need to guide your wisdom is hard to find. Look at Crosby Stills and Nash's 'Cathedral'. I paused to recite the song's punch-line:

'Open up the gates of the church and let me out of here.
Too many people have lied in the name of Christ for anyone to heed the call.
So many people have died in the name of Christ that I can't believe at all.'

"Look at the Church's history of persecution and suppression of knowledge. Look at the extent to which they have manipulated human awareness in the hope of maintaining the level of ignorance that their survival depends on. Take Galileo – persecuted horribly for suggesting the world was not as flat as the Church maintained. The Church behaves like a mafia protection racket, controlling a monopoly on spiritual considerations, you either bend over and pay them or they do you in.

"The worst part of religious subjugation is that it removes the individual's right to choice. Spiritual growth relies on the exercising of choice. It's only through exercising choice that the process of growth prospers - the action and reaction arising from cause and consequence. Exercising choice and facing the consequences of those choices is how we refine the choice process, without which there can be no spiritual growth. The Church obstructs this process with dire consequences. It is a logical dead-end. It presents a finite number of possibilities, which can only ever lead to one outcome. The philosophy that makes every non-believer wrong can only end in confrontation, war and death. This is the nature of polarising, divisive philosophy built on the bedrock of intolerance. And that's the hypocrisy that characterises your blind faith in Christianity. Your imaginary friend is not, as you have told me repeatedly, a God of love but a guarantor of death. He who is not for me is against me. Just take a moment to consider on this day of all days, your birthday, the crap you have been spouting at me for the past year.

Yours is a belief system designed to subjugate and dominate the ignorant and weak-willed, not to nourish and encourage. It's led you to look at someone like me who doesn't readily succumb to your will and conclude the appropriate explanation must be that I am the Devil. Where do you think you will end up if you carry on peddling this philosophy of hatred, intolerance and self-righteousness to people in reduced circumstances who would believe the earth was flat if you bullied them enough? You, Gerald, have happily swallowed the greatest lie ever sold. What you do, trying to exploit and victimise the weak-willed and vulnerable, is the worst kind of wrong."

That was as much as Gerald could take. He stood up and left without a word. We never spoke again. I don't think he ever so much as looked me in the eye during the remaining three months when we saw each other almost every day.

The next Ad-Lib gig was at the Afrikaans University, Tukkies, on the 27th September, dinner dance for third year medical students and memorable because it was my last day as a teenager. This was another private gig arranged by Pete and myself, featuring Mario as the lead singer. It paid 350 Rand, split five ways. We were playing a long version of 'On Broadway' when the clock struck midnight and I began my 20th year playing a guitar solo with a great sounding band thinking to myself, things could be worse. I could have been one of the third year medical students on the other side of the stage.

To test the choice and consequence theory I had developed through my forced association with Gerald, over-ridden by the fact that I was now smoking at least 30 cigarettes a day, I decided to stop smoking on my birthday. I didn't think this through in any great detail but just decided that smoking as much as I was couldn't be a good thing and as an exercise in self-discipline, I would stop.

Day one of abstinence was a real torture and illustrated the dimensions of the challenge. Until then I had not properly appreciated the addictive power of tobacco. I'd have walked a mile on my hands for the Camel pain to stop. The first day was a struggle from the moment I got out of bed and avoided the usual first post-breakfast cigarette of the day. I eventually ended up spending most of the day in bed trying to sleep off the withdrawal pangs. The second day, a Monday, was even worse. I had to be at Entertainments in Pretoria at eight o'clock.

Until I gave up, I would normally smoke two Camels during the 30-minute drive to Pretoria. By the time I reached the unit that morning I was in an agitated state. Matters did not improve as the day wore on and I barely made it through until closing. By the time I reached my bed that night, I felt sick, anxious, distracted, nauseous and agitated, classic symptoms of withdrawal from addictive substance dependency. I doggedly maintained my abstinence for the rest of the week, by which time I was unable to do anything other than divert all my energy and attention into not smoking.

Stuck inside of Greytown (with the Camel blues again)

Our next gig was in Natal. On Saturday we were due to appear at the Greytown Town Hall for another prestigious army function. Almost invariably, the functions we were booked for would be described as 'prestigious'. I was never quite sure if they were prestigious and therefore we were booked to play, or that we were booked to play and thereby the gig became prestigious. Greytown was some distance away and we drove there in one of the unit's brown Combis with Gerald, the only one of us who held or would want a military driving licence, at the wheel.

To the first time visitor, Greytown looked like a typical Afrikaner country town. It was the birthplace of another famous Afrikaner leader, Louis Botha, and its clean and well-ordered main street was lined with Dutch style buildings redolent with Boer War imagery. There was a statue of an ox-wagon in the town centre and occasional glimpses of Boer paraphernalia in the windows of the stores, like models of ox wagons and framed sepia pictures of Boer Voortrekkers. As we drove through it, Greytown looked picture postcard pretty in the summer sunshine. For the duration of the drive towards Greytown I was aching with the ongoing symptoms of withdrawal. I found that by going into a virtual state of hibernation I could just about carry on, but with show-time approaching and the adrenaline rush that this thought promoted, I could see the front line of my resistance crumbling under the ceaseless assault of pain bombardment courtesy of R.J.Reynolds, cigarette manufacturer. My resistance was finally reduced to a single thread and when the time came to check the sound system, it snapped. I faced the utterly galling reality that my will was vanquished.

While the others started lugging the gear into the Town Hall by the back entrance I went into the nearest store and bought a pack of Camels. Within seconds I was standing in the town square inhaling deeply and feeling the rush of bright white anaesthesia surging through my veins as the pernicious cocktail of designer drugs that make up a Camel cigarette effortlessly wiped away the programmed pain they had inflicted on me to keep me loyal to their brand. I felt I had made the acquaintance of a formidable foe in the chemistry-graduate employees of the cigarette companies. Addiction had won this battle and all I could take away from the encounter was the resolve to one day win the war.

Buoyed by the abundance of energy suddenly available now that I was no longer engaged in the draining fight against my own craving, I was in particularly good spirits. I felt especially in tune and enjoyed the few songs I sang in the set more than ever and, in the short term at least, I noticed an interaction between singing and smoking.

After the show, we stayed overnight in another of the cheap hotels that proliferated in the outlying country towns. The following morning we enjoyed the traditional breakfast that ended with the customary 'moer' coffee enjoyed with the first of the day's cigarettes before setting off for the town of Newcastle, a few hours drive to the south east.

Coals to Newcastle

Newcastle, being a larger town, had more hotels on offer than Greytown and we found ourselves in the Holiday Inn, an experience made especially memorable because this hotel had a Space Invaders machine in the lobby. Such entertainments were scarce and I did not miss any opportunity to play on this machine. Sucking away on Camels between screens, I spent every available moment playing. I couldn't wait for the gig to finish in order to get back to the hotel to take on the Space Invaders once again. I was still there at 3am, blasting furiously at the falling blobs, chain smoking and thinking to myself that this is as good as it gets.

That week, the army newspaper 'Paratus' published a picture of Ad Lib, along with a short though enthusiastic piece about the band. When the paper came out, several Permanent Force members came over to congratulate us. It was the first time I had seen a picture of myself in a newspaper.

Our set list was growing every week. Whenever a popular new hit arrived in the South African charts we would play a cassette of the song in the band room and take a decision on whether to add it to the set. Current hits of that week were 'Coming up' by Paul McCartney, which had a guitar riff that was fun to play and 'All for Leyna' by Billy Joel, that we eventually had sounding just like the record. This song summed up the 1980s musical mentality perfectly and was sufficiently musically challenging to keep us interested. A yellow Boss fuzz-box, very trendy amongst guitarists at the time, enabled a close approximation of the sound for the guitar part. The band had been playing together for almost a year now, rehearsing or performing on most days. Philosophical differences notwithstanding, we were turning into a reasonably impressive musical unit.

October 1980 was another busy month for the band, with ten confirmed bookings. We appeared in Bloemfontein City Hall on the 17th to play a four-hour Variety Show backing various artists. Before the show, I walked over to the Military Hospital where just over a year earlier I had lost so much energy. I felt a chill in my bones just looking at it.

The city of Bloemfontein had sinister reverberations, as if the very soil I stood on transmitted messages up through my feet relaying the dark nightmares of the tortured souls who had passed through there. I could not relax for one second, so much so that after the gig ended at one in the morning I agitated enough to get a Combi for the drive back home rather than stay overnight in that unhappy place.

I kept remembering the doctor I had seen for the tribunal appointment who, instead of being a reasonable human being on the occasion of our first meeting, had instead made it necessary for me to lose so many months in getting back to the reclassification board. As if that wasn't enough for him, he had then sent me to Ward 5 for a week of psychiatric evaluation that left me with an insight into a world of spiritual and ethical necrosis that I had not imagined existed. Although he had somehow qualified as a medical practitioner, Hippocrates himself would have felt very little but contempt for the malignant Dr. Muller.

Socially, this period was very lively. Being in a band carried with it an attractive status and although I was still in the army I was in effect working as a professional musician. I had made a choice and, against considerable odds, I was playing music all the time and had achieved a degree of respect within the army. As a result, I had seemingly become untouchable by the thing I found most offensive which was military authority. The outward effect of this inner confidence meant I was able to interact rewardingly with whoever I chose to interact with.

Although the politics of the band were polarised with Pete and myself on one side and the rest in obeisance to the special South African style Jesus who ignored racism, I enjoyed a cautious friendship with Nick, grandson of the revered author of the classic South African novel 'Cry the Beloved Country', Alan Paton. When Nick invited me to his home in Parktown for tea with his grandfather I was quick to accept. Alan Paton must have been approaching 80 when I was introduced to him. He was certainly an estimable character, a grand old man famous for his intellect and a rare beacon of light in that he was able to speak out against the Afrikaner regime and yet remain alive, uncensored and unburdened by house arrest. The conversation revolved around day-to-day issues and though I have no recollection of any great profundities being discussed or wisdom delivered it was nonetheless a privilege to spend a short time with a hallowed South African thinker whose works will be read by future generations. I came away inspired by the evidence that if you were sufficiently intelligent and capable of articulating your position it was possible to live by principle and survive without being overwhelmed by the hostile attentions of the Afrikaner political Establishment. Neil Aggett had not been so fortunate.

The following day, the 25th October, we travelled to Middleburg for a Saturday night show in the Town Hall. Middelburg was another significant Afrikaner town that I would not have ever visited but for military conscription. Formed originally by the Voortrekkers in 1694, it had a large Dutch Reformed Church in the centre and was the location of another of the infamous British concentration camps in which some 1,380 women and children died during the Boer war. Awareness of this situation came to characterise many of the heartland gigs we did and a theme developed around Dutch Reformed churches, stories of famous Afrikaners from Voortrekkers to Boer war fighters and all kinds of reminders of British atrocities in the Boer war. The story of little Lizzie van Zijl, the nine year-old Afrikaner girl who was allowed to starve to death in a concentration camp by a British doctor as her Kommando fighter father would not surrender was an especially poignant reminder of the inhumanity that war promotes in otherwise reasonable men. **(See note 6.)**

As a footnote to the tragedy of the British concentration camps, it should be remembered that countless thousands of black South Africans, considered too insignificant by the British to warrant their names or their numbers being recorded, also perished in the camps.

Mariepskop Military Base

On Thursday, 31st October, we were booked to perform for officers and men at Mariepskop military base. Also booked on this show were two popular acts, Fernando Coelho with his troupe of Spanish dancers and Sias Reinecke with whom we had already performed on our Border tour. Because of the distance to Mariepskop, a plane was sent to collect us and a Dakota duly arrived to pick us up from Waterkloof airfield.

Flying in a Dakota was a real thrill. This legendary plane, the McDonnell Douglas DC3 to give it its full name, is a twin-engine propeller plane first flown in 1935 and the most widely used troop transport plane in World War Two. The one we flew in had benches down the side and was incredibly noisy as the thin exterior did little to mitigate the roar of the engines. I imagined that the one we were in might have been used in World War Two and speculated that paratroops sat on the very benches where we sat just before swallowing their terror and leaping into the fray. The pilots appeared thrilled to have our troupe of musicians and dancers on board, especially the giggling Spanish dancers with their shiny red lipstick. The flight to Mariepskop was great fun with landmarks being pointed out from the air. I had a flutter of youthful ego at the thought that I was a musician being flown to gigs by private plane. We landed at Mariepskop, almost two kilometres above sea level and the highest peak in the Northern Drakensburg, the obvious site for the radar equipment that monitored South Africa's northern border. On a clear day, Mozambique's capital city, Maputo, can be seen shimmering on the horizon from Mariepskop. The surrounding area with its sheer, verdant cliffs and canyons is a breathtaking sight.

The Mariepskop gig was a triumph for the band. We were on top form and it was a real thrill to be a part of such a successful show. It was the first time I had appeared with sexy dancing girls and had seen how helpful this was in terms of getting a crowd on its feet.

We were particularly well looked after in terms of hospitality and the following morning after loading our gear into the Dakota for the return leg, we were treated to a low level flight over the Blyde River canyon, the third largest canyon in the world.

The sight of the brilliant blue Blyde River winding between the deep green heaving curves of the Drakensburg on either side from inside this legendary historic aircraft was thrilling to a 20 year-old. The pilot of the Dakota seemed to have decided to entertain us in return, in the way he knew best. At one point he flew us directly towards three towering spirals of rock. "These are called the Three Rondavels," he shouted above the roar of the engines as he flew the plane straight at them, waiting until the last possible moment before banking the plane steeply to one side as we turned. The journey to and from Mariepskop in a classic aircraft and the success of the performance were two of the few occasions upon which I felt able to describe the times I spent in military uniform as exhilarating.

Hoedspruit

Just two days later we were back in the same area when we were flown to Hoedspruit for the air force's Prestige Ball. We flew in a different DC3 and this time there were no dancing girls on board, just our band and Sias Reinecke. Hoedspruit is a small town near the Kruger Park and close to the Mozambican border. In previous years, military intelligence identified this area as the prime location to set up a northern border defence position and so, in 1978, they built a state of the art runway attached to a highly protected wartime base. As we landed, I noticed what looked like garage doors leading up onto the runway. There was a feeling of high energy about Hoedspruit. When we left the Dakota we were welcomed into the base by the kommandant who was extremely friendly and seemed keen to answer any questions. I asked him about the doors leading onto the runway.

"Yes, we are very proud of our facility here. Would you like a guided tour?"

The tour started on the runway.

"We are in an area that is filled with wildlife. In fact, all around us there are game reserves. This presents a problem for airplanes coming in to land. Wild animals seem to like standing on the runway and we were seeing too many accidents where pilots swerved to avoid buck and so forth, so what do you think we did?" he asked, pausing for effect.

"We introduced three cheetahs from the Kruger National Park and let them set up home on the runway. This has reduced accidents involving animals by 90 per cent."

He led us up flights of stairs into the main command centre. Hoedspruit was the location of the largest radar system in South Africa. Inside the main radar room we were shown round screens with circling lines that illuminated white blips in ghostly light. Several officers stood by, casually monitoring proceedings on the screens.

"See that dot?" the kommandant asked, pointing at a blip halfway down from the top of the screen. "That is a small plane taking off from the airport at Maputo. From there it would take him 20 minutes to fly over here. We monitor all air activity in this region. Anything that looks suspicious and we launch Mirage fighters well in advance of it becoming a problem."

The efficiency of the system was mesmerising. The control room had a long open expanse of window that looked out from its aerie on the mountaintop across a wide expanse of cloud below. We were, quite literally, above the clouds. The kommandant walked us outside to a viewing area from which the cliff face melted into a fluffy white cloud below.

"This is where Jamie Uys filmed the scene from 'The Gods must be Crazy,'" he told us. We made our way to the canteen for coffee where the kommandant carried on explaining the workings of the base.

"If we spot a plane taking off that does not correspond to any flight plan we recognise, we go to the first stage of alert. We will try to make radio contact. If nothing happens to reduce the alarm, allowing for the maximum speed of current aircraft we will always have at least ten minutes warning before any hostile plane could enter South African air space. That will give us ample time to launch planes to intercept."

"Ten minutes doesn't seem like a long time but we need a lot less than that," he said.

"Those hangar doors you saw on the runway. Behind those doors are fully equipped underground hangers, where we have Mirage fighters, armed and ready, with engines left on permanent standby. Pilots are kept on standby footing, kitted up ready to go at any time. They do a four-hour rota system, 24 hours a day, 7 days a week. If signalled a 'go' order, they will be in their cockpits ready to take off within two minutes. Two minutes after that they will be at 20,000 feet fully armed and ready for just about anything."

Despite my indifference to anything the SADF did, I must confess that this visit to Hoedspruit left me feeling that there were some special skills being employed to a high level of excellence here. This was 1980 and fully armed supersonic jet fighters could be airborne and in attack mode within four minutes of the alarm being raised, any time within the 24-hour cycle. As far as I know this expensive expedient was never employed at any time. Twenty-one years later the failure by the US Air Force in 2001 to launch a plane for over 30 minutes after the 9/11 alert reminded me of our visit to Hoedspruit.

The Hoedspruit gig was less impressive than the environment. The audience seemed irreparably depressed by their isolation and appeared to be hell bent on getting drunk as rapidly as possible. Our drummer, Al Debbo Jnr, had been having a running argument with Sias ever since we boarded the plane. Evidently there was some history of disagreement between Sias and Al's father, Al Debbo. Sias was not at his best on this occasion, visibly slowed by drink. At the beginning of the break after the second set, Al came over to me and said flatly, "I've had enough. I am not playing with this idiot." He walked out, leaving Pete, Tony and myself to work out how to continue. Gerald couldn't play any instruments and was in any case more or less irrelevant by this stage of the evening as Sias was by now not to be separated from the microphone, crooning maudlin Afrikaans love songs to a bleary eyed audience. I found the whole thing quite disgusting but the show had to go on. I volunteered to play drums and we started the third set as a piano, bass and drums trio. Such was the alcohol intake that I don't think anyone even noticed the change in the line up. A good bash on the drum kit worked wonders for the soul and made the evening pass more quickly. I never found out what Sias could possibly have said to offend the otherwise gentle Al to such an extent.

Counting down

There was a tradition in the SADF off celebrating 40 days before the end of national service. My '40 days' landmark fell in November. I didn't bother with the usual piss-up with one's mates, but I did pause long enough to reflect that the end was now truly in sight and that I had no clear plan as to what direction my life would take after military service.

The last few gigs for Ad Lib were lined up for the weekend of the 14th December. Ironically, we were booked to return to Kimberley for two shows, returning to the scene of the crime. The first gig was on a Friday night in the Kimberley City Hall and Ad Lib was the featured band. The return to Kimberley was an emotional roller coaster. On one hand, I felt like a returning conqueror, having struggled so desperately to escape this appalling place and find my way to the Entertainment Corps. On the other hand, I felt overwhelmingly depressed when seeing this miserable place for the dump it really was and thinking back on just how much energy I had expended on such small endeavours. The gig in the Town Hall was frankly dreadful, possibly because I made it so. I found the people revolting and found myself besieged by unpleasant reminders of the time wasted in Diskobolos. Returning to Kimberley with some possession of my faculties and in control of my own agenda was very different from the way I had first arrived. I felt that performing well on this night was below me. In boxing parlance, I threw the fight, launching into guitar solos at any opportunity and pointedly turning my back on the audience. We finished the gig and returned to our hotel lodgings early.

After breakfast on the Saturday morning, with some time on my hands before the gig, I made a point of visiting the Big Hole for the first and perhaps the last time and making some effort to find out more about the place.

I learned that Kimberley only exists because Erasmus Jacobs found a diamond on the banks of the nearby Orange River some time in the 1870s. News of his find quickly spread and a rush of prospectors began. A large diamond was found on a hill and, before long, digging prospectors had turned the hill into a hole and that hole grew wider and deeper until it became known as the 'Big Hole'. The hill that had became the diamond-mining camp went through various name changes in its progress including Vooruitzicht, Colesberg Kopje, De Beers, New Rush and eventually in 1873, Kimberley, which attained city status in 1912.

Although the area was to be a part of the Boer-controlled Free State the British, true to form, annexed the diamond field. Cecil John Rhodes used De Beers, his personal company, to exploit this opportunity. Such was the region's prosperity that Kimberley became the first town in the southern hemisphere to install electric street lighting. Black people came from far and wide to provide the cheap labour required to dig for and extract many tons of diamonds on behalf of De Beers. Laws were invented to prevent the black labour force from moving freely, creating conditions of virtual slave labour and setting an early precedent for what would later become the unfortunate 'Group Areas Act' of the apartheid years.

At the start of the second Boer War in 1899, Kimberley was one of the first targets for the Boers who laid siege to it for four months, inflicting heavy losses on the British relief effort and trapping Cecil Rhodes in the town for an uncomfortably long time. Later in the war Kimberley was to be the location of a British concentration camp. Many black people died digging for Kimberley's diamonds for slave wages for the enrichment of the British-owned company.

Several of the biggest diamonds in the British crown jewels, including the Star of Africa, came from Kimberley. Because of the association between Kimberley, diamonds, cruel and inhumane exploitation of impoverished labour and colonial avarice, vanity was never more grotesque to me than in the guise of the wearing of diamonds.

'*Diamonds are forever,*' whispered the sexy voice hired by De Beers to foment demand.

"And so is the memory of those faceless, countless thousands who lived so poorly and died so miserably for your profits," I thought.

Following my Saturday afternoon visit to the Big Hole, having a few hours to kill, I decided to drive to 11 Kommando and pay my lack of respects, continuing my tour guide's approach in bringing to life for the band the story of my time at 11 Kommando. We drove into the Diskobolos camp and up to the HQ. It all looked different this time around, much smaller and much dirtier. I felt waves of real black despair looking at the sights around me, as if I were a victim returning to the scene of a crime in which part of me had been stolen. I felt like accusing someone. I wanted to confront the nearest sergeant major and shame him with the evidence of his evil, but common sense prevailed. The faces in Dislobolos were all unfamiliar and I decided not to stay too long and decided against going to see whether the Kommandant or Whiteley were still in the HQ.

Last days

We drove back to the hotel to prepare for what we knew would be our last gig as Ad Lib in the Kimberley Boys' High School Hall. I could not get over the tremendous coincidence that brought me to the same venue for my final show in uniform as where I had played one of the first gigs near the start of my conscription. "Of all the gigs in all the world, how did it come to be this one?" I ruminated, pondering what possible significance Kimberley had in my life beyond being the place where it so nearly ended. In the hotel room, the thought occurred to me as we dressed for the gig that I didn't need to wear the regulation army outfit. After all, who was going to try and confront me at this late stage, and so I left for the gig still in my jeans T-shirt and trainers outfit, my final moment of rage against the machine. No one said anything about my appearance in civilian clothes and the gig went particularly well. The sound was right, the set list worked, the players were all on form and the crowd was thrilled. This was as good as the band would ever be. Word had got around that we were in town and a few old faces from my Kimberley days showed up at this gig to say hello leading to several rounds of drinks in the hotel after the gig, where we sat talking and smoking until 4.20 in the morning. During this late night interlude, I heard from one of the former troops that the Kommandant had been suspended and was no longer running 11 Kommando. There were rumours that he had been caught stealing army provisions and was to face court martial. I laughed inside at the thought that he might face a court martial using the same procedural handbook in the same room as the one where I had so enjoyed my own court martial. Remembering the many gigs to which we had travelled along with various items belonging to the military loaded in the back of many a Bedford truck, it suddenly made perfect sense. It also dawned on me that most of the gigs we had done whilst at 11 Kommando were paid for and that I for one had certainly not seen any of the money. I knew Whiteley's thieving character from the night he intercepted and pocketed the jar of money collected for the band but it seemed the Kommandant had been using his position of authority within the military to maintain a profitable business sideline. It was obvious now that he had wanted to keep me in Kimberley because he was making tidy money out of the band's musical services. On all those occasions where he sat in the front at Church service, holding his cap in his hand and looking reflective while the Dominee prayed for the nation's success in the war against Communism and the black peril, Kommandant Van Rensburg may well have suppressed a quiet little snigger of gratitude.

Although it was extremely late and we had overnight accommodation in Kimberley, I was desperate to get away from there and convinced the rest of the band that the drive back to Johannesburg was a good idea. With the dawn just an hour away we set off once again in the brown, army Combi.

New morning

There were just a few weeks left before the big last day. In that calming period during which those of us due to clear out counted down the few days, I was standing outside the band room smoking a cigarette when a car pulled into the parking area. A small grey-haired, middle-aged woman stepped out. She approached the building and asked where she would find Major Hayden. I directed her to his office and shortly afterwards Major Hayden escorted her to the band room where he introduced her as Edith Goldstein, a theatrical agent, who had a specific requirement. Major Hayden told her that she should speak to either Gerald or me as one of us might be able to help her and we were introduced. Edith began by describing a venue where the resident musician needed to take a night off. Her mission, she said, was to locate a solo entertainer who could deputise on the night, performing to a sizeable crowd in what she described as one of the top music bars in South Africa.

"Not something I would do," said Gerald primly, who by this stage in his military service seemed to be distancing himself from developing his musical interests.

"The gig pays 180 Rand," said Edith. My ears pricked up. 180 Rand was then a useful sum. It was several times an Army monthly salary. I think she spotted my look of interest and encouraged me further.

"Why don't you go and have a look at the venue? It's in Hillbrow. You have been playing lots of shows and George Hayden says you can do it, so go on, why not give yourself a chance?" My heart was beating faster at the thought of 180 Rand for one night. She handed me her card. I assured her that I would go and check out the venue and the following Friday night I found my way to the 747 Bar in the Crest Hotel.

Hillbrow in 1980 was a bustling spread of high-rise buildings located next to Johannesburg's city centre, being the major residential sector for Johannesburg's multi-cultural work force. Many foreign immigrants would start their South African experience by renting accommodation or business premises in Hillbrow, giving the area a cosmopolitan feeling with colourful restaurants, cafés and boutiques lining the sidewalks below the towering high-rise buildings. The Crest Hotel was a tall building and the 747 Bar was located on the top floor. The bar occupied the entire floor, offering spectacular views of Johannesburg's then bustling Central Business District. As I walked in I felt a lurch in my stomach. The place was heaving, packed with a lively crowd numbering many hundreds. On the stage, raised some five feet above the ground and bathed by the light from a swathe of multicoloured spotlights, a single musician was performing. The sound emanating from the stage, however, sounded nothing like the range of sounds commonly associated with a solo performer. This sounded like a full band with bass, drums and lots else in between. I was intrigued and manoeuvered myself into a better position to see how he was doing it.

The performer's name was Allan Gold. He was sitting centre stage on a bar stool, playing an Ovation guitar, the first acoustic guitar to offer a built-in electronic pickup system, which was plugged into a guitar amplifier and then fed into a huge PA system. At ground level in front of his left foot was a set of organ bass pedals, on which he was tapping out the bass line. With his right foot he operated a pedal that triggered a drum box, turning it on and off but also, when appropriate, triggering a drum fill. It was a Korg KR55 drum machine, the first time I had ever seen such a device. All of this was fed into the biggest sound system I had ever seen, much more powerful than the Shure Vocal Master that was the commonly used PA of that period. The result was that he really did sound like an entire band.

There, in the 747 Bar, I experienced another epiphany. This was the clue I had been looking for. I had not been sure about what to do when I left the army, how to pursue my musical ambitions and make a living at the same time, as the appeal of playing in bands was always tempered by the recurrent problems of working alongside other musicians who would almost inevitably introduce time-consuming complications or personal idiosyncrasies into any gig. Here was a skill I could acquire and direct to my own ends, offering complete musical autonomy. When the musician stopped for a break I went over and introduced myself, confirming that I would be prepared to stand in for him the following week. It was not until much later that I realised that Edith Goldstein, who had recruited me from inside the army base, was his mother.

In the interim, I worked hard at preparing an appropriate set of songs. Most of the band's repertoire went out of the window as songs that worked in the context of a band did not always lend themselves to solo arrangements. Much of the folksy repertoire I had developed was equally unsuitable, being too calm in attitude. Finger-picked guitar songs like the 'Streets of London' would surely get drowned out and lost in this setting. I needed to find three hours' worth of well-known, up-tempo tunes that would lift the mood of the drinkers. Standard songs that I knew would work well in this environment included Don MacLean's 'Bye Bye Miss American Pie', something of an anthem on the pub circuit at that time, 'Cocaine' by JJ Cale and 'Lying Eyes' by the Eagles.

My preparations for the big night were complicated by the fact that I had no drum machine of my own to rehearse with and so I used a metronome to identify tempos that worked for the various songs, writing them on the set list. I had never played bass pedals before and didn't have any to practise with, so I experimented with moving my foot as if I was playing a bass line. The demands on my coordination made it clear that putting all these elements together to sound like a fully functioning one man band was going to be anything but easy.

All too soon, Friday the 22nd November arrived. I drove to

Hillbrow early in the afternoon to check the sound and familiarise myself with the drum box and bass pedals. When I stepped out of the elevator on the top floor I felt an enormous rollercoaster of nervous energy start its journey through my solar plexus. At best I had about half an hour's worth of arranged material that could be considered suitable. Taking on the challenge had been an act of lunacy. I had no clue as to how the bass pedals would work, had never played with a drum box before and didn't even own an acoustic guitar, showing up instead with my Ibanez electric.

   I arrived at the venue in mid-afternoon to set up and familiarise myself with the equipment. What got me through the first stage of wanting to walk away there and then was the excitement at having the use of Allan's expensive sound equipment. I lost myself in playing about with the various bits, trying out different drum patterns and setting up a range of guitar sounds. I soon established that playing the bass pedals was not going to be an option as I would have to concentrate so hard on which note to stand on that I would lose track of the guitar arrangement, if not my entire life. I also found that playing along to a drum box was quite different from playing with a human drummer. Nevertheless, after an hour of rehearsal I at least had some control over the sound and had worked out a list for the first set that included all the songs I thought might stand half a chance of working. With two hours until starting time, I decided to go out for a light meal and return in time for kick off at 8.30pm.

   At 8.15, as I rode the elevator filled with exuberant revellers up to the top floor and stepped out into the jam-packed venue, I experienced a shock wave of gut wrenching terror. Almost a thousand people were milling around, drinks in hand, buzzing with excitement as they waited for the musician to take the stage. I was crazy to have agreed to what was now being revealed as a complete nightmare.

   The stool in the spotlight that beckoned me was about as tempting as an executioner's chair. There was just no way I could pull this off. I was mad to even think of taking the gig. In the blind panic of the moment, quite suddenly a flash of brilliance calmed my wildly raging mind. There was only one thing for it. I decided to call in a bomb scare. That way I might still be able to get paid without losing face. In my panicked state I actually got as far as asking a bar maid where the nearest pay phone was before my fortunes took another abrupt turn when I bumped into a group of friends who had arrived to support me. Boosted by their presence, I recovered a semblance of self-confidence and made my way to the stage.

Of all the gigs I had ever done this was the first time I had experienced real heart-racing, knee-shaking fear. It was, after all, a top dollar professional gig where a paying public numbering many hundreds was used to a high standard of musicianship and was drunk enough to make their disapproval known if I blew it.

The pay for one night was four times what army conscripts earned in a month and the reason for that was because it takes a considerable degree of specialised skill to entertain a room with around a thousand white South African drinkers on a Friday night. In the course of my experience in the three army bands I was usually the second singer and was able to sound convincing for a few songs a night but I was certainly not used to the vocal demands of singing at top volume at a high energy level for four hours while being at the same time the lead guitarist, rhythm guitarist, bass player, drummer and sound engineer. Remembering the old adage - start strong and finish strong and what goes in between doesn't really matter - I began with *All along the watchtower*, a popular favourite at the time and a song that was amongst the most plausible on my set list for the night. A group of my friends had filled a table quite close to the stage and as the song came to an end they burst into a round of raucous applause that started a chain reaction in the room. The terror that had accompanied me to the start of the song turned to exhilaration and the night passed in what seemed like the blink of an eye before I was announcing the final encore to a bar packed with drinkers all cheering, clapping along and shouting for more.

Starting with the terror beforehand I had never experienced as much of an adrenaline overload as I did that night. If that was solo performance, I was hooked. It was also the most money I had earned in my life.

As a result of that night, my destiny had undergone a shift. I had seen that with just a few components in the right order, a sound system, a set of bass pedals, a drum box, and a liberal measure of the single most important quality for anyone seeking to make a living as a performing musician, known in the trade as 'schmurgle', anything was possible. Although I didn't know it at the time, the schmurgle was the magic key that would enable a solo entertainer to put on a show that could match the interest factor of a band.

With previous experience in putting on a show and with the growing range of musical skills within my reach, I had a sight of how I might be able to make a living out of solo performance. I would be playing music without having to submit to the approval of or be affected by the moods and weaknesses of other musicians. I could see myself as a musician for hire with a one-man-show. But that would have to wait until I had finished my national service, or the other way around. Although the end of my two-year sentence was finally in sight, this was not the end of my legal obligation to the South African military. The demand for fighting men on the border required that all national servicemen would have to return for annual camps lasting 30 days a year for the next 10 years. I knew with all certainty that I would not be doing that. I would swim to America before that day arrived. This meant that I would have to find a way of becoming exempt from doing camps until such time as I could emigrate. Returning to full time studies provided the only reliable means for achieving this exemption and so I put my name down for three years of Computer Science, starting just three weeks after my uitklaar in January 1981. That would keep me out of army camps while I pursued the skill set to progress the musical ambitions which would in time enable me to emigrate.

When asked at that time: "What do you want to do when you leave the army," my standard answer was: "Leave South Africa."

The final flourish

The last day of my life in military uniform dawned on 18th December 1980. The clearing out process entailed driving to Pretoria to the Quartermaster's building where I had to return a box load of various military items and complete the paperwork for the uitklaar. I parked the green Peugeot on a side street and went into the building carrying a cardboard box filled with the items needing to be returned. As I walked down the corridor in the Quartermaster's section, a sergeant major coming from the opposite direction stopped me with a roaring bellow.

"Jou rooif! Waar's jou houding?"

He launched into me, yelling that my houding was not appropriate and that I had failed to strek him in recognition of his rank, all the while employing the traditional sergeant major's delivery which involved vitriol laden spittle spraying on my face.

"You're a disgrace. Look at your beret. It's like a fokken pancake. Your boots have not been boned. Your hair is too long. Your browns have not been ironed. You haven't even shaved. What the fuck is the matter with you? You're in the army now, ROOIF! You had better start waking up. What have you got to say for yourself?"

I was overwhelmed by the urge to burst into hysterical laughter at the scale of this no-contest. I wanted to say "You have no clue whatsoever" but I waited politely for a few seconds, staring straight into his rheumy eyes and then with a courteous smile intended to infuriate as much as confuse, I dismissed him with a loaded, wide-eyed stare before walking on towards the counter. I don't know what he did next as I didn't turn to look but I took tremendous reassurance from the fact that on my final day in the army a sergeant major had mistaken me for a new recruit.

Perhaps my walking away tactic succeeded as well as it did during my service period because in the SADF at that time there were many 'bos-befok', crazed troops coming back from the border in a psychotic state that made them capable of extreme and unpredictable violence. I suspect I had by then achieved some success in mustering the look of one such and this was why I managed to get away with much of the behaviour that would probably have given rise to a court martial for insubordination in any other army. On this occasion the sergeant major was so dumbfounded that he watched me walk away without saying another word, unprepared by any former experience to deal with silent eye-contact dismissal by someone he had mistaken for a potential victim.

  Soon my remaining few bits were packed in the Peugeot and I went in to say my final farewells at the unit. Uppermost in this memory was the genuine sadness I felt saying goodbye to George Hayden. I went into his office for the last time and told him that without his efforts, both in maintaining the high quality of the Entertainment Unit as well as in his personal interest in my circumstances, I might not have survived being called up. He wished me good luck in life and told me that I had a great future ahead as a musician, welcome words of encouragement that carried disproportionate weight at that time. It may have been a misty-eyed moment for him too though he must have seen many a troop come through his door with a grateful farewell speech. Gerald was nowhere to be seen as I made my round of handshake goodbyes with the rest of the unit. And then, focusing on breathing deeply, I drove out of the camp for the last time. The great moment had arrived and yet I felt strangely numb. As Voortrekkerhoogte shrank in the rear-view mirror and the certainty of the unknown lay stretched before me, an Afrikaans colloquialism from army culture came into my head.

  'Ek voel vere.' I feel feathers.

  I didn't realise then that there was more to come.

Lost and found

Returning to civilian life presented a new set of challenges. Although I was back in the same room in the same house in Bryanston as the one I had left two years previously, I found I was no longer similarly acquainted with the person returning. There were new colours on the canvas of my personality not of my choosing or of my understanding. As the days of my new post-army life rolled by, I became increasingly familiar with a number of uncomfortable truths about my outlook on life. Personality maladies that I was not properly equipped to deal with or even to reliably identify, would reveal themselves in unexpected ways, the most common of which were sleep related. I simply did not slow down enough to approach the appropriate weariness of pre-sleep. When I did eventually fall asleep the slightest noise would wake me and I would be unable to get back to sleep. Once asleep, I experienced unpleasant dreams, almost always revolving around a central plot wherein I would find myself in the custody of the Afrikaner authorities.

One of the dream themes involved members of the South African Police in sinister dark blue outfits handcuffing me and forcing me into a car whilst shouting in Afrikaans that I was now going to the border to fight properly. Another variation would involve being woken up in my bed by screaming policemen – also bellowing in Afrikaans – dragging me off into the steel caged rear compartment of a Land Rover for a bumpy journey to the notorious torture chambers deep in the soulless heart of darkness I imagined the inside of John Vorster Square to be. I had never been inside John Vorster Square but my experience of being locked inside a military police cell in the Kimberley guardroom had provided my subconscious with a thoroughly convincing insight into incarceration within harsh concrete and metal bars. I had driven past John Vorster Square and the image of that evil building, the spiritual heart of the Christian Afrikaner regime, formed another powerful building block in my subconscious. The images from the Detention Barracks, where I had visited Sean, would return and I would find myself inside the walls, chatting away with Sean as prison buddies sharing a Camel cigarette before a uniformed Afrikaner thug would once again drag me away for further torture. The blue overalls worn by the Jehovah's Witness prisoners in detention barracks made frequent appearances in many of those dreams, ghastly ghostly apparitions of stolen squandered youth.

Another dream would start in Kimberley, where I would be waiting in uniform in a line, smoking while Afrikaans officers drifted past shouting at me. I would eventually reach the boarding steps of a Hercules aircraft destined for Walvis Bay. Officers' faces, blended from aspects of Whiteley, the Kommandant and the odious Dr. Muller, would point quivering blood-stained fingers at me as they unleashed venomous accusations with assurances of impending malice. In all those dreams I was always the victim, never once able to defend myself or strike back. On many occasions I would wake up gasping in terror, coated in sweat with my heart hammering.

My outlook on humanity had shifted. I had seen how easily an innocent could be turned into a mindless killer on command and it had shaken my faith in the inherent goodness of man. Mostly, my first impressions of the people I was meeting at this time was of weak-willed victims who lacked a moral compass.

To compound this paranoia I was increasingly meeting and working with musicians and characters from Johannesburg's alternative culture, some of whom were black and some of whom were known agitators who may well have been on security police watch lists or among the informers with which South African society was saturated at that time. The possibility that I might be marked as a threat to the system became so real to me that something had to be done. I was becoming increasingly, unmanageably depressed as the lack of proper sleep, the endless battle with the fears arising from mistrust of the people around me and the growing anxiety at the hopelessness of existence, all of which conspired to leave me feeling constantly on edge. Gradually, I realised that in the absence of some firm and decisive remedial action I was in danger of losing my tenuous grasp on the one constant hope that sustained me and that had become at that time my single-minded focus in life, the hope I would find a way of escaping from the nightmare that life in South Africa had become for me.

Edith Goldstein, the agent I had met at Entertainments, had kept my phone number and shortly after my release from the army had called to enquire if I would like her to represent me. After a successful audition, Edith secured a three-month solo entertainer's contract for me at the Quirinale Hotel in Hillbrow where I would perform from Thursday through to Sunday from eight until midnight. The pay was good and the number of regular patrons who followed my performances soon began to build. One night, Mike, one of the friendly regulars who lived in Hillbrow and would come in for a drink almost every night, failed to show up. The following night he was absent again and I asked after his whereabouts, to be told that he had disappeared. Eventually my persistent enquiries revealed that he had been detained by security police under the notorious Internal Security Act. Mike, as it turned out, had an interest in trade unions. As the Security Act provided for 'detention without trial', Mike had not been charged, nor did he have any rights as a prisoner including the right to anyone knowing where he was. The security apparatus of the Christian Afrikaner regime had the legal power to detain anyone they suspected of being a threat to national security on the whim of individuals empowered as security police officers. No charges had to be brought for at least 60 days and even then the individual could be released then re-arrested as soon as they left the building to be detained for another 60 days, and so on. Within a few weeks of Mike's disappearance, I heard that he was dead. As I never saw him again, this was quite possibly true. Mike's disappearance in this disturbing way became a turning point for me. Something had to change. I could not continue to live in fear of being picked up at any moment and I could not pretend this iniquitous behaviour was not a part and parcel of the society in which I lived. My mistrust of the people I came into contact with was becoming an all-pervading limitation to the pretence of a normal social life. Even musical fans at my gigs would be looked at on a scale of probability that they might be security police informers gathering information on me.

My army experience had left me with a powerful disregard

for the intelligence of the uniformed Afrikaner. 'Afrikaner Police Intelligence' was to my mind an oxymoron. Rightly or otherwise I felt a battle of wits favoured me strongly and this was my starting point in addressing the fear that oppressed me constantly. I set about formulating a two-part battle plan. The first strategy involved secrecy and misinformation designed to minimise the chances of being exposed as a subversive. I began by avoiding any loose talk especially to strangers whilst feeding as much misinformation on my intentions as possible. The second involved preparing as deadly a defence as possible, which I began to develop by establishing a safe perimeter around myself which I would protect by force if necessary and which excluded all but invited guests. I needed to establish the means by which to defend myself in the event that I was approached by sinister elements, which in my mind would most likely be plain-clothed members of the security police alerted to my dissident thinking by a traitor among my acquaintances. One of the conversations I had around this time in the Quirinale Hotel, which was something of a meeting place for foreign visitors seeking work in the mercenary soldiering business, was with an English former SAS soldier then resident in South Africa and employed by the army. He provided me with a wise and memorable piece of advice:

"If they arrest you under Internal Security, they can hold you without charge and do whatever they like because you are outside of the legal system. You have more chance of falling out of the eleventh floor of John Vorster Square than being heard in a courtroom by a Judge. So, you're better off shooting a few first. That way they have to charge you with manslaughter at the very least and that means they have to keep you alive to get you to court."

This insight reverberated on many levels and provided a concrete absolute which was both within my means and which would enable me to draw a line under the constant weight of powerlessness that was dragging me ever further downwards. The first thing I did was apply for a firearm licence. Inside the safe at my mother's

Bryanston home was my father's World War Two officer's handgun, a 1917 Browning 9mm pistol, a beautiful weapon by the standards by which these things are measured, that was as much a work of art as a gun. The Browning was of petite and compact design, conceived primarily for ease of carriage. It was not a high calibre stopping machine like, say, the Colt 45 or a Magnum 357, but was more an instrument of finesse designed for close range protection. It was ideal for my purposes.

In a short space of time, the licence was issued and I was legally entitled to buy ammunition. As an indication of my intent, my first purchase was for 1,000 rounds. "Are you going to start a war?" asked the jovial salesman as he handed over the small but weighty box.

By this time, with the increased income available to me from the residential gig, I had moved out of my mother's Bryanston home and into a rented farmhouse in Chartwell which I shared with a musician friend, Jose Fernandes. The farm, some 20 minutes drive out of the northern suburbs, backing onto a Lion Park, had 500-acre grounds providing an anonymous secure location far from prying eyes as well as a large sand wall that would serve as a private shooting range. And so, on this patch of sandy ground in the grounds of the Chartwell farmhouse, my handgun training commenced.

Armed with the 9mm Browning with six rounds in the magazine and a further two loaded magazines in readiness, I propped up a beer can in front of the sand wall and stepped back 10 metres. Aiming directly at the centre of the can I squinted through the sighting on the barrel, holding the weapon just as I'd seen shooters in movies do. I fired. The can did not budge. I aimed with more determination and fired again. The same thing happened. I couldn't even see where the bullets were going. It was immediately apparent that my plan to shoot a few policemen before they arrested me was in need of considerable skill enhancement. Over the next few months, I fired many thousands of rounds. Starting from two metres behind the tin can and working backwards I shot almost every day, often hundreds of rounds in a day, buying ammunition in boxes containing a thousand rounds at a time which on occasions would be spent within a week.

After a few months, the signs of progress began to emerge. I established that there was a feel to sighting a target and once I could see where the bullet would hit before I pulled the trigger, I started to experience to joys of increasing accuracy. From five metres away I could hit the can six times in a row and then from ten metres. Eventually my relationship with the gun become so secure I could confidently expect to hit anything the size of a beer can from 15 metres six times in swift succession. At my best, I could fire six shots into a can that was still moving from the previous strike from a distance of five metres. The Browning accompanied me at all times, even at night it when it went under my pillow. By this time I slept so lightly that even a creaking door would wake me. My plan was that if the police came to arrest me, and I knew that this would usually take place at around three in the morning when the science of these matters determines that one's resistance is at its lowest, I would be prepared to shoot the first six officers right between the eyes. I would joke with friends that, "If they come, they better send seven officers, because I have a six round mag and I'm good for six head shots. The soft tissue between the eyes - that's the target point. The 9mm doesn't provide an especially powerful impact so a shot to the skull won't necessary penetrate, especially if it's a thick skulled Dutchman, so the kill shot has to find the gap right between the eyes where the shell goes straight through the soft tissue for a little brain splat."

I was likely to trot out some variant on the 'soft tissue between the eyes' phrase if I was talking to a stranger who I imagined might in some way be untrustworthy. If this information was somehow fed back to those considering a visit, I reasoned, it might make them less inclined to show up at three in the morning.

Some nights I would fall asleep visualising the scenario of a 3am raid, which involved snap shots and intuitive aim and curiously, with this image in mind, my sleep pattern improved, the fear of attack being allayed by my controlling interest in the remedying alternative. My paranoid delusion was starting to yield dividends as a coping mechanism.

Not long after the move to Chartwell, I moved the two German Shepherd dogs, Apollo and Cindy from my mother's house to roam the perimeter and provide early warning of any intruders. Apollo was a fully attack-trained young male who would have charged at a galloping rhino if I had given him the order. The dogs would provide an early warning in the event of an unwelcome visit. When I went to gigs, the Browning was located in my jeans, held in place by my belt. I first bought an under-shoulder holster but soon discarded it as the compact size of the 9mm meant it was much more convenient to slot it into my jeans when I got dressed each morning. Carrying the gun with me wherever I went soon became second nature. I never considered that my behaviour was extreme or even unusual. Showing up at lectures with a 9mm in my trousers didn't even warrant a thought. Similarly, I saw no irony in being on stage singing a tender love song to a crowd of happy music lovers who were unaware that I had a loaded 9mm behind my belt. Gene Simmons sang with a sock down his trousers. I sang with a 9mm down mine for very different reasons.

Many of the people I knew carried guns, although not all of them took an attack trained German Shepherd in the passenger seat of their car when going out for groceries. Apollo loved going in the car, insisting I open the window so he could enjoy the scenery with his head sticking out of the window. Fifty kilometres-an-hour was the speed at which wind resistance buffeting made him return his head back into the car. Often I would keep my speed down to 40 so he could continue enjoying the outside view.

Strangely, once I had established the presence of a loaded gun within my lifestyle, many of the pressures that gave rise to its need were lifted. In that sense it was a balancing remedy to the events surrounding me. Instead of going to sleep in fear at what might happen next, I could go to sleep knowing that I was in a position to react should something happen. This was a liberating power and carried with it an educational benefit: I had learned the first rule in a gun-carrying lifestyle, which is never to take out your gun unless you are going to use it. This lesson translated well as a metaphor for future behaviour and I would never make a threat without the intention of carrying it through. As fortune would have it, I never had the occasion to draw the gun and perhaps this failure of any threat to materialise was because I had the gun there to draw.

During the three years of study that started within weeks of my leaving the army, I worked almost continuously as a musician, sometimes doing 10 gigs a week whilst maintaining a pass grade as a full time student. Admittedly, my attendance at lectures was extremely poor, declining as I became busier with musical work. In 1982, during my second year, I held down two resident gigs. Six nights of the week, from Monday until Saturday I did the cocktail session at the Sunnyside park hotel from five until eight, which entailed performing three 45-minute sets to a crowd that often numbered over a thousand. Then, from Thursday through Sunday, I performed from nine until one in the morning at the New York Strip Grill House in Braamfontein. Whilst a full time student, I was performing ten gigs a week totalling around seven hours a day as well as loading and setting up equipment in two separate venues as well as being the solo road crew and sound engineer. The intensity of my work effort related directly to my intention to leave. The harder I worked, the more likely I would be able to go when my studies ended. I turned down no work, even when I was so tired I needed a 10-minute cat-nap during my 15-minute break in sets just to keep going. On many occasions, I acknowledged that the army lesson of Vasbyt had served me well. I am not sure I would have mustered that dogged, unbreakable determination to see things past the pain barrier without the army experience. I can think of no comparable life experience that would provide the lesson of Vasbyt.

    Three years passed in what memory now serves as a rapid blur. Then, with the date of my final exam in place and with enough money saved up to enable a basic start abroad, on the day after my final exam I booked a flight to London despite the fact that I had no more than the address of a vague acquaintance to aim for and no contacts at all to guide my prospects.

I had, by this time, adopted a degree of sanguine detachment regarding events in my life which felt a bit like holding my breath. I held my personal ambitions largely in abeyance until such time as I might find myself in a free society where I would not be subject to the kind of malevolent attentions prevalent in South Africa.

I came across a Taoist parable during this period that I would recite to all and sundry and which served my patience well during the wait to graduate and leave. It is the story of the Farmer and the Horse:

'This farmer had only one horse, and one day the horse ran away. The neighbours came to console him over his terrible loss.

The farmer said, "What makes you think it is so terrible?"

A month later, the horse came home, bringing with her two beautiful wild horses. The neighbours became excited at the farmer's good fortune. Such lovely strong horses!

The farmer said, "What makes you think this is good fortune?"

The farmer's son was thrown from one of the wild horses and broke his leg. All the neighbours were very distressed. Such bad luck!

The farmer said, "What makes you think it is bad?"

A war came, and every able-bodied man was conscripted and sent into battle. Only the farmer's son, because he had a broken leg, remained. The neighbours congratulated the farmer.

"What makes you think this is good?" said the farmer.'

The one up side I found in my experience came with the understanding that bad experience is a far more efficient teacher than good.

On the eve of my departure, I said very few goodbyes. South Africa for me was stained beyond redemption by events leading up to that point. In the light of my virulent overview of their homeland and my tendency to hold everyone who didn't protest the iniquitous system as complicit in its existence, there seemed little point in saying goodbye to those who would be content to stay behind. The Browning was returned to the safe at my mother's house and I sold the green Peugeot for 50 Rand to her gardener, who even in those days was still known as 'the garden boy'. I had offered it to him for nothing but he insisted on paying me. In my argument with him over not wishing to accept the money he indicated his strong desire that I should take it because I would need money to get overseas, a moving gesture of support.

   Almost exactly five years to the day after my life had been hijacked by P.W. Botha and his gang of delusional thieves, on a cold grey December morning I landed at Heathrow, with a Greek passport and £1,500 - the maximum cash allowance by South Africa's emigration-deterring foreign exchange regulations - and the burning, lasting ambition never to return.

Notes:

Note 1. Eugène Marais

The costly obstinacy of the Afrikaner is typified by the story of Eugène Marais (1871-1936). Marais was a lawyer, a naturalist and a gifted writer who, had he not suffered from the dishonesty of the Belgian plagiarist Maurice Maeterlinck as well as from his own tribalistic arrogance, would probably have been recognised as one of the great thinkers of his time.

While a law student in London, Marais was interned as a hostile alien when the Boer War started. This experience, combined with his outrage at the treatment of the Afrikaans prisoners of war by the British, embittered Marais to the point where he refused ever to speak English again. He returned to South Africa on his release and spent two years studying the habits of a tribe of baboons, living in close proximity to them as he observed their behavioural patterns. He started by sleeping a safe distance from the tribe, before very slowly, over a period of six months working his way closer to them until he was able to work himself into their midst without causing alarm. In the process, he developed a rapport with baboons that could be compared with the remarkable work of the late Dianne Fossey and her extraordinary relationship with Central African primates. At the time when the writings of Charles Darwin were making an impact, though Marais worked in isolation and obscurity, his studies provided an insightful, impeccably researched corollary to the theory of evolution.

One of the conclusions Marais reached was that baboons are able to connect cause and effect and that they not only have a logically constructed social order but they are also able to determine their own individual behaviour. Marais' view of evolution differed from Darwin's in a significant area; whereas Darwin viewed evolution as a matter of the survival of the fittest, Marais held that it represented the line of least resistance. In a Bible-dominated creationist state such as South Africa was at the time, Eugène Marais' stance, like that of Charles Darwin, was dangerously revolutionary.

Marais' work on baboons was never completed but his fascinating work on termites, 'Die Seel van die Mier' ('The Soul of the White Ant') in which his studies of termites led him to the conclusion that the colony should be considered as a single organism, was undoubtedly a masterwork years ahead of its time and was published in an Afrikaans journal where it was spotted by the predatory and amoral Maurice Maeterlinck. Being Belgian and thus Flemish- speaking, Maeterlinck had no difficulty in translating Marais' work into English from the original Afrikaans and, knowing that Marais would never allow his work to be translated into the English language and confident that Marais would never sue him in an English court, published it under his own name. Maeterlinck shamelessly intercepted the kudos due to Eugène Marais and when he was awarded the Nobel Prize he accepted it without acknowledging the source of his plagiarism.

Marais was addicted to morphine for most of his adult life having developed a taste for opiates as a young man and his addiction was to affect the course of his life until in 1936. Whilst attempting to break the cycle of his decades-long addiction, Marais succumbed to depression, insomnia and bleak despair at having been robbed of his rightful intellectual status. Unable to cope, he visited a neighbour from whom he surreptitiously borrowed a shotgun with which he fired one round into his chest before placing the barrel's end in his mouth for the second shot. He was 65. Marais' undoubted brilliance had been undermined not only by his drug addiction but also by his prejudice against the English language.

Note 2. Steve Biko
Stephen Bantu Biko was born in King William's Town, in the Cape Province of South Africa in 1946. After being expelled from his first school, Lovedale, in the Eastern Cape for 'anti establishment behaviour' he was transferred to a Roman Catholic boarding school in Natal where he finished his schooling. From there, he enrolled as a student at the University of Natal Medical School.

Biko began visiting black campuses around the country where he propounded the emergent Black Consciousness philosophy. During 1968, he founded the South African Students' Organisation (SASO) and was elected its first president a year later. At the end of his third year at university, he was expelled as a result of his political activities.

In 1973, under constant surveillance and harassment from the security police, a banning order was imposed on Biko restricting him to his hometown. In the same year, he was instrumental in forming the Black Peoples' Convention (BPC), as an umbrella political movement for groups sharing the ideals of the Black Consciousness movement.

During the disturbances following the Soweto riots of June 1976,

Soweto leaders demanded that the government negotiate the country's future with three black leaders, namely the leader of the African National Congress, Nelson Mandela, the leader of the Pan Africanist Congress, Robert Sobukwe, and Steve Biko.

Biko was first charged with breaking his banning order in 1974. In August 1976, a time of nation wide mass demonstrations following the Soweto massacres, Biko was arrested together with a reporter from the East London Daily Dispatch and held in solitary confinement for 101 days. The terms of his banning order prevented any statement by him or any account of his detention from being published. After being released in March 1977, he was again arrested but was later released but in July 1977 he was re-arrested and charged before being released on bail.

On 18th August, 1977, Biko was arrested at a police roadblock under the Terrorism Act (No 83 of 1967) and interrogated by officers of the Port Elizabeth security police including one Major Harold Snyman, later denied amnesty by the Truth and Reconciliation Commission for non-disclosure before evading incarceration by dying of lung cancer in 1997. Biko's other interrogator and the man widely regarded as his killer was Gideon 'Notorious' Nieuwoudt, later accused of causing the deaths of three other black activists, referred to as the "Pebco Three", in 1985.

Section 6 of the Terrorism Act allowed anyone suspected of anything that might 'endanger the maintenance of law and order', to be detained without trial for an indefinite period on the sole authority of any senior police officer. Since there was no requirement to release information on prisoners being held, people subject to the Act tended to disappear. It is estimated that at least 80 people died while being detained under the Terrorism Act.

The interrogation of Steve Biko, which took place in the Police Room 619 and lasted 22 hours, included the torture and beatings leading to the head injuries which rendered him comatose. While in police custody he was also chained to a window grille for an entire day.

On 11th September 1977, Steve Biko, naked, restrained in manacles and virtually unconscious from the prolonged torture and beatings he had received at the hands of Snyman and Nieuwoudt, was loaded into the back of a Land Rover and began the 1,191 kilometre journey to Pretoria. Although he survived the arduous journey in the steel cage of the Land Rover's rear compartment in the stifling summer heat, Biko died shortly after arrival at the Pretoria prison on 12th September, 1977.

Denying any wrongdoing, the police claimed Biko's death was the result of 'an extended hunger strike' despite an autopsy which revealed that after suffering multiple bruises and abrasions he succumbed to a brain haemorrhage caused by massive head injuries.

Steve Biko was 30 years old when he died and was survived by his wife and two children. His funeral, conducted by the Right Reverend Desmond Tutu, was attended by more than 15,000 mourners. Though thousands more South Africans were prevented from attending by the apartheid government's security forces, 12 Western countries sent representatives to the service.

The truth behind the circumstances of Steve Biko's death was exposed by newspaper editor Donald Woods and journalist Helen Zille, later a political leader in the Western Cape. The following year, on 2nd February 1978, the Attorney General of the Eastern Cape stated that he would not prosecute any of the police officers involved in the arrest and detention of Biko.

On hearing of Biko's death, the Minister of Justice and Police, Jimmy Kruger, infamously remarked: "It leaves me cold".

Note 3. The laws that made South Africa the pariah of the world.
The principal "apartheid laws" all enforced by draconian means and lengthy jail terms, were:
  * **Amendment to The Prohibition of Mixed Marriages Act (1949)**
  * **Amendment to The Immorality Act (1950)**
    This law made it a criminal offence for a white person to have any sexual relations with a person of a different race.
  * **The Population Registration Act (1950)**
    This law required all citizens to be registered as black, white or coloured.
  * **The Suppression of Communism Act (1950)**
    This law banned the South African Communist Party as well as any other party the government chose to label as 'communist'. It allowed the government to ban any 'communist' simply by naming them as such. It made membership of the SACP punishable by up to 10 years' imprisonment. The South African minister of justice, R.F. Swart, drafted the law.
  * **The Group Areas Act (27 April 1950)**
    This law partitioned the country into different areas, with different

areas being allocated to different racial groups. This law represented the very heart of apartheid because it was the basis upon which political and social separation was to be constructed.

* **Bantu Authorities Act (1951)**
  This law created separate pseudo-government structures for black people.
* **Prevention of Illegal Squatting Act (1951)**
  This law allowed the government to demolish black shackland slums. This is how it became legal to transform Sophiatown into 'Triomf', so named as it was seen as a triumph for apartheid.
* **Native Building Workers Act and Native Services Levy (1951)**
  This law forced white employers to pay for the construction of proper housing for black workers recognised as legal residents in 'white' cities.
* **The Reservation of Separate Amenities Act (1953)**
  This law prohibited people of different races from using the same public amenities, such as drinking fountains, restrooms, park benches and so on.
* **The Bantu Education Act (1953)**
  This law brought all black schooling under government control, effectively ending mission-run schools.
* **Bantu Urban Areas Act (1954)**
  This law curtailed black migration to the cities.
* **The Mines and Work Act (1956)**
  This law formalised racial discrimination in employment.
* **The Promotion of Black Self-Government Act (1958)**
  This law set up separate territorial governments in the 'homelands', designated lands for black people where they were allowed to vote under the claim that these homelands or 'bantustans' would eventually become independent of South Africa. In practice, the South African government exercised a strong influence over these separate states even after some of them such as Bophutatswana became 'independent'.
* **Bantu Investment Corporation Act (1959)**
  This law set up a mechanism to transfer capital to the homelands in order to create jobs there.
* **The Extension of University Education Act (1959)**
  This law created separate universities for Blacks, Coloureds and Indians.

* **Physical Planning and Utilization of Resources Act (1967)**
  This law allowed the government to stop industrial development in 'white' cities and redirect such development to homeland border areas. The aim was to speed up the relocation of blacks to the homelands by relocating jobs to homeland areas.
* **Black Homeland Citizenship Act (1970)**
  This law changed the status of the inhabitants of the 'homelands' so that they were no longer citizens of South Africa. The aim was to ensure whites became the demographic majority within South Africa.
* **The Afrikaans Medium Decree (1974)**
  This law required the use of Afrikaans and English on a 50-50 basis in high schools outside the homelands.
* **General Law Amendment Act No 39 of 1961**
  Provided for twelve-day detention. existing Acts that were amended included:
  The Arms and Ammunition Act 28 of 1937 regarding the issuing and cancellation of firearm licences:
  The 1955 Criminal Procedure Act regarding powers of the Attorney-General to prohibit release on bail or otherwise.
  The 1956 Riotous Assemblies Act. Commenced: 19 May 1961. Sections 6 and 7 repealed by the Internal Security Act No 74 of 1982.
* **Indemnity Act No 61 of 1961**
  With retrospective effect from 21st March 1960, this Act indemnified the government, its officers and all other persons acting under their authority in respect of acts done, orders given or information provided in good faith for the prevention or suppression of internal disorder, the maintenance or restoration of good order, public safety or essential services, or the preservation of life or property in any part of the Republic. Commenced: 5th July 1961.
* **Terrorism Act No 83 of 1962**
  According to Horrell (1978: 473), this Act signalled the beginning of the struggle against 'Red arms' as opposed to purely 'Red ideology'. It authorised indefinite detention without trial on the authority of a policeman of or above the rank of lieutenant colonel. The definition of terrorism was very broad and included most criminal acts. No time limit was specified for detention; it could be continued until detainees had satisfactorily replied to all questions or no useful purpose would be served by continued detention. Fortnightly visits by magistrates

were provided for, 'if circumstances permit'. No other visitors were permitted. The Act was operative retrospectively to 27th June 1962 and also applied to South West Africa retrospectively.

The Terrorism Act differed from the 90-day and 180-day detention laws in that the public was not entitled to information relating to the identity and number of people detained under the Terrorism Act

All sections except section 7 were repealed by section 33 of the Internal Security and the Intimidation Amendment Act 138 of 1991.

* **General Law Amendment Act No 37 of 1963**

Section 17, the 90-day detention law, authorised any commissioned officer to detain - without a warrant - any person suspected of a political crime and to hold them for 90 days without access to a lawyer (Horrell 1978: 469). In practice, people were often released after 90 days only to be re-detained on the same day for a further 90-day period.

The Act also allowed for further declaration of unlawful organisations. The State President could declare any organisation or group of persons which had come into existence since 7th April 1960 to be unlawful. This enabled the government to extend to Umkhonto we Sizwe and Poqo the restrictions already in force on the ANC and the PAC

Commenced: 2 May 1963, except ss 3, 9 & 14, which came into effect at different times. Sections 3-7 and 14-17 were repealed by the Internal Security Act No 74 of 1982.

* **General Law Amendment Act No 37 of 1963 (commenced 2nd May)**

This allowed a police officer to detain without warrant a person suspected of a politically motivated crime, to be held for 90 days without access to a lawyer. When used in practice, suspects were re-detained for another 90 day period immediately after release. This Act also introduced the Sobukwe clause which allowed people already convicted of political offences to be further detained (initially for 12 months). The Sobukwe Clause was so named because it was used to keep PAC leader Robert Mangaliso Sobukwe (who was originally arrested in 1960 and sentenced to three years) on Robben Island for an additional six years.

This act was amended by the General Law Amendment Act No 80 of 1964 which allowed the Minister of Justice to extend the Sobukwe Clause as desired.

Note 4. The Universal Soldier Reproduced with grateful thanks to Buffy Sainte-Marie.
Words and music by Buffy Sainte-Marie.

He's five foot-two and he's six feet-four,
He fights with missiles and with spears.
He's all of thirty-one and he's only seventeen,
Been a soldier for a thousand years.
He's a Catholic, a Hindu, an Atheist, a Jain,
A Buddhist and a Baptist and a Jew.
And he knows he shouldn't kill,
And he knows he always will,
Kill you for me my friend and me for you.
And he's fighting for Canada,
He's fighting for France,
He's fighting for the USA,
And he's fighting for the Russians,
And he's fighting for Japan,
And he thinks we'll put an end to war this way.
And he's fighting for Democracy,
He's fighting for the Reds,
He says it's for the peace of all.
He's the one who must decide,
Who's to live and who's to die,
And he never sees the writing on the wall.
But without him, how would Hitler have condemned him at Dachau?
Without him Caesar would have stood alone.
He's the one who gives his body as a weapon of the war
And without him all this killing can't go on.
He's the Universal Soldier and he really is to blame,
His orders come from far away no more.
They come from here and there and you and me,
And brothers can't you see?
This is not the way we put an end to war.

Note 5. The two Anglo-Boer Wars.

The first Boer War started in 1880 when Benjamin Disraeli, the British Prime Minister annexed the Transvaal and the Orange Free State, known since 1877 by their inhabitants as the South African Boer Republic. The Boers had already trekked their way northward from the Cape and Natal in their dislike of British domination, an arduous journey in ox wagons across plains and mountains in the course of which they fought several bloody conflicts with hostile black tribes.

Having fought and suffered to establish what they perceived as their God-given homeland, the Boers were not happy at the prospect of it falling under the rule of the Queen of England. Paul Kruger, President of the Transvaal, stood firm against the imposition of English law and secured a limited degree of self-government for his people. Provoked beyond recall by what they considered arrogant British colonial aggression, the Boers revolted in 1880 and began to attack British garrisons, starting a campaign that was to change the face of armed resistance to a greater and more established power.

The Boers had no standing army but instead they formulated a kommando system under which the men were organised into mounted militias. Boer recruitment instructions required burghers to bring their own rifles, ammunition, horses, saddles and bridles to their mustering point as well as enough food for eight days. Without a formal military uniform they dressed in the colours of the land, mostly khaki. Travelling light and striking their targets at speed, they made the maximum use of the element of surprise.

Despite the recent inglorious massacre of the Light Brigade during the Crimean War, the British army responded using their traditional, unrevised tactics which were to prove both outmoded and extremely costly. The uniform tunics traditionally worn by some British regiments were bright scarlet and provided a perfect target against the muted colours of the African landscape. The Boers were renowned for and took pride in their marksmanship and with their well maintained Mauser rifles, acquired by President Kruger from his German allies, found the bright red targets presented by British soldiers difficult to miss even from a distance, enabling a spectacularly successful new military policy of 'aim at the bright red slow moving target, shoot, reload and repeat until there are none left'.

The British military leadership, headed by the arrogant intractable and, as many thought, moronic Lord Kitchener, seemed to have no idea as to how to contend with this modus operandi. The use of military intelligence by the British was inadequate and their response to the Boer raids was compromised by a dire lack of planning and co-ordination. British soldiers, many of whom were volunteers, found themselves armed with standard issue single shot Martini Henry breech loading rifles. They were ordered to keep in tight formation and to show discipline at all times whilst, concealed invisibly in distant cover, Boer marksmen were able to pick them off virtually at will.

After a series of humiliating defeats at the hands of the Boers, the turning point for the British army was the Battle of Majuba Hill on 27th February 1881 when British troops under General Sir George Colley were forced to defend their position atop Majuba Hill while Boer fighters stormed them from below. Boer marksmen targeted the British lookouts and signallers with great success, ensuring that the commander on the hilltop had no intelligence to guide his reaction to the Boer onslaught. In the ensuing battle, one Boer fighter was killed and 405 British soldiers were vanquished. The commander of the British regiment was killed and 180 British soldiers were taken prisoner. A rag-tag, amateur army composed mostly of farmers and lay preachers using their own weapons and riding their own horses had defeated a regiment of one of the world's most powerful armies. To the astonishment of his killers, the corpse of Major General Colley was seen to have been wearing tennis shoes.

The British military command went back to the drawing board. Utilising one of the many lessons learned from their enemy, new uniforms were issued this time made from khaki drill, and along with new weaponry – and more importantly, new thinking - preparations for the avenging of British honour began in earnest.

With the discovery of gold and diamonds in the Boer Republic in 1884, the British including Cecil Rhodes and his cabal had sought to control the huge mineral wealth seen by the Boers as being rightfully theirs. As if revenge for their ultimate defeat and humiliation during the war was not a sufficient incentive, expropriation of the Boer's wealth certainly was. The British began to muster the largest army the world had yet seen and the Boers could read the writing on the wall. Faced with the inevitability of British subjugation the Boers decided to strike first and launched what would become known as the second Anglo-Boer War.

In October 1899, the Boers, with a population numbering less than 100,000, again attacked the British, whose army would employ 448,435 officers and men in the conflict. British forces at Ladysmith, Mafeking and Kimberley were surrounded and besieged. The General Frederick S. Roberts was given command of the British forces and organised counter-attacks to relieve the towns under siege. As Boer resources dwindled, the British with the huge resources of Empire to call on, were able to keep steady supplies coming in.

Despite this, the guerrilla tactics invented and honed by the Boers continued to frustrate the British. Boer kommandos moving swiftly on horseback would strike unexpectedly with their customary speed before withdrawing as suddenly as they had appeared, evading capture by living in the wild. So successful was this technique that for a time the British objective of the total elimination of the Boers seemed unattainable until the British army, by then under the joint command of Kitchener, Milner and Roberts, contrived a two pronged tactic that was to turn the tide of the conflict.

The kommandos had been supplied with food and with horses from Boer farms which in the absence of the men were kept operational and productive by their wives and children. Those farms were ordered to be razed to the ground, all livestock and poultry slaughtered and the means of re-supplying the Boer fighters thus terminated. Kitchener's plan was to flush out the guerrillas in a series of systematic drives organised like sporting shoots with their success defined in a weekly 'bag' of killed, captured and wounded, and to sweep the country bare of everything that could give sustenance to the guerrillas including their women and children. It was the heartless clearance and the ignominious liquidation of civilians - in effect the uprooting of a small nation - that would come to dominate the final phase of the war.

Faced with the problem of what to do with the now homeless women and children, the notorious solution was to arrange the first military use of two words that have subsequently taken on an even more sinister meaning.

The British administration built the first concentration camps during the Boer War. Although their purpose was not primarily to exterminate the inmates, cold winter nights, inadequate diet and poor sanitary management conspired to produce a horrendous death toll; around 27,000 women and children died, of whom some 22,000 were below the age of 16 years. The people who died represented around 25 per cent of the total Boer population. In an attempt to force the men to surrender, the wives and children of Boers known to still be fighting were given reduced rations, which in many cases led to their dying of starvation.

As a footnote to the tragedy of the British concentration camps, countless thousands of black South Africans, treated even worse than the Boer prisoners and regarded by the British too insignificant to warrant their numbers being recorded, also perished in the camps. Estimates as to this death count range from 14,000 to the admittedly unlikely figure of over half a million.

The scorched earth policy and the setting up of concentration camps ultimately prevailed. The Boers surrendered and Britain claimed victory. Rudyard Kipling wrote that the Boer War had taught the British 'no end of a lesson', adding perceptively and ironically that it had done them 'no end of good'.

It is estimated that 22,829 British troops were wounded in the course of the two Anglo-Boer wars and that another 20,000 lie buried in South Africa, the majority of their deaths having been caused by disease. Estimates on Boer losses in the fighting range from 3,000 to 6,000.

The British ethnic prejudice was not limited exclusively to the Afrikaners. When Field Marshal Roberts took Johannesburg on 31st May 1900, he had already prepared for immediate action to rid the town of 'Jews and other riff-raff'. On orders issued by Roberts within hours of seizing control of Johannesburg, some 300 Mediterraneans and Central Europeans were summarily arrested and deported. Two days after the town was taken, the British administration gazetted an order re-imposing the Pass Laws of the ZAR, the Afrikaner government led by Paul Kruger, to control black inhabitants and effectively outlaw the presence of any unemployed or self-employed black man. This proto-racist legislation secured the workforce needed by the army and the mines and within a few years the gold mines of the Transvaal were on the way to becoming the world's richest, providing for the spectacular growth of the South African economy. The economic success of the mines relied entirely on the exploitation of virtually unpaid workers that was undistinguishable from slave labour. In their pursuit of mineral wealth, both the Boers and the British were guilty of shameful abuse of the black population.

Note 6. Emily Hobhouse

One story that shines as a metaphor for this dark chapter in South Africa's relationship with Britain was that of Emily Hobhouse and a young girl named Lizzie van Zijl.

Emily was born and raised in Cornwall. Educated at home, she remained caring for her bereaved father until the age of 35 by which time her political interests had gravitated towards women's rights. As a Liberal she was opposed to the Boer War and once she became aware of the suffering of the Boer women in British concentration camps, Emily travelled to South Africa at the age of 39, driven by the need to address this injustice.

In October 1900, Emily founded the Relief Fund for South African Women and Children, an organisation set up 'to feed, clothe, harbour and save women and children - Boer, English and other - who were left destitute and ragged as a result of the destruction of property, the eviction of families or other incidents resulting from the military operations'. Very few people were willing to contribute to this fund.

Emily visited the British concentration camps and was horrified by what she saw, attempting to highlight the plight of the victims to her fellow citizens. In South Africa she directed the attention of the authorities to the inadequate sanitary accommodation and inadequate rations but was dismissed without consideration. Outraged, Emily returned to England determined to persuade government to bring an end to the British army's scorched earth and concentration camp policies. The Minister of War was unwilling to take any action and when the issue was raised in the House of Commons, few members showed any sympathy for the plight of the Boers. Emily later wrote:

'The picture of apathy and impatience displayed here, which refused to lend an ear to undeserved misery, contrasted sadly with the scenes of misery in South Africa, still fresh in my mind. No barbarity in South Africa was as severe as the bleak cruelty of an apathetic parliament.'

It was Emily Hobhouse who made famous the story of young Lizzie van Zyl, who died in the Bloemfontein concentration camp. Pictures of this child's pitifully thin body were circulated to highlight the inhumane conditions in the camps.

'She was a frail, weak little child in desperate need of good care. Yet, because her mother was one of the 'undesirables' due to the fact that her father neither surrendered nor betrayed his people, Lizzie was placed on *the lowest rations and so perished with hunger that, after a month in the camp, she was transferred to the new small hospital. Here she was treated harshly. The English disposed doctor and his nurses did not understand her language and, as she could not speak English, labelled her an idiot although she was mentally fit and normal. She died soon after.'*

In 1921, having spent most of her life campaigning unrewarded for victims of war and now in her 60s, in recognition of the work she had done on their behalf during the Boer War the people of South Africa raised and sent Emily £2,300, the price of a cottage on the Cornwall coast for her retirement years. Referring to this gift she wrote:

'I find it impossible to give expression to the feelings that overpowered me when I heard of the surprise you had prepared for me. My first impulse was not to accept any gift, or otherwise to devote it to some or other public end. But after having read and reread your letter, I have decided to accept your gift in the same simple and loving spirit in which it was sent to me.'

Note 7. The Border War

In 1979, when I was conscripted into the SADF the Border War was at its height. Fighting began in 1966 continuing until 1983, a war lasting 23 years that would become the world's most significant conflict of the age whose legacy would affect South Africa's political landscape for generations to come. Billions of dollars were spent prosecuting this war, on one side by the Russian-backed Cubans who were supporting groups opposed to the South African government, most notably the ANC and SWAPO. On the other side, the South African government, in pursuit of white Christian-Afrikaner led dominance, squandered the mineral wealth that during that period had made the South African economy one of the world's strongest.

The theatre of operations for the Border War straddled Northern Namibia (formerly South West Africa) and Southern Angola, the so-called 'Operational Area' or 'Border'. By keeping the conflict out of sight of the populace in a way that would not have been possible had the war encroached onto South African sovereign territory, the Government was able to maintain an illusionary status quo where life went on as normal with very little reference given to military operations in South West Africa. Even by the late 1970s, visitors to South Africa were unlikely to realise that the country was at war. Considering the scale of the Border War in terms of its duration, the casualty rate and the overall economic cost, it remains amazing to me that so little is known of this conflict outside of the relatively closed circle of those directly involved.

The operational area was vast, stretching over a distance of 1,600 kilometres along the South West Africa/Angolan border and several hundred kilometres deep on both sides of the international border. By 1980 the SADF had about 18,000 troops stationed within the operational area, of which the vast majority were national servicemen. Only about 3,000 of these were deployed at any one time on cross-border operations. The majority were occupied in patrolling the operational area, doing base duties or in training.

Background to the Border War

With the signing of the Treaty of Versailles at the end of World War One, South Africa, then a British dominion, was given 'mandate' rights by the League of Nations over South West Africa, previously a German colony. At that time, the four provinces of South Africa were Natal, Transvaal, the Orange Free State, and the Cape Province. South West Africa effectively became a fifth province of a country populated by some four million whites who by virtue of their unique legal system enjoyed a special status at the expense of the 30 million blacks. When the National Party subsequently referred to as the apartheid regime won power in the election of 1948 led by the Dutch Reformed Church Minister Daniel Malan, they soon began to impose apartheid on South West Africa and the seeds of rebellion were sown. Local anti-South African opposition began with the formation in 1960 of the South West Africa Peoples Organisation (SWAPO) and its military wing PLAN (Peoples' Liberation Army of Namibia). By the 1960s, SWAPO emerged as a military organisation staging basic guerrilla attacks on South African military interests. SWAPO originally operated from bases in Zambia until 1975 when pressure from the South African government made the Zambian option untenable. Thereafter they operated from Angola where SWAPO formed an alliance with the Marxist 'Popular Movement for the Liberation of Angola' (MPLA). South Africa would go on to stage several military campaigns against SWAPO and the MPLA in Angola from its territory in Namibia. SWAPO never managed to establish permanent bases in Namibia during its military struggle, apart from the initial base at Ugulumbashe which was destroyed in 1966 by a SADF raiding party, marking the commencement of the Border War.

Whereas South African military records suggest SWAPO/PLAN suffered about 11,400 casualties due to SADF action, the SADF claimed to have suffered 1,659 (combat and non-combat) casualties during the 23-year Border War. There is no accurate record or assessment of the psychological consequences borne by the youthful participants. There is little doubt that this conflict changed the circumstances of an entire generation on both sides and cast a long dark shadow over the future of South Africa.

The breakdown of conscience in the conduct of participants in this war was a defining aspect in the zeitgeist of modern South Africa. SWAPO tactics followed those of the Warsaw Pact armies during the cold war under which members would be spirited out of the country to attend training camps in Russia, East Germany and Tanzania. Armed groups ranging from a mere handful to several hundred returned from their training armed with light weapons such as AK 47's, RPG 7's, mines and grenades for operations originating from SWAPO bases deep inside Angola. These groups infiltrated South West Africa mainly during the rainy season, since the scarcity of water in the semi-desert region made it difficult to move across long distances without carrying large water reserves. Terror activities conducted against the SADF and the local population included ambushes, the mining of roads, the terrorising of members of the local population who showed support for the SADF and the recruitment by kidnap of new PLAN members.

The Portuguese factor

During the early 1970s, Portugal was fighting three costly civil wars within its colonies, namely Angola, Mozambique and Guinea Bissau. Portugal being one of the poorer European countries, the cost of those wars became prohibitive and local resentment against the wars increased due principally to the recruitment of young Portuguese citizens to fight in colonies the mother country could no longer afford to sustain. With a peaceful coup of the Caetano Government in 1974 a military government took over in Portugal and established the rapid withdrawal of Portugal's military from Africa and the granting of independence to its former colonies. This created a power vacuum as a result of which Angola went spiralling out of control, torn between three freedom movements, often fighting each other.

Those three movements were:

1) **The MPLA** (Popular Movement for the Liberation of Angola), the strongest, led by the Marxist-orientated Agostinho Neto and fielding a semi-trained militia of around 4,500 fighters who formed the armed wing of the MPLA known as FAPLA (Forças Armadas Populares de Libertação de Angola, or the People's Armed Forces for the Liberation of Angola).

2) **The FNLA** (National Liberation Front of Angola) under Holden Roberto with its stronghold in the northern Bakongo region supported by the USA and Mobuto sese Seko's government in Zaire with approximately 7,000 men under arms.

3) **UNITA** (National Union for the Total Independence of Angola) led by Dr. Jonas Savimbi who was pro-Western and was supported by South Africa and the USA. UNITA controlled the central, south and eastern Uvimbundu parts of Angola.

The presence and controlling influence of the Portuguese had previously prevented SWAPO from establishing secure bases in Southern Angola. With the departure of the Portuguese and the growing Russian/Communist interest in the area, the South Africans became increasingly concerned at Angola's instability and the threat of SWAPO gaining a meaningful foothold within the South West African border. Finally, in 1975, with elections that would determine Angola's fate imminent, the South African military decided to mount Operation Savannah. South African forces invaded Angola, escalating what had formerly consisted of a series of skirmishes into a full blown war. The timing of the operation was chosen with the first Angolan post-colonial elections, scheduled for 11th November 1975, in mind. The main purpose was to clear Southern Angola of MPLA presence and support Jonas Savimbi's UNITA towards controlling the southern and eastern parts of the country.

Although Angola's civil war was still raging on Election Day, the MPLA had driven the opposition out of Luanda and had unilaterally declared independence. Portugal hastily recognised that independence and Agostinho Neto became the first non-Portuguese President of Angola. At the same time, South African troops were fighting their way north towards Luanda. Thirty-three days after Operation Savannah began the

SADF taskforce had advanced a distance of 3,000 kilometres into Angola and was standing poised to take control of the new nation. Advance paratrooper regiments landed north of Luanda while the advancing force from the south stood ready within artillery range of the capital. The power to assume control of Angola lay firmly in the hands of the South African government.

Operation Savannah was to prove to be too ambitious as the logistics of holding a country three times the size of Iraq under military control were not feasible. Just before Christmas 1975, six weeks after the hijacked Angolan election, the decision was made not to enter the Angolan capital but rather to scale back the operation from a full-scale conflict to one of creating a buffer zone and defending the bottom third of Angola which bordered on South African territories, an approach comparable to that of the Israelis in Lebanon.

Neither FNLA and UNITA recognised the MPLA-declared independence of Angola and with covert help from South Africa and the USA, Angola's civil war raged on. It was in South Africa's interests to keep Angola in a destabilised state since the prospect of a Communist-backed regime in power in Angola offering support to anti-South African forces camped right on the border of South West Africa would surely compromise South Africa's national security. The USA too had a vested interest in undermining the ascension of a Communist government in Angola and the destabilisation of Angola became a matter of policy.

Following the withdrawal of the South African forces, UNITA was supported only to the extent of ensuring that the MPLA and Cuba could not establish bases in the lower third of Angola. Holding this area ensured SWAPO could not establish permanent bases from which to launch incursions into South West Africa. With the MPLA backed by Communist Russia and their proxy Cuba, and UNITA by the Capitalist West, the conflict became a sub-plot in the on-going Cold War.

South Africa had the covert support of the USA until 1975 when American policy shifted, affected by the anti-apartheid lobby and the US Senate voted to withdraw all anti MPLA support. This withdrawal and the subsequent embargo on all arms sales was instrumental in encouraging South Africa to expand its own armaments industry, Armscor, one that grew, as is widely accepted, to include nuclear capability.

Operation Savannah ensured that UNITA maintained a strong presence in Angola's emerging political landscape. With on-going SADF and Western support throughout the Border War UNITA remained the dominant freedom movement in South Angola until the end of the Border War. The situation in Angola however deteriorated from 1975, plunging the country into a bitter civil war that lasted until August 2002.

Addressing ridiculously inflated Cuban propaganda claiming victory against Operation Savannah, Colonel Dean Ferreira, the SADF commander in Angola reported that

"South African losses were 31 men, 3 tanks, 5 armoured vehicles and 3 aircraft. FAPLA and the Cubans lost 4,600 men, 94 tanks, 100 armoured vehicles, 9 aircraft and other Soviet equipment valued at more than a billion Rand."

Cuba and Russia

Cuba started sending military support to Angola as early as 1975. By March 1976, there were 36,000 Cuban military personnel in Angola. By 1989, the figure had grown to 55,000. In the course of war, approximately 350,000 Cubans were to visit Angola as military personnel of whom around 2,000 died there.

Though South Africa became increasingly isolated from the international community as a result of its apartheid policy, it was still seen as pro-western and enjoyed the silent blessing of most Western governments, in particular the Conservative British government led by Margaret Thatcher and the Republican US administration headed by Ronald Reagan. Worldwide popular awareness of apartheid and all that this word represented had not yet come about and many influential conservatives in the US and the UK still applauded the Afrikaners' racial policies and admired their firm stance against Communism.

At the start of the Border War in 1966, the SADF was mostly equipped with outmoded equipment dating from the Second World War vintage and was reliant on arms purchases from Britain, America, France and Belgium. Operation Savannah caused the SADF to realise how outdated its weaponry was and the consequent need to develop an independent arms industry led to massive investment in Armscor.

In 1977, the international community imposed military and economic sanctions against the apartheid regime and after unprecedented spending

Armscor became a highly efficient producer of war weaponry, among which were the following:

1) The Ratel ICV (Infantry Combat Vehicle) armoured personnel carrier providing armoured transport in all terrain, its V shape design base offering excellent protection against land mines. The Ratel was developed from a prototype used by the Rhodesian army against guerilla forces formed by Ndabaningi Sithole and Joshuah Nkomo before credit for the liberation struggle was hi-jacked by the non-combatant Robert Gabriel Matabiri Mugabe.

2) The G5 155mm artillery system, a mobile, easy to use cannon that could fire a shell with great accuracy for up to 70 kilometres. The G5 was a key weapon in the Border War, designed in direct response to the SADF artillery being outgunned and outranged by the Soviet D30 and M46 152mm guns during Operation Savannah.

It was often repeated during training that the G5 could 'hit a car in Pretoria from Johannesburg'. Because other 155mm guns only have a maximum range of 25 to 40 kilometres, the G5 subsequently became a best seller at Arms shows around the world.

The story of origin the G5s is of interest. The technology to build an advanced weapon capable of superceding the best the Russian arms industry could offer lay beyond the skills of South Africa's ballistics experts, besides which arms sanctions prevented South Africa from acquiring the technology with which to build state of the art weaponry.

Enter the notorious Canadian ballistics expert Dr. Gerald Bull. Disgruntled by American failure to encourage his work and keen to put his skills into practice, in defiance of the UN arms embargo Bull sold his services to Armscor and worked with them to develop the G5. Once American intelligence got wind of this 'fabulous' weapon, Bull was arrested and served a year in prison in 1980 for breaching the UN arms embargo by working with Armscor. Following his release and now firmly embittered against the US, Bull went on to work with Saddam Hussein's regime in Iraq for which designed the so-called 'Super Gun'. Had it been completed, this gun would have given Iraq the ability to launch shells all the way into Israel.

In March 1990, whilst resident in Brussels, Bull died a gruesome death after being shot five times in the back of the neck while entering his apartment. No one heard the shots and no one saw the gunman though

Bull's assassination was widely attributed to the Israeli secret service. Although the Iraqi super gun was destroyed, Bull's twisted expertise lives on in the form of the G5.

The Border War officially ended in 1989 as dialogue with the ANC advanced, heralding the release of the former 'terrorist' leaders, who would go on to form the first post-apartheid government and proclaim the Border War as their war of liberation.

Glossary of terms:

Aangekla (Afr): Put on a charge.
Afkakkamp (Afr): A camp where you shit yourself. 8 SAI which lost quite a few troops to abuse and heat exhaustion was legendary as an afkakkamp. Walvis Bay was another.
Afkak parade (Afr): Shitting off parade, usually a punishment or fucking around session, sometimes on a company or platoon level.
Al Debbo Jr: Drummer with Ad Lib Band.
Al Debbo: The rubber faced comedian and star of the Afrikaans Country market.
AWOL: Absent Without Official Leave.

Basics: Basic training, usually lasting about 10 weeks and supposedly the worst part of your army career, where the individual was broken down and the soldier created from the detritus.
Bedford: The British-made general-purpose workhorse truck used by the SADF. Many of these vehicles dated from the 1950s.
Beskadiging van Weermag Eindom. (Afr): Damaging military property. This was considered a serious offence and could encompass something like breaking a leg or not taking malaria pills.
Bim Schtunk: A humorous play on the words 'Bum stinks'.
Bokkop (Afr): Infantryman. The insignia of the infantry was a springbok. A rifleman was called a bokkop (buckhead).
Bombadier (Eng): The artillery equivalent of a corporal.
Boshoed (Afr): The nutria-coloured bush hat so beloved of many nostalgic ex-soldiers.
Bossies/ Bosbefok (Afr): Crazy, mad, usually suffering from shell shock/ PTSD. Literally 'bush-fucked'.
Bom Verband (Afr): A bomb bandage. This was a packaged bandage carried in a pocket by every border soldier. It was a first line of treatment for the wounded.
Bren: The BrNo 7,62mm machine gun which was used as a platoon weapon. Most were of World War Two vintage and very temperamental. They used the same 20-round magazine as the R1.
Buffel (Afr): Buffalo. A mine-proof troop carrier. Another Armscor product.
Burger Sake (Afr): Civic Action, an attempt to win over the local

population. Similar to a 'hearts and minds' campaign.
Buddy/Chommie/Maatjie: Friend, fellow platoon member, mate.
Budgie Club: South African Air Force.
Budgie: The cap badge of the Air Force.

Casevac: Casualty Evacuation.
Casspir (Afr): A mine proof vehicle used by the police in anti-terrorist and anti-riot ops.
CB: Confined to barracks.
CF: Citizen Force. The CF consisted of mostly civilians who were called up to do camps. The norm was that after you had served two years national service, you were liable to 10-12 camps over the next 10 years, theoretically the camps were supposed to alternate between a one month camp and then a three month camp.
Chicken Parade: Picking up litter and stompies (cigarette butts) in an area. Aka 'policing the area'.
CSM: Company Sergeant Major.

Dankie Tannie Organisations: The Southern Cross Fund and similar organisations. An organisation founded to provide support for families of those on the border as well as provide comforts for the troops. Troops leaving for the border received a "Dankie Tannie" ('Thank you, Auntie") package with writing pads, envelopes, a pocket knife/nail clipper, Chesterfield cigarettes, sweets, a letter from Mrs. Botha, a pen, presented in an embossed fake leather folder.
Darachlor: A brand of anti-malaria pills which taken weekly while on the border. Legend had it that these would make you turn yellow and that you wouldn't be able to tan.
DB: Detention barracks
Dixie: Two Square aluminium 'plates' which were kept in your webbing and which were used to eat out of. They fitted inside each other and with the firebucket and pikstel formed your eating kit when in the bush or border.
Dog Tags: The two metal plates worn on a chain around your neck which indicated your name, army number, blood group and religion.
Drol (Afr): Turd. Usually describing somebody, eg "Hy is 'n drol!".
Doppies (Afr): The cartridge cases left over from shooting.

Firebucket: The metal water-bottle holder which was in the water-bottle pouch. It had a folding handle and doubled as a cup/pot/shaving dish. It held about half a litre and was often blackened with soot from being put over a fire.

Flossie: The C130 Hercules aircraft used as a troop transport. These were not military aircraft but were operated by SAFAIR.

FAPLA. Forças Armadas Populares de Libertação de Angola (People's Armed Forces for the Liberation of Angola).

FNLA: National Liberation Front of Angola.

George Hayden: Major in charge of Entertainment Corps.
Gerald Sharpe: Unpopular Evangelist member of Ad Lib Band.
George Constantinides: Duty driver, 11 Kommando, driver of Bedford which went over my right foot.
Grant Enfield: Troop who stabbed an officer in shoulder with bayonet resulting eventually in the discontinuance of bayonets as standard issue
Grootsak (Afr): The big knapsack which was worn on your shoulders.
Gunner (Kanonier (Afr): A private in the artillery.
Gyppo: Avoiding duty. A sly deceit to get around fulfilling a duty. Any idle time or sitting around was considered gyppoing.
Gyppo guts: The runs. An upset stomach, sometimes known as the squibbling shits.
G3: An older 7,62mm assault rifle, used in the Air Force, South West Africa Territory Force (SWATF), interpreters, and in some citizen force units. It was originally made by Heckler and Koch and also known as the R2.

Hardegat (Afr): Hardassed, stubborn, non-conformist.
Houding (Afr): Physical reflection of conformity to military standards. Identified by bearing, attitude, appearance and military discipline.

January intake: There were two intakes each year, one in January and one in July.

Klaarstaan (Afr): The period just before and after sunrise and sunset. Also known as 'Stand To'.
Koevoet (Afr): The South African Police anti-terrorist unit.
Kort Diens (Afr): Short service. These were guys who had signed on for

three years in the army as opposed to the usual two, they ended up doing fewer camps and were often hated as much as the PF's were.

Loopas Mars (Afr): Double time/on the double.

MAG: A 7.62mm belt-fed machine gun used as a platoon weapon on the border.
Min Dae (Afr): Few days. Only a few days left.
Mike Selborne: Singer, guitar player with Ricochet, Kimberley Band.
Mynie Grove: Singer, entertainer who toured the Border with Ad Lib in 1980.

NAAFI: No Ambition, And Fuck-all Interest.
NDP (Afr) NSM (Eng): Nationale Dienspligtige. National Serviceman. Somebody who was doing their two years national service.
Neil Aggett: Trade Union organiser, doctor and inspirational activist, killed by the Christian Afrikaner regime in 1982.
NG Kerk (Afr): Nederduits Gereformeerde Kerk. The Dutch Reformed Church, the official religion of the SADF.
Nick Paton: Guitar and saxophone, Ad Lib Band, grandson of South African writer Alan Paton.

Ou Manne (Afr): Old Men. Anybody who had at least six months to go was an ou man. Theoretically anybody who had been six months in the army was an ou man too.

Permanent Force (PF's): PF's were the career soldiers and generally despised by conscripts who they treated badly.
Pete Sklair: Bass player in Ad Lib Band.
Puma: A general purpose helicopter used by the air force. The workhorse of the air force, it was used in a variety of roles eg: Casevac, search and rescue and VIP transportation.
Pikstel (Afr): A shovel and pick set. This was a fork and spoon which slid into the handle of the knife.
P. W. Botha: The South African Prime Minister, head of the apartheid regime, Dutch Reformed Church Christian and slaphead. Botha was a former Nazi supporter whose mother was interned in a British concentration camp and was largely responsible for increased

conscription and commitment to a military defence of apartheid. One of his many unaffectionate nicknames was Piet Wapen.

Ratel 20 (Afr): A locally produced armoured personnel carrier which was armed with a 20mm cannon, three X 7,62mm Browning machine guns and four smoke launchers. It could carry eight infantrymen or a section. A Ratel 90 mounted a 90mm turret mounted anti-tank gun, while a Ratel 60 had a turret mounted 60mm mortar. They were very fast and very agile. The crew consisted of a driver, with a gunner and commander in a manually operated turret. Ratel is the Afrikaans name for a honey badger.

Richard van Lijr: Troop in Jan Kemp Dorp in 1979 who slashed his own wrist artery and was punished for damaging government property.

Ride Safe Sign: Many troops hitch-hiked home when they went on pass and many were killed standing in the middle of nowhere waiting for a lift. It was decided to create a road sign which showed the silhouette of a soldier and these were placed at strategic points along the main roads where troops could hitch-hike from. The hitch-hikers were also issued with a dayglo sash to wear when hitching.

Rockspider/Dutchman: A derogatory term for an Afrikaner.

Rondfok (Afr): Fuck around.

Roofie Ride (Afr/Eng): A very bumpy and often fast ride on the back of a vehicle. Your initiation into military transportation was usually on the back of a Bedford along a bumpy road.

Rowers/roof (Afr): Rowers or Roofs (Afr) were newbies... anybody who still had at least 18 months to go was a rower or roofie.

RP's: Regimental Police, aka 'Rat Packs', or 'Roomys Polisie'.

RSM: Regimental Sergeant Major.

RTU/Return to unit: Sent back to the unit that you came from.

R1. The 7,62mm assault rifle which was used by the SADF. It was basically a South African made FN Rifle.

R4: The 5,56mm calibre assault rifle which replaced the R1. It was based on the Israeli Galil. The civilian version of this rifle is known as the LM4.

R5: The 'parabat' version of the R4.

SADF: South African Defence Force.

SAM: Sergeant Major.

SAP. South African Police.

Samewerking/saamwerk (Afr): Co-operation, teamwork.
Santa Marias: Army issue underpants.
Sapper: A private in the Engineering Corps (Genie (Afr)).
Sak vir tien/vyvfig: Drop for 10/50 pushups.
Seven Single: A very large and misformed beret, lacking in appropriate houding.
Sean Wege: Bass Player in Ricochet, Kimberley band.
Sias Reinecke: Afrikaans singer who performed shows with the army band in the 80s.
Sien jy daardie boom? Is jy al terug? (Afr): "Do you see that tree? Are you back yet?" Instruction to make troops run over a distance.
Skiet Piet (Afr): The beret badge of the Commandos.
Skieter (Afr): Rifleman, a member of the infantry.
Skyf: Smoke.
Snotneus (Afr): Snot Nose. The American M79 grenade launcher used on the border.
Soutpiel/Rooinek (Afr): Pejorative reference to non-Afrikaans origins. One foot in Africa, one in Europe with his dick hanging in the salt water. Salt dick. Not committed to the Afrikaner cause.
Slap and Paraat (Afr): A person who was 'slap' was lazy or untidy or dirty, whereas 'paraat' was the exact opposite.
Staaldak (Afr): The heavy steel helmet which the SADF used. It had a liner called a 'morsdop' or 'doiby'.
Staaldak, webbing en geweer (Afr): Helmet, webbing and rifle
Staan Op Troep! (Afr): Literally: Stand up soldier! Usually used when entering a bungalow of sleeping troops or when entering a room. Always bellowed at the top of the voice.
Suurstof dief (Afr): An oxygen thief, one who is such a waste of space, they are seen as stealing air from the healthy.
SWA: South West Africa, the name formerly given to Namibia.
SWAPO: South West Africa Peoples' Organisation.
SWAPO Airforce: Any flying beetle or insects.

Tampax Tiffie: Slang term for a medic.
Tein Ops (Afr) Coin Ops (Eng): Teen Insurgensie Operasies. Counter Insurgency Operations.
The Kas (Afr): The cells in the camp.
Tiffie: A member of the TSC/TDK (Tegniese Diens Korps/Technical

Service Corps).
Toby Steyn: Drummer Ricochet, Kimberley band.
Tony Drake: Keyboard player in Ad Lib.
TJ Numberplate: The old Johannesburg number plates carried the prefix TJ. When hitch-hiking back to Jo'burg, a car with a TJ plate usually meant a ride all the way.
Tree Aan! (Afr): Form a squad.
Trommel (Afr): A heavy lockable steel trunk which lived at the bottom of your bed.

Uit klaar, Klaar-uit (Afr): Clear out. Leaving a camp or finishing your national service.
Uitpak inspeksie (Afr): Inspection where your kit is laid out on your bed.
Uittree (Afr): Dismiss. Opposite of 'Tree aan'.
UNITA: (National Union for the Total Independence of Angola) led by Dr. Jonas Savimbi
Vasbyt (Afr): Bite Fast. Hold tight through the pain barrier.
Voorwarts Mars (Afr): Forward march.

Webbelt: The general purpose greenish belt which was worn with your browns. It had press studs on it and the buckle lip had to always point in the same direction. It also formed the basis of a stripped down webbing.
Weerman (Afr): Private. Usually applied to tiffies, clerks, cooks, also members of the air force.

2,4: 'Two comma four' The standard army fitness test. 2.4km run.
40 days: Based on the popular song by Cliff Richard, it referred to the long awaited time when you had 40 days left before you kla-ed out.
50 Browning: Pronounced "five oh". The .50 calibre Browning heavy machine gun.
Zol: Cannabis.

Acknowledgements

There were several invaluable contributions without which this book would not have developed as it has. My wife Charlotte's constantly confident and supportive encouragement is of course at the genesis of the whole process. Always showing enthusiastic and consistent interest in a subject from far away without even once requesting respite is a special and invaluable quality without which the book would almost certainly never have been completed. How lucky am I.

After two years spent drinking a lot of coffee and completing a 150,000 word manuscript, the first reader was Ray Galton whose thoughtful critique gave me cause to reflect on the magnificent good fortune I enjoy in the matter of my friendships. Rays guidance helped focus the early direction of the book.

Mike Popham read the revision and was encouraging and generous with his encyclopaedic knowledge of South African history. Meeting Mike as a result of writing this book has been a tremendous privilege.

The third reader whose comments I invited was John Oakley Smith, who found the time from his remote location among the blue hills of Zimbabwe to send a 2,000 word synopsis of his thoughts on the book, reminding me once more of how tremendously fortunate I am to have such gifted friends. Since John's familiarity with the subject matter is immense, I could think of no one better to edit the manuscript and was thrilled when he agreed to fulfil this most tedious of tasks. John's edit helped establish the spine of the story based more on my Greek heritage than my South African experience and, to my mind, has defined the flow of the book quite beautifully. He also suggested the title.

Stuart Catterson helped with both the design of the cover and ongoing encouragement.

My deepest acknowledgement is to Neil Aggett, who I met only once and who, despite not being from Sfakia, changed the way I understand courage, conscience and consequence, and whose story shaped the course of mine.

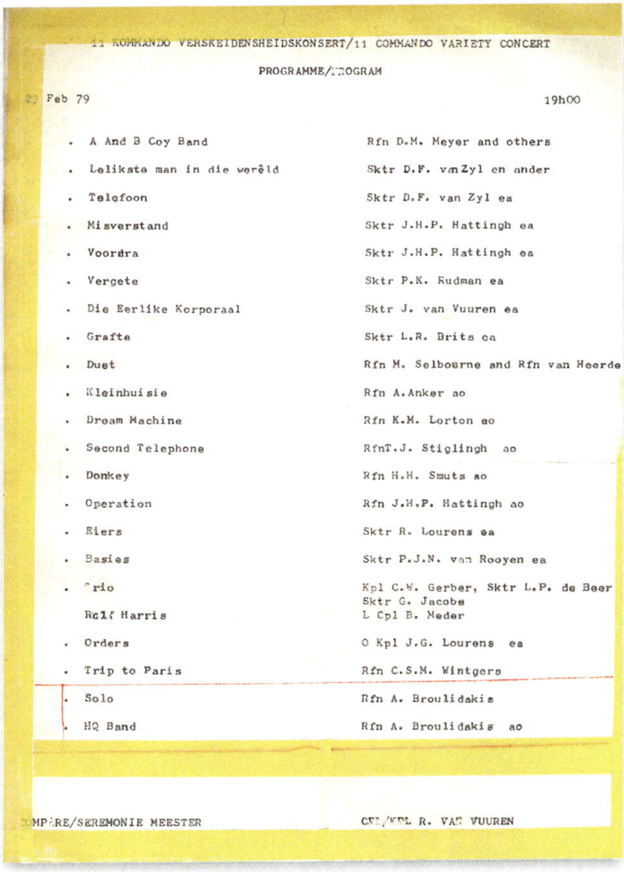

11 KOMMANDO VERSKEIDENSHEIDSKONSERT / 11 COMMANDO VARIETY CONCERT

PROGRAMME/PROGRAM

23 Feb 79   19h00

- A And B Coy Band — Rfn D.M. Meyer and others
- Lelikste man in die wêreld — Sktr D.F. van Zyl en ander
- Telefoon — Sktr D.F. van Zyl ea
- Misverstand — Sktr J.H.P. Hattingh ea
- Voordra — Sktr J.H.P. Hattingh ea
- Vergete — Sktr P.K. Rudman ea
- Die Eerlike Korporaal — Sktr J. van Vuuren ea
- Grafte — Sktr L.R. Brits ea
- Duet — Rfn M. Selbourne and Rfn van Heerde
- Kleinhuisie — Rfn A. Anker ao
- Dream Machine — Rfn K.M. Lorton ao
- Second Telephone — Rfn T.J. Stiglingh ao
- Donkey — Rfn H.H. Smuts ao
- Operation — Rfn J.H.P. Hattingh ao
- Eiers — Sktr R. Lourens ea
- Basies — Sktr P.J.N. van Rooyen ea
- Trio — Kpl C.W. Gerber, Sktr L.P. de Beer, Sktr G. Jacobs
- Rolf Harris — L Cpl B. Meder
- Orders — O Kpl J.G. Lourens ea
- Trip to Paris — Rfn C.S.M. Wintgers
- Solo — Rfn A. Broulidakis
- HQ Band — Rfn A. Broulidakis ao

COMPERE/SEREMONIE MEESTER   CPL/KPL R. VAN VUUREN

The bill for my first army show, playing to 1,000 rooifs, first as a folk solo and then with the band.

My service and Pay book.

Sean smoking a two toke in front of the parade ground at 11 Kommando

Outddor gig in Jan Kemp Dorp, 1979, playing my new Ibanez guitar.

R1 rifle. Standard issue for infantry in 1979. Exactly like the one I was issued and Court martialled for losing.

AK47. Don't start a revolution without one.

In the days before conscription was a twinkle in my worst nightmares eye, aged 15, playing with my band Hobo.

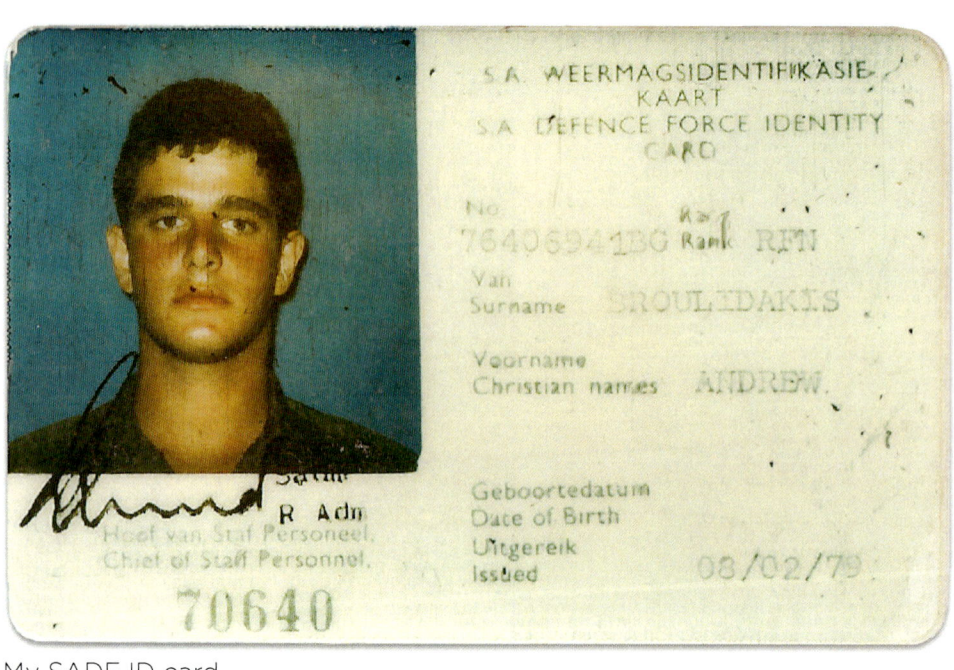

My SADF ID card

When we started, the crowd was all white, when we finished, all the whites had been replaced by Black faces.

Sidewalk in downtown Kimberley. Maybe the first time most of this audience had heard western style music performed live.

Aged 18. Imagine this - singing 'Get up stand up' to a crowd of Black folk - while wearing the uniform of the army, with an Afrikaner officer glaring at you trying to work out whether what you told him about this song being a medical lullaby for crippled soldiers seeking improved pension terms, is in fact true.

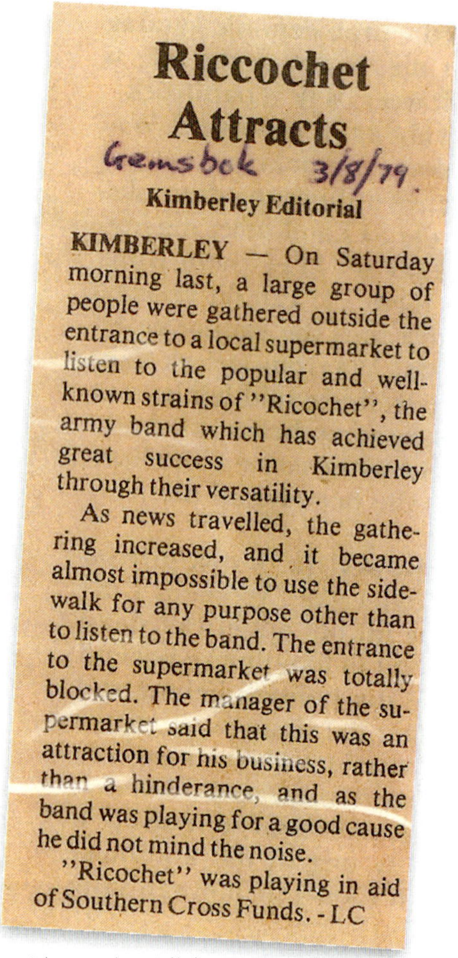

Riccochet Attracts

Gemsbok 3/8/79

Kimberley Editorial

KIMBERLEY — On Saturday morning last, a large group of people were gathered outside the entrance to a local supermarket to listen to the popular and well-known strains of "Ricochet", the army band which has achieved great success in Kimberley through their versatility.

As news travelled, the gathering increased, and it became almost impossible to use the sidewalk for any purpose other than to listen to the band. The entrance to the supermarket was totally blocked. The manager of the supermarket said that this was an attraction for his business, rather than a hinderance, and as the band was playing for a good cause he did not mind the noise.

"Ricochet" was playing in aid of Southern Cross Funds. - LC

I love the 'did not mind the noise' comment.

Dobson in front of the infamous bookstore at 11 Kommando, shortly before his Uitklaar.

Alleviating the boredom at long gigs by playing drums.

Major George Hayden. Founder of the Entertainment Corps. Saviour of many a musician.

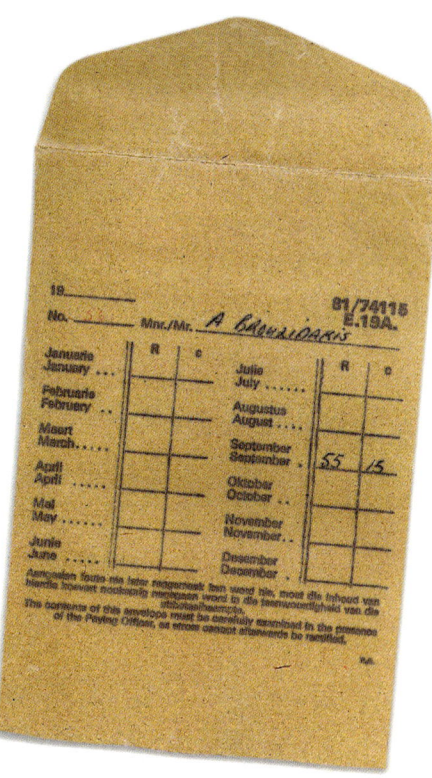

Paybook

Ricochet live at Jan Kemp Dorp Golf club. From right to left: Toby Steyn - drums, Mike Selborne - guitar and vocal, me, and behind me Sean Wege on bass.

AdLib. Our official press photo.
From top left:
Tony Drake (keys),
Pete Sklair (Bass),
Al Debbo (Drums),
Nick Paton (Guitar, sax)
Gerald Sharpe (Vocal) and myself on the only occassion of Moustache, playing a major 9 chord.

Here was are stopped on side of road on Caprivi strip for Photo Op. Behind us is Angola.

Fame at last.

Aged 18. Folk club acoustic set - playing 'Don't think twice its alright' during a weekend pass. 1979.

Mynie Grove. Promo pic from our Border tour 1980.

Shortly after my arrival at Entertainment corps - in front of the main band room section. Me on the left, Lloyd Martin, Nick, Tony, Pete kneeling with his Fender bass and Gerald looking on benignly. The doorway on the right leads to the band room.

This is me drinking a can of coke inside 32 Battalion camp during set up for our show.

Our Band posing in a active bunker at Omega Base during the border tour of 1980. Left to right: Al Debbo, Pete Sklair, me, Gerald Sharp, Tony Drake, Nick Paton.